MAMA LIEU'S KITCHEN
劉媽媽給孩子們的台菜/中菜食譜

A Cookbook Memoir of Delicious Taiwanese and Chinese Home Cooking for My Children

By Ruth Wu Lieu

吳淑幸

with Tina Lieu

Photos by Derek Lieu

Mama Lieu's Kitchen:
A Cookbook Memoir of Delicious
Taiwanese and Chinese
Home Cooking for My Children

First edition, published 2015

By Ruth Wu Lieu, with Tina Lieu

Copyright © 2015, Ruth Wu Lieu

Cover design by Bill Asher
Photos by Derek Lieu
Calligraphy by Ruth Wu Lieu

ISBN 978-1499766493

For my children, Tina, Clara, and Derek

Contents

劉媽媽給孩子們的台菜／中菜食譜

CHAPTER 1

憶兒時美味

My Life in Food

Taiwan (台灣) is a small island with a large mountainous area in the center located off the southeast coast of China with a population of 230,000. It is 245 miles from north to south and 89 miles from east to west (from Wikipedia). The island is shaped like a yam. In the 19th century, my ancestors came from Fujian Province (福建省) located in southeast China. Most Taiwanese came from the area surrounding Fujian. The cooking style is similar to that of southern Chinese, mostly stir fry and a lot of soup dishes, as the weather there from May until October is hot and humid. The temperature can easily reach 90° to 100° degrees Fahrenheit.

From 1885 to 1945 Taiwan was a colony of Japan, thus the cooking is also influenced by Japanese cuisine. There are dishes like sushi, sashimi, and tempura. A very high concentration of Japanese restaurants can be found around the island.

Following World War II in 1945, CHIANG Kai-Shek (蔣介石), defeated by MAO Ze-Dong (毛澤東), came to the island with his army after the Japanese left Taiwan. They brought their assortment of Chinese cooking styles to the island as well. Those soldiers came from all regions of China. They eventually retired from the army, settled in Taiwan, and opened up numerous eateries and restaurants. As a result, today just in the city of Taipei alone, Taiwanese people can enjoy food from all regions of China: Canton, Shanghai, Sichuan, Beijing, Shandong, Northeast China, and even Mongolia.

Taiwan, especially the City of Taipei with its cosmopolitan flair, has come to embrace everything outside of Taiwan. Every internationally known food chain has established branches there with numerous storefronts. Local restaurant owners have also adapted to the new trend and rushed to cook "Western." However in the countryside, local restaurant owners still retain the traditional way of cooking. It's an island where you can enjoy all sorts of cuisines especially in Taipei.

1. Home Cooking

I was a teenager in Taiwan during the 1950s, and it was not a time of abundance. My father was an elementary school teacher with just enough to get by. My mother opened a small grocery store in front of our house in order to supplement the family income—or put it more practically in her own words—so the family would not go without food for a while if anything happened like World War II.

When my mother was busy with the grocery store, I was the one to fix dinner. My brothers and sisters were all working. We had an enormous family wok sitting on a charcoal-heated brick stove built by a mason. It took skill to start a fire. The first layer is newspaper, then twigs and wood charcoal, similar to starting a fireplace, except for the difference between wooden logs and wood charcoal. After starting the fire, the heat has to be maintained until the cooking is done. It takes patience to keep the charcoal burning. Before I even started the actual cooking, my hands and face were all covered with smoke and soot.

I would first put a couple of Taiwanese yams (purplish red in color) (蕃薯)[1] inside, next to the charcoal to "bake." Most of the time, the yam would be baked beyond recognition; the skin turned to black charcoal. But the taste of the yam inside was unbelievably good, fluffy and piping hot. A well-designed stove built by a mason would ensure the smooth burning of the fire. Some masons were well known for designing stoves to make the stove fire burn evenly. We had to offer to the God of the Stove (灶神) many special dishes once a month, like a whole cooked chicken, a fried whole fish, and other dishes with meat to keep the God of the Stove happy and the stove easy to start. Those were the few times we could have a feast with tasty meat. On regular days, one pound of meat would feed a ten-person family. Meat was primarily used as flavoring to enhance the taste of the vegetables, not as a main dish. So we all loved to "bai bai" 拜拜 (pray to Buddha).

As there were many Buddha, well-known ones and obscure ones, they took turns having birthdays or festivities, so we had many times in a year to celebrate. Before the celebration, my mother would prepare many dishes.

She would first kill a chicken or duck she was raising in our yard. When I was in elementary school, one of my chores was helping to kill the chicken. My mother asked me to hold down the chicken while she held the head of the chicken with one hand and a knife in the other. Before she slit the chicken's neck, she would murmur blessings to the chicken: "It is not an end[2] to be a chicken or a bird, in the next life you will be the child of a wealthy family." (做雞做鳥無了時，　富貴家庭做兒女。) When the neck was slit, the chicken's blood was caught in a bowl of uncooked rice. When the blood coagulated with the rice, it was steamed into a chicken blood rice cake. Nothing was wasted in those days.

After the chicken was killed, boiling water was poured over the whole chicken, making it easier to pluck the feathers. Plucking feathers was also my job. Then my mother would finish up the butchering by cutting open the chicken to remove the innards. My mother raised chickens, ducks, geese, and pigs in our yard. All the animals responded to her when she started the meal calling: "Wo, goo, goo, goooo!" My mother made this noise when she called the chickens and ducks to dinner. The chickens, ducks, and geese flapped their wings, jumping and flying to her. She fed them rice husks (米糠) mixed with leftover food.

Even the fat pig would get up from its cozy nap and stick out its head at my mother's call. The pig was fed vegetable scraps from the meal preparation, and the water we washed the rice with. I hated the smelly animal odors especially from the pig. My mother always said that I was very ignorant, not knowing where food came from.

When the pig was big enough, she could sell it for money. When the duck, chicken, or goose was big enough, she would kill one for the Buddha's birthday festival meals. My mother always designated each

---

1   It's strange. In 2006, I was back in Taiwan and could not find those purplish Taiwanese yams with red skin and white flesh. The farmer's market vendor told me it's because they are harder to grow and less profitable, so the farmers simply abandoned growing that kind of yam. There is only the golden yam like the one available in U.S. supermarkets now. However, the Chinatown grocery stores and Japanese stores still carry the red skinned yams.

2   After the chicken is killed, the chicken will be born again to be a human being or other kind of animal according to Buddhism.

chicken, duck and goose for a specific festival when they weighed one or two pounds.

The hen would sit on the eggs dutifully everyday for about one month until the eggs hatched into little chicks. It was really fun to watch a chick pecking its way out of the eggshell. It took several months to raise a chicken, duck, goose, or pig.

Besides Buddha's birthday festival, there is also a festival for ghosts on the seventh month of the lunar calendar (around August). People have to "feed" the hungry ghosts to make peace with them in order to have a good year. That month no weddings are held. People who had recovered from a serious illness would put on an ancient restraining device for prisoners and parade with Buddha on the street to redeem their "sin" that supposedly caused their illness. (This combination neck cuff and hand cuff was placed on prisoners in the old days when officials transported them on foot to a remote area where they would not be able to escape, or to be exiled.) Then we would feast. Our meager daily meal would be replaced by dishes of chicken, duck, and pork on festival days.

2. Cooking on Special Occasions

The first day of the fifth month of the lunar calendar is the birthday of the God of the Underworld 地藏王誕辰. For this occasion, thousands of people converged on my hometown Sing Zhuang (新莊) to feast on their local hosts who would provide them with the most elaborate dishes the host could produce.

I don't know how that custom started. It was a terrible custom. For wealthy merchant families, it was a time to show off to their guests or give thanks for their patronage. For poor families, it was torture. For the sake of "saving face," poor families saved all year to splurge on a one-day feast for their relatives and family friends. This event happened in many towns on different days. In Taipei it's the 13th day of the fifth month of lunar calendar.

Those guests could be acquaintances, relatives, or friends of the family who came to feast. (Luckily, the custom has since been abolished.) I hated that day. I could not do too much cooking. My mother usually hired a caterer to come to our house.

The chef would come equipped with his own utensils, two large half-moon ladles with long handles, one of which had holes like a colander, just like the one Iron Chef CHEN Kenichi (陳建一) uses on the TV show. He would come with one or two assistants to chop, cook, and serve. I always sat next to the chef and watched him making Taiwanese *shao mai* (燒賣) (Taiwanese-style dumplings) and other dishes. He would let me have a couple of *shao mai* first. I still can taste the tender dumpling skin and the delicious crunchy fillings he made. (They were definitely filled with fresh water chestnuts.) The taste is etched in my memory; I have never found any *shao mai* that tasted better. I still have yet to work out the right combination for that *shao mai* skin. Maybe since the taste is combined with this bygone memory, I cannot duplicate it.

The festival food for our guests was all served banquet style with 12 or more courses—always an even number, as they are supposedly lucky numbers. From each course, guests would spoon out a small amount. One dish was served to ten guests at one round table in a communal way. Nowadays there is a lazy Susan in the middle to make serving easier. One slight turn and the food moves to the next guest.

The first course was usually the cold platter consisting of Smoked Fish 熏魚 (xun yu) ***** (page 130), Drunken Chicken 醉雞 (zui ji) **** (page 102), Pickled Cucumber, Easy Squid Salad 涼拌墨魚 (liang ban mo yu) * (page 140), or Fried Pork Chunks. Then it would be followed with a few dishes. About halfway through the meal, there was Fried Rice 炒飯 (chao fang) *** (page 169) or Cold Noodles 涼麵 (liang mian) (page 168), served as a filler for guests. When the Fried Whole Fish 炸全魚 (za quan yu) (page 128) came out, it signified the end of a banquet. Dessert that followed was icy soup with lychee or canned pineapples. As the weather in Taiwan is quite hot, dessert is usually a cold, mixed drink.

At the end I was the one who had to wash all the dishes in a huge pot when all the guests were fed and gone. That's why even after I had my own family, I didn't like entertaining at home. It gave me goose bumps just to think of all the dishes to be washed afterward. For that chore, the dishwasher really comes in handy nowadays.

3. Food During World War II

During the Second World War, Taiwan was occupied by Japan, so U.S. B-29 aircraft bombers often bombed Taiwan on their way to the Philippine Islands. My hometown, Sing Zhuang (新莊) was located in the north of Taiwan, in a suburb of Taipei (台北). U.S. aircraft would fly over Taiwan from Keelung Harbor (基隆港) to the North. Once the bombers were spotted over Keelung Harbor, it only took a few minutes for the U.S. bombers to reach my hometown.

I was only five years old at the time, but one vivid scene is still clearly etched in my mind like yesterday. I was having lunch at home with my family. Everyone had finished lunch but my mother and I. When the air siren sounded—meaning U.S. B-29 had been spotted coming toward Taiwan—my father WU Chang-Lang (吳滄浪), being the nervous one, rushed everybody to the outdoor shelter as soon as he heard the siren.

I was always with my mother WU Chen Mai (吳陳買) as I am the youngest. She told me to finish my bowl of rice first and not to rush. She always told us that the farmer had to work very hard for every grain of rice. No one should ever waste any. She said if we did not finish the rice in our bowl, when we grew up we would end up with rice grain-like spots on our face. We never dared to leave any food in our bowls. When we finished lunch, my mother was holding my right hand and standing at the threshold about to step outside to go to the shelter (dug underground in the yard), when suddenly a U.S. aircraft swooshed down so low, I could see the pilot inside the cockpit. I still remember the pilot in the cockpit. That aircraft flew over the Dan Shui River (淡水河) located behind our house. Later on, we were told that many neighbors had been killed by that plane, which had sprayed bullets as they stood on the riverbank watching the B-29 bomber swoosh by.

In case of nighttime air raids, my mother made a backpack for each one of us. Inside the backpack, besides a few necessities like clothing, there was a bottle filled with flour cooked with sugar that my mother made. During a raid, we could survive by mixing boiling water with the cooked flour. Besides the backpack, we each had a cotton-padded hood to protect us from head to shoulder. During the night when the siren sounded, after we dressed, we would run to the outdoor shelter.

My eldest sister Shun-Hua (舜華), who was in her early 20s, was the only one who refused to go to the shelter at night. She would bury herself in a thick blanket and stay in her bed. I thought it was fun and exciting whenever the air siren sounded. I wanted to taste the cooked flour with sugar. I always opened the bottle and sneaked a handful while we were snuggled up inside the dark and crowded shelter.

During the war, the only way to obtain any food was through food rations. My second oldest sister Shu-Ying (淑英) told me that she was about elementary school age when my mother sent her to wait in the ration line. My oldest and second oldest brothers Jian-Si (建熹) and Jian-Yu (建燠) and oldest sister Shun-Hua (舜華) were working or in school at that time. My third oldest brother Jian-Ming (建銘) was always nowhere to be found. My third sister Shu-Shu (淑姝) was too young like me to handle any chores yet.

People had to line up before the meat stand even opened. If they were there too late, the meat might be sold out when they got to the butcher counter to take their turn, and it would be another two weeks before they could get meat again. The line was long, stretching from the entrance to the rear end of the market. My sister Shu-Ying was tiny and was always shoved and pushed by the other adults, but she kept her position in the ration line steadfastly. After about one hour or so, my mother would come to take her place and receive the ration. My sister was too young to carry the heavy load home.

Photo courtesy of Ruth Lieu

Family photo taken in 1966 on my father's 70th birthday. Back row: (left to right) Leo Lieu (wearing necktie), 4th in back row Jian-Ming (建銘) (with glasses), my third eldest brother, 7th in back row Shun-Hua (舜華), my eldest sister (to the right of man with glasses); 11th in back row Shu-Ying (淑英), my second eldest sister (to the left of man with necktie); 13th in back row Shu-Shu (淑姝), my third eldest sister. Front row seated (left to right): myself, Jian-Yu (建燠), my second eldest brother; 4th seated WU Chen Mai (吳陳買), my mother; 5th seated WU Chang-Lang (吳滄浪), my father.

To receive rations, every family had a wooden plaque indicating the number of people in that family. They had to present the wooden plaque, the family registry book, and the head of family signature seal to verify how much food they should receive. A few families formed a unit to receive rations. Each family took turns waiting in line and bringing food back to distribute to everybody. When it was their turn to stand in line, they would collect money from each family.

Once every two weeks, each person in each family could receive about 4 ounces of meat. For fish, they went to the fish stand. There were only two kinds of vegetables that were not rationed since they grew easily and plentifully in Taiwan. One is the "hollow heart vegetable" 空心菜, and the other one is like romaine lettuce with smaller leaves and a bitter taste 野仔菜, also called "A菜." In present day Taiwan, these two kinds of vegetables have become a favorite among the Taiwanese as they are supposedly good for health.

With the scarcity of rationed rice, my father would go to his farmer students to sneak in a bag of rice. He would strap the rice to his back with a baby-holder strap to make it look as if he were carrying a baby. Sometimes he would bring home a few duck eggs from his students, too. If the authorities had found out that my father was circumventing the ration system, he could have been prosecuted.

The rice my father got from the farmers was a rough, whole grain rice with only the outermost hull beaten off by a machine run by a foot pump at the farm. It was what we would call brown rice today, but even rougher! My second oldest brother Jian-Yu (建燠) would use a stone mortar and pestle to pound off the rice's outer layer with two hands. Or, my second sister Shu-Ying (淑英) said that they would fill a bottle halfway with the whole grain rice and then put a stick into the bottle to hit and pound off the outer layer of the rice to get at the white rice underneath.

In those days, the daily meal was one of rice porridge with cabbage; rice porridge with dried yam sticks—yam cut into strips, then dried in the sun to keep it from spoiling—rice with yam; or sometimes only yam without any rice, due to the shortage of rice. There were few other dishes to accompany the porridge, maybe only some salted turnip.

Taiwan grows a lot of yams. There were a lot of dried yam sticks. My mother would grind those dried yam sticks into powder. The yam powder would be mixed with water to form small, ball-shaped dumplings to be cooked in soup. There was not enough rice to feed all of us if it was cooked the regular way, so my mother would add a lot of water to make rice porridge to make a little rice go farther and feed the whole family.

At that time, my eldest sister Shun-Hua (舜華) was in high school. Her lunch box had to be arranged to look like a Japanese flag (during the Japanese occupation). In the middle of a bed of white rice was a Japanese *umeboshi* (a salted red plum), resembling the Japanese flag, which has a white background with a red circle in the center. She had to hide the vegetables under the white rice so as not to ruin the flag design.

After the war in 1945, when Chinese Nationalist CHIANG Kai-Shek took over Taiwan, the economy was very bad all the way to the 1950s and 1960s. On top of that, the old Taiwan dollar was replaced by the New Taiwan dollar. NT$1.00 was equal to old NT$40,000. Every family became instantly poorer. A middle-class family income could no longer feed a family decently.

With my father's meager income, my mother had to struggle to feed our family of seven kids. Every morning, there were eight lunch boxes (including my father's) to be prepared. To boost the volume of rice, she boiled the rice with more water and then after being cooked, strained the rice using a sieve.

With the rice, she would pack an "eggplant glob" and an egg mixed with chopped, dried, salted turnip made into egg pancakes. Eggs were a luxury item at that time. Eggplant was cheap and abundant. We had eggplant all the time, boiled or cooked mixed with cornstarch into eggplant glob. That's why I am not fond of eggplant. Other times she made Brown Eggs (page 147), Eggs with Salted Turnip, Eggs Over Easy, Eggs with Salted Pickle, Salted Fermented Black Beans with Chopped Pork, or just salted pickles and salted fermented black beans. There was always something salted to make the plain rice more appetizing.

Cabbage was usually the vegetable packed in the lunch box because it could stand the heat of the steaming lunch box better. Only when there was "bai bai" (拜拜), a praying to Buddha festival, would meat would show up in our lunch box.

Besides receiving food from rations, my mother also got a helping hand from her sister who had a noodle eatery. My aunt received more food because of her noodle eatery, and passed on extra food to help feed us. After the war, my aunt fell onto hard times, and my mother not only took care of her, but her kids, too. Whenever they came over, my mother always told them to stay for lunch or dinner. I would pick out a few items from our grocery store and cook up a few extra dishes for the never announced guests.

As we had the grocery store, any guest who dropped by our house was always guaranteed that we would have enough food to feed them. There were rice sticks, flour, eggs, mung beans, red beans, tree ears, tiger lilies, dried tofu sheets, and many other items like wood charcoal, pickled tofu, pickled cucumber, home-made black bean sauce, and salted eggs. My mother also made the best sour bamboo shoots.

We had a tenant farmer who farmed land my parents owned in a mountainous region. My father visited him once in a while and would come home with newly cut bamboo shoots with mud still clinging to them. Bamboo shoots have to be cut off very early in the morning before the sunrise in order to get the tender shoots. My mother would cook the best bamboo shoot soup that I had ever tasted. It was juicy, crunchy, and sweet with the freshest aroma. It didn't need any condiments, just bamboo shoots, water, and salt. The leftover bamboo shoots would be boiled and soaked in water in a few large ceramic pots to let it turn sour. When cooked with the meat, sour bamboo shoots are simply delicious. It is so appetizing that I would eat an extra bowl of rice.

My father started his teaching career immediately after graduating from Taipei Teachers School (台北師範學校) during the Japanese occupation. He had only learned Japanese, but when Chiang Kai-Shek took over Taiwan, suddenly all the Taiwanese had to learn Chinese, an entirely different language and writing system than Japanese—except for a few Chinese characters that the Japanese use in their writing.

By the time, I was in elementary school after the war, he had had students from all over. They came to visit us quite often and they would bring freshly picked vegetables or live poultry raised in their farms in Lin Kou (林口) where my father started his teaching career. Those students would stay for lunch or dinner before they took the long mountainous bus ride back home.

We had seven kids for dinner. My mother always cooked up a huge pot of soup and a large quantity of dishes. There were always leftovers. Before she went to bed, she would heat up all the leftover dishes so they would not go bad the next day as there was no refrigerator in those days. The first refrigerator we got was a real icebox, with a space in the top section to hold a block of ice.

The peanuts sold in our store were "stir-fried" by my mother. My mother didn't deep fry them, rather she would cook the raw peanuts with a lot of salt to evenly distribute the heat through the peanuts, so they would not burn. The peanuts were kept in a glass jar. When customers came, we would weigh them on a scale. But most of the time, we ate a lot of them ourselves. My eldest brother Jian-Si (建熹) always grabbed a handful to eat when he came home from work. One time, when his daughter Ling-Ching (吳玲卿) was about three or four years old, she put a peanut into her nose! It was a scare. She had to be taken to a nearby doctor's office to have the peanut removed.

In the grocery store we had three huge wooden barrels filled with rice: one with new-crop short grain rice, one with older-crop short grain rice, and one with long grain rice. The long grain rice was cheaper. It is good for making rice cakes. Families on a meager income would buy the long grain rice for their meals. I don't like long grain rice; it is hard and dry. We only cooked the older-crop short grain rice for ourselves, even though the new crop rice was more tender and delicious. The new-crop rice cost more and produced less in volume when cooked because it has more water content.

4. Grocery and Consulting

Besides selling food, our grocery store also served as a neighborhood "consulting" center. At the time, quite a few people were illiterate. In the afternoon, when business was slow, neighbors would come to our store to ask my mother for advice on their family problems.

Most of the time, they would ask her to read their *qian* (簽), a piece of pink paper they obtained from the temple when they went to *bai bai*, (拜拜) by burning incense to worship the god in the temple. Each worshiper got a *qian* by picking from a small wooden barrel container with about a hundred thin sticks of bamboo, each with a number. After you *bai bai* and tell the god what kind of problem you are looking to resolve, you shake the wooden barrel filled with bamboo sticks and pull one out or let a stick fall out. To get the god's answer, you throw a pair of slender crescent-shaped wooden *bie* (茭) on the floor. The *bie* are flat on the bottom and rounded on top. If both land with the rounded side face up, that is a "no"; if one is up and one is down that is a "yes"; and if both land with flat bottoms up, that is a "smile" which means the god is not sure, and you have to try it one more time to get a "yes" or a "no." If you get a "yes," that number on the bamboo stick is yours, otherwise you choose again. Once you have the right stick, you look up the number, and find the numbered *qian* that matches your numbered stick. There are hundreds of *qian* hanging on the wall of the temple, and sometimes you have to ask the temple clerk to get it for you.

Each *qian* has four lines of ambiguously written poetry. People coming to consult would show the *qian* to my mother and tell her what kind of family problem they had. My mother pretty much knew their family situation, so she would interpret the *qian* to tell them how they should handle their problem in order to resolve it.

Especially before an exam in school, I would go to the temple to get a *qian* to see if my exam would come out all right. Most of the time, believe it or not it was quite accurate!

The mother of Mr. Shi (施振榮) the founder of a Taiwanese computer company Acer, always consulted with the temple whenever there was a problem that needed to be resolved. The mother of the former President of Taiwan CHEN Shui-Bian (陳水扁) also did the same thing. Their mothers all struggled through hard times, and it is still a very popular way for people in Taiwan to seek psychological assistance in this manner.

As a school girl, I would just *bai bai* with incense. But for my mother, with every *bai bai* she would cook up a few fancy dishes to offer to the gods to seek their help. We were delighted on those occasions to have a feast.

The *qian* poem is usually very ambiguous. You have to figure it out yourself. One *qian* poem is "Deep in the mountain, there is a tiger/The big ocean has to collect water from the streams/ Trouble rises from opening your mouth/Misery results from forcefulness." There is one *qian* I like very much: "Take one step back to look at things/One lone cloud and wild crane have their ease/Wind on the pine tree travels here and there/Bow to the bright moon on the mountain top with a smile." (萬事無如退步人，孤雲野鶴自由身，松風十里時來往，笑揖峰頭月一輪。)

Some of our customers were so poor, they would receive goods from the store and pay at the end of the month if they had money. My mother had a blackboard about two feet by one and a half feet where she wrote how much each person owed. The blackboard was so full of numbers, only my mother could read her own handwriting. When my mother passed away, the blackboard was wiped clean, and the debts disappeared with my mother.

5. Specialty Items

One specialty item in our store was salted duck eggs made by my mother. She used a special kind of red mud from the town of Lin Kou (林口) in a remote mountainous region. (Since the highway was built, Lin Kou has become a bedroom town outside of Taipei.) The red mud becomes very sticky when it is mixed with water. My mother would mix the sticky mud with a lot of salt and coat each egg and leave it for 30 days. The porous egg surface draws in the salt turning the egg yolk a brilliant orange color when boiled. In the recipe for Salted Egg 鹹蛋 (xian dan) ** (page 204), I use saturated salt water, which produces pretty much the same result. Salted eggs can be served with rice or rice porridge for breakfast, or steamed with meat for an exotic dish, Salted Egg Steamed with Ground Pork (page 83).

The other specialty item was fermented black bean sauce. My mother used fresh pineapple as a sweetener. It was a very tedious process to make fermented black bean sauce. The black beans have to be boiled, drained, and then dried in the sun inside a large, round bamboo tray until it is dry but not too dry in order to let the mold grow. It's then left in a dark place to grow moldy, then mixed to remove the mold. After that, mix black beans and salt in even portions, alternating layers of black bean, salt and fresh pineapple chunks. Finally, everything was sealed in a huge ceramic pot for about one month. The opening was covered with parchment paper tied with a "salted grass" (鹹草). Then a cloth bag filled with sand was placed on top of the parchment paper to ensure the opening was sealed until the fermentation was completed.

When the pot was opened, there was a distinctive aroma which is hard to describe. It was really aromatic with a pineapple fragrance. Since there were no plastic bags or containers available to hold wet food, customers would bring a bowl to buy a cupful at a time. Black bean sauce can be cooked with fish, meat, or tofu or served alone with rice porridge.

As most products were not packaged, except for bottled soda, we made paper bags. Glue was flour and water cooked in the wok. Out of the rectangular shaped newspapers, we made triangle shaped bags after the store closed at night.

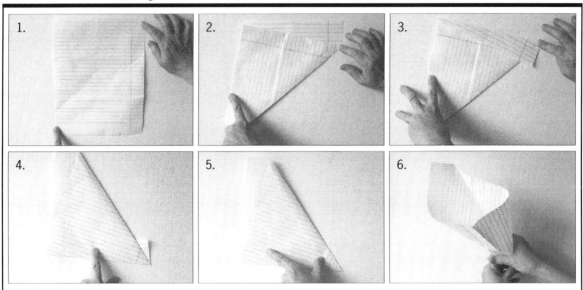

1. Position the paper with the short ends at top and bottom.

2. Fold up the lower right corner to within a half-inch of the upper left corner. Along the top edge of the paper, smear a half-inch swath of glue (made from cooking flour and water), so the bag is sealed in the next step.

3. Fold down the top flap along the edge of the top sheet of paper.

4. Then, flip the paper towards yourself.

5. Fold the lower right flap downward over the edge of the top layer and glue the corner down.

6. The bag is now done and ready to be filled with dry products like peanuts, sugar, rice etc. Very few things were pre-packaged at that time. To close the bag, fold down the open flap and seal.

6. Late Night Snacks

After finishing the bags, I was always hungry. There was a noodle eatery in our neighborhood, about four or five houses down. My sisters would give me money, and I went to fetch the noodle soup. There were no take-out containers, so I would bring a couple of bowls with me. The shop had a good-sized, round, tin pot to boil the noodles in. It was divided into two half-moon-shaped compartments. One side was filled with stock-based soup, and the other side with boiling water.

The shop owner, a skinny, short guy with a faint smile on his face, would move slowly and ask how many orders I wanted. The place was dark and dingy with four or five seats for customers, but I was so hungry that the uninviting environment did not deter me. Close to midnight, there were always quite a few customers waiting, holding bowls in their hands.

When I was there, all I saw was the boiling water and the aroma coming out of the stock. The shop owner would pull a bunch of fresh noodles and put them in a small bamboo basket with a long handle and immerse the noodle into the boiling water for about five minutes. Then he would take the bamboo basket out of the water, and flip the noodles onto my bowl in a dome-shaped half ball. Then he used a ladle to pour the stock over the noodle and place three thin slices of deep fried Taiwanese style red pork (台灣紅燒肉) on top of the noodle dome. To me those three thin slices of Fried Red Pork (page 94) represented heaven to me. I could not wait to go home to eat them. I would usually sneak one piece on my way home. Then my sister would say "Oh, oh, you ate one piece already!"

There were other midnight snacks, too. Vendors holding two baskets full of food balanced on the ends of a bamboo pole across their shoulders would be out close to midnight with delicacies like Sweet Sticky Glutinous Rice Cake (甜糯米糕) in a tin can tube; Glutinous Rice with Pork Fillings wrapped in bamboo leaves, called *zong zi* (肉粽) (page 160), Rice Cake with Taro Root (芋頭糕) (page 202) and Taiwanese Turnip Rice Cake (蘿蔔糕) (page 199). I would never go hungry. Those vendors would call out their wares from far away as they walked by. I had to decide what to get real quick. If I missed them, I had to go running after them, shouting to catch them.

7. The 1950s and 1960s

It was frugal living during the 1950s and 1960s. There was not too much meat available for every family. Meat was expensive. My mother would purchase about one pound of pork to cook dinner for our family. There was no shortage of vegetables, but meat and oil were not abundant. From the one pound of pork, the fatty part was cut off to fry in a pan, rendering the oil for cooking. After the oil came out from the pork fat, the cracklings leftover from the burned fat were very aromatic and sometimes added to the vegetable dishes. The lean part was used for cooking with vegetables. Each vegetable dish only had a few pieces of pork. One egg would be added to make a luxurious dish. The aroma of eggs in a dish was intoxicating when I cooked it.

Our grocery store carried duck eggs. The only chicken eggs available were from our own hen. At that time, people would buy just one egg at a time. Eggs were a luxury item. I would usually sneak one egg into whatever I was cooking. The feeling was so satisfying that I felt like I was having something special that day. My mother tried to prevent me from cooking with even one egg as it was considered an expensive item, but I usually sneaked one into a vegetable dish.

During my junior high and high school years, I took a 35-minute bus ride and walked 15 minutes to my school. Getting to school took one hour or more each way, depending on if the bus was on time. Our school got out at five o'clock. By the time I got home, it was well past six o'clock, and I would be really hungry. My mother would be cooking the rice in the wok. I would scoop out a bowl of rice and mix it with some pork lard and a spoonful of soy sauce. It was very satisfying.

First thing every morning, my mother would cook boiled rice to fill our lunch boxes, so we rarely ate rice porridge (稀飯) like other families in the morning. Salted pickled white turnip egg (菜脯蛋) was a daily lunch box item for a lot of people during the war and after the war in 1950s and 1960s. This dish has become a symbol of the hard life endured during that time.

During my high school years, my classmates and I took turns bringing all the tin lunch boxes to the school kitchen to be heated up in a gigantic steamer. Each lunch box was marked with the classroom number and student's name. One time, my lunch box was lost or stolen. I looked all over the school kitchen in vain. So, I had to buy lunch from our school cafeteria that day.

The school cafeteria served a few items like noodle soup and rice stick soup. They tasted pretty good. Once in a while I would skip my lunch box and buy a bowl of noodle soup at the cafeteria. I had a classmate WENG Mei Rong (翁美容) who lived in my town. School ran from 9 a.m. to 5 p.m. during the week and 9 a.m. to noon on Saturdays. Before we started home after school, we would pass through Chong Ching South Road (台北重慶南路), which was lined with bookstores and small eateries, to reach the bus station for the bus home.

Mei Rong loved Beef Noodle Soup (牛肉麵). She would ask me to go eat with her. Most of the time, I did not have that much money in my pocket, so I could not go every time, but sometimes she wanted to go and insisted on paying for me. She came from an affluent family. Her mother had a maltose sugar factory. We would enjoy the Beef Noodle Soup (page 61) with the sour pickled cabbage. It was hot, spicy, and delicious.

My mother never cooked beef at home. The only chance to eat beef was at a restaurant. At that time, the cows in Taiwan helped farmers till the fields. It was considered too cruel to eat its meat after the cow had spent its lifetime laboring for human beings.

8. Modern Day Taiwan

Life has greatly changed in Taiwan since then. I returned home in 1988 after a 20-year absence to visit my family in Taipei. My three young nieces CHANG Wan-Zhen (張婉貞), CHANG Wan-Wan (張婉娩) and CHANG Wan-Hui (張婉慧) took me to a place high in the mountains to enjoy "exotic" dishes. Those dishes turned out to be what we tried to avoid during the war: rice with yam (蕃薯飯) and one vegetable called hog vegetable (蕃薯葉) and rice porridge (稀飯). How times have changed!

After that experience, I told my nieces to spare me that kind of restaurant food. I only order dishes that I do not know how to cook. Later they took me to Ning Ji Hot Pot Restaurant—"Genuine Sichuan Taste" on Fu-Shing South Road in Taipei (寧記麻辣火鍋店,正統四川風味燙,台北復興南路). That was really something. As customers sit down around a round table, a piping hot Mongolian Hot Pot (火鍋) is brought to the table. The pot is divided into two halves: one side is a spicy red stock soup, the other side is a regular-type stock soup. It is called Lovers' Pot (鴛鴦鍋). That restaurant is well known for the stock soup. As you eat, the stock soup evaporates and the waiter brings out more stock to fill the pot. It is a fun way to eat—especially on a cold day. My nieces told me that the restaurant is constantly packed even in hot summer weather.

9. The College Years and My First Job

I always loved learning something new and exciting. I took cooking classes with a professor chef in a cooking class full of housewives in Taipei during my college years. The teacher was a deft and great chef. The most memorable dish from his class was Squab Wrapped in Lettuce (see Chicken Lettuce Package 生菜雞鬆 (sheng cai ji song) ** (page 99). He would chop a whole tiny squab with bones in no time using his gigantic cleaver. When the dish was finished, it was wrapped in a crispy lettuce leaf trimmed into a bowl-shape and served. It was the best dish I have ever tasted. Not only was the lettuce crunchy but the chopped squab was too. Today when this dish is prepared, the squab is usually replaced with chicken.

After I graduated from college, one of my college classmates LIN Abe (林景煌) found me a job teaching English at a rural junior high school. He was leaving the position so he had to find a replacement. I was reluctant to go there because I had to change buses twice to get there, and the bus route did not run too frequently. However, my mother pushed me to take the job. This classmate was also our family friend. This job forever changed my life. It was a small private junior high school called Gu Bao Middle School (穀保中學). There were only about 10 classrooms. I met my future husband, Leo there.

One weekend, it was my turn to watch the school. The teachers took turns staying in the school each Sunday when there was no class in session. It was for the security of the school as the classrooms were open, not like schools in the U.S. that can simply be locked up. So, I took my niece CHANG Wan-Zhen (張婉貞) along to keep me company. After an early lunch, a math teacher invited me over for a lunch that he had prepared himself.

He lived in the school's makeshift housing. That morning when he found out that I would be at the school, he had ridden his bicycle 30 minutes to the neighboring town of Lu Zhou (蘆洲) to shop for food. Then he rode another 30 minutes back with the food hanging off his bike handles and in his backseat basket. He chopped and cooked making five or six dishes. Unfortunately, my niece and I had already eaten, so I ate a little bit not to disappoint him. I don't remember what dishes he prepared except the Sha Cha Beef, but his efforts really impressed me.

10. Working for the Americans

Later I changed jobs and worked at NAMRU-2, a U.S. Navy tropical disease research center. I worked as a secretary in a physiology laboratory with six technicians, three or four American G.I.s, a scientist, Dr. Love, from England, and my boss Dr. Mitchell.

They did experiments on monkeys, frogs and other animals. There were always leftover frogs. Someone would take the frogs home and cook them. At that time, I had not heard that frogs were considered a delicacy. At the end of each year, the Namru people would have a Taiwanese *bai bai* blessing ceremony, and burn incense to those animals sacrificed on the laboratory table. I remembered the head of Namru named Captain Neptune was a very nice old man with a gracious and mild manner. He was always holding a cup of coffee and smiling to everybody on his way to his office.

There were quite a few American G.I.s in Taiwan during the 1960s. The political turmoil in Vietnam had just started. There was a lot of G.I. traffic between Taiwan and Vietnam. Namru G.I.s were sent to Vietnam cities like Da Nam and Saigon. The G.I.s in Taiwan had a really good life. A G.I.'s pay provided for a very comfortable life in Taiwan. One U.S. dollar was NT$40. A bowl of beef noodle soup cost only NT $5. They simply loved Taiwan. In Namru, there was a lunch dining hall for the Taiwanese staff and two dining tables reserved for American service people. They would place a lunch order and the service staff would bring lunch to them. One thing I noticed was when they had soup, it was placed in a shallow plate. And when they ate the soup, they spooned away, instead of toward themselves. That was really strange to me. Our custom was to place soup only in a bowl, and spoon the soup towards ourselves when eating.

After work, Leo would wait for me across the street from Namru. We would go eat first. There was a sidewalk eatery well known for goose meat. We would order one plate of goose meat, chopped into chunks with some ginger julienne on the side and a small dish filled with homemade dipping sauce. It was really tasty. The business was really good; sometimes we had to wait for seats. Customers squeezed onto the only two long benches placed next to the eatery stand.

Another eatery was well known for its clear beef soup. They cooked a big chunk of beef with the bone for a long time. Then the beef was cut up into small pieces. The beef was tender and the tendon was soft yet chewy in texture (嚼勁). It was simply terrific.

The 1960s was a glorious age for the United States in Taiwan. American dollars were strong, and G.I.s were everywhere They lived in Taiwan like kings and queens. In Tien Mu (天母) and Yang Ming Mountain (陽明山), an exclusive area in the suburbs of Taipei, American-style houses were built for them.

11. Going to the United States

A lot of Taiwanese college graduates dreamed of going to the U.S. Leo could not resist the pull and wanted to go, too. His high school teacher's wage was not enough to support himself with rent and food. I was very reluctant to go to the U.S. There were articles describing the hard life of the overseas students in the U.S. Many students had to survive by working in Chinese restaurants, washing dishes in dingy kitchens and working as waiters between school semesters. My mother was also worried that I would not survive the harsh life here. She had us get engaged in Taiwan before we left. She gave me all her savings, U.S. $2,000, to bring with me.

I left Taiwan with Leo from Song Shang Airport (松山機場) in Taipei one hot summer morning. All the passengers were students going to the U.S. via a Flying Tiger freight flight fitted with temporary passenger seats. It was a mad scene. Everybody was being pushed or shoved by somebody. My father pushed his way to the airline counter for me. That was the last time I saw him. He passed away three years later in 1969 at the age of 71.

Besides my luggage, I took with me the indispensable Tatung rice cooker (大同電鍋). At the same time, Leo had to borrow flight fare from his eldest brother Ken Liu (劉志賢). He paid back his brother as soon as we landed in the U.S. We arrived in Berkeley, California. My college classmate Cindy Chen (陳杏仔) and her husband Ralph Lai (賴維敏) picked us up. We stayed with them for a few days enjoying the cool weather of California in August.

We bought $99 Greyhound tickets to go across the country to New York. It was a tiring journey, but the worse part was the food at the bus stop cafeterias. The only food available was tuna fish sandwiches, ham sandwiches, or pizza. To me it was like chewing wax. One thing that I found out though, was that I could enjoy the chicken noodle soup.

In order to save money to live together, we had a simple wedding ceremony arranged by Leo's brother Ken (劉志賢) and his wife Susan (曾淑容) in New Haven, Connecticut. I guess it was a difference in custom, but the local florist arranged an all-white bouquet. I was so petrified to see the bouquet in white that I had to insert a red flower in the middle. White flowers are only used for funerals by Chinese. Chinese wedding flowers have to be pink or red, or even yellow or orange, but not white.

12. New York City

The fall of 1966, Leo was accepted by the University of Massachusetts. The first semester he had no scholarship. We had to rely on the money I brought with me. I was scared to death seeing the savings account dwindling day by day.

One morning I took a bus and left for New York City. With another college classmate Stella Liu (劉富美) and the help of her then-boyfriend (and future husband) Mike Weng (翁正男), he found me an apartment with two girls in Brooklyn Heights, New York. The next day I went for a typing test (typing 61 words per minute) and got a job as a typist at CNA Insurance Company on Wall Street, for $2.50 per hour.

Leo had to take me riding on subway several times from my apartment to office before I felt secure enough to ride alone myself. I started to pack sandwiches for lunch without a lunch box. On Friday, lunch was unofficially one hour. Maria, who worked at the office with me would take me window shopping, all the while we munched on our sandwiches to save time for the lunch break. The other weekdays, lunch break was only 30 minutes. Luckily Leo received a scholarship from the second semester onward, so I stayed in New York for only half a year.

13. Culture Shock

It was a real challenge to come to the U.S. in the 1960s. Jumping from the colorful restaurant culture in Taipei to the quiet small town of Amherst in Massachusetts was unimaginable. The market closed at 6 pm and on Sunday nothing was open. I felt totally helpless. I had no transportation except for walking or asking friends for a ride. It was such a culture shock.

When we first got to Amherst, we rented a room in an old lady's house. She only allowed us to heat up hot water in the kitchen. We could not use the kitchen to cook anything. However, the rice cooker I brought from Taiwan was put to good use. With it, we cooked without using any frying pan. I would use the rice cooker to cook white rice first. Then the rice cooker was used as a steamer. Meat marinated with soy sauce together with green beans and mushrooms on the side were steamed in the rice cooker. Later we moved into Lincoln Apartments—graduate student housing at UMass. There we met quite a few fellow students from Taiwan. With them, we exchanged ideas on cooking and dined together with everybody's homemade food.

14. Cooking Community

In the town center of Amherst, there was a medium-sized supermarket called Louise. We found that chicken hearts, liver, gizzard, and pig feet were very inexpensive. I would cook up a pot of Red Cooked

Pig Feet/Pork Butt 紅燒豬蹄/蹄膀 (hon shao zhu ti/ti pang) *** (page 69). By mixing the pig feet with soy sauce, sugar, black pepper and wine, I could cook up a very decent tasty dish.

Once in a while we would get a ride from fellow students to go to a larger vegetable stand to buy fresh produce. We found produce new to us. I had never liked the skinny string-like celery in Taiwan. Celery in the U.S. is gigantic and good. We never had broccoli in Taiwan at that time, but here the broccoli is fresh and crunchy. The only problem was the rice. The "River" brand short grain rice is okay. Besides that, there was only long grain rice and the Uncle Ben-type rice. I could only look at the rice with a sigh. At UMass, students from Taiwan would frequently get together for potluck parties. They were real homemade feasts for everyone.

We made tofu, getting the coagulating agent, calcium sulfate, from the school chemistry laboratory or a local pharmacy. After experimenting a few times, it turned out all right. A few times when we started making tofu, the soybean milk boiled over. Being mostly protein, the soybean milk made the stove a mess and the burnt protein was hard to clean. We also made our own bean sprouts, but the sprouts frequently were long, skinny and purplish instead of short, fat and white because they had not been kept in total darkness.

Later Leo started a one-man Chinese grocery operation. He took Chinese grocery orders from fellow students. On the weekend, he drove our boxy green/white Volkswagen station wagon to Chinatown in New York City and came back the same day with food. He rented a space on the campus and everybody came to pick up their orders that night. He made a small profit. For a while he solved the food supply problem for the Taiwanese students at UMass. I was delighted to have fresh Chinese vegetables and ingredients to cook with.

We often invited some singles to our place for dinner. A few times I would prepare filling and dough for everyone to make Jiao Zi Dumplings or Guo Tie Pot Stickers (page 196). While making dumplings, everybody talked about their experience living in the U.S. and gossiped while busily making dumplings. Some liked the dumplings pan-fried and some preferred boiled. Everybody was happy.

On weekends when there was a sporting event, we would cook some dishes like Cold Noodles 涼麵 (liang mian) *** (page 168), Fried Rice 炒飯 (chao fang) *** (page 169), brown eggs (page 147), fried wontons (page 58) and so forth for a picnic. Sometimes there were several cold noodle dishes from different families. Even though they were all cold noodles, each person's dish had a distinctive flavor. There was no Chinese restaurant in the neighboring towns good enough to spend our money on. When we wanted to eat something, we had to think of a way to prepare it ourselves. Sometimes I spent a lot of effort cooking something delicious but my first daughter, Tina, loved to eat only white rice when she was little.

When the war with Vietnam started, and people protested by throwing eggs, it was a shocking sight for me. How wasteful those people were! Imagine back home that I had to sneak an egg from my mother just to add it to a dish.

15. Cooking With This Book

Somehow I survived by improvising and utilizing whatever could be found in the market. After 30 years of home cooking experience in the U.S., I wanted to write down some tips for my children and at the same time, share the experience with my readers. During the writing of this book, I was lucky to live very close to Chinatown in Boston. The ingredients listed were available to me. If there are some ingredients that you cannot get, you can either skip it or replace it with available items. However some ingredients cannot be substituted. I have indicated where an ingredient cannot be substituted. For something like shark fin you have to have the real thing. Man-made shark fin made from some kind of starch exists, but it is tough and not good at all. After watching on TV how they cut off the fin from the fish and discard the remaining body into the ocean, I don't eat shark fin any longer.

Most Chinese dishes do not call for a sauce as in French-style cooking. Chinese food tries to bring out the natural flavor of the ingredients. Here I have tried to put together recipes for dishes with an authentic flavor. I did some research and tried to also explain the origin of those dishes to my readers. If you have an opportunity to visit Asia, such as Taiwan, Hong Kong and China, you should feel at home when you see those dishes on a menu there. It is like you are seeing an old friend in a faraway land.

When I cook at home, I never measure. It's funny when I try to measure with teaspoons and tablespoons, sometimes the taste does not come out right. Just like anything else, you have to cook a dish a few times to get the hang of it. Your kitchen is your best friend. When you feel the "flow" in cooking, the dishes will come out right. Chinese food home cooking is quite easy except there is a lot of chopping beforehand. The big difference is the use of condiments. We use a lot of soy sauce and some ginger, garlic, scallion, shallot, and wine. The bean sauce, sesame paste, and black bean sauce are only used occasionally.

The level of difficulty of each recipe is rated out of five stars, with one star being the easiest. The preparation time varies depending on how you follow the steps. As a rule of thumb, a quick stir fry dish should not take more than 30 minutes from start to finish.

My intention in writing this recipe book is to teach my children how to cook some dishes that I have made for them. Those homemade dishes do not require elaborate preparation, yet are genuinely easy and delicious. As a mother, I don't think too much ahead of time. When I go to the market I usually just get whatever vegetables are fresh and liked by my family. About one hour before dinnertime, I open the refrigerator and see what's inside, then conjure up 2-3 dishes in my head. I start to cut, slice, mix, and finish in the 60 to 90 minutes before dinnertime.

On a rare occasion, for a special dish, I will make a special trip to get an ingredient; otherwise, most of the ingredients are ones I keep at home normally.

When I started planning this cookbook, I wanted to have dishes made from easily found ingredients. As I progressed with the writing of recipes, my plan started to change. Quick, stir-fry dishes for frequent daily use such as Fried Noodles, Fried Rice, Chicken with Spinach, Curry Chicken with Potato, Pan-Fried Salmon, and Chicken with Bean Sprouts are only one part of my repertoire.

Sometimes when I have more time, I indulge myself and cook up some dishes that I have read about in a Chinese cookbook, dishes I had at someone's house, or eaten at a restaurant in Taiwan, Hong Kong, New York, Boston, or somewhere else. Most Chinese cookbooks only write down the concept of a dish without bothering to write down specific measurements, so I have to try it out a few times to get it right. Frequently, the measurements given have to be adjusted. The Chinese are known for ambiguity in writing and conversation. That trait also applies to cooking recipes. If you ask someone how to cook a certain dish, he or she will tell you roughly how to assemble the ingredients together. They will never tell you how much of each ingredient you need. They all figure that you should have some knowledge of cooking already.

Missing some ingredients is usually not a big deal. It's not a laboratory experiment. Sometimes, missteps can create unexpected results. Once I was following a recipe for baking oatmeal cookies, but somehow I forgot the oatmeal. Still, the cookies turned out so wonderful, everybody was asking for the recipe. Trust your instincts. Make friends with your food, kitchen, and cooking utensils.

Where relevant, I have done some research to give a sense of how a dish was created, such as for Kun Pao Chicken, Ma Po Tofu, Bang Bang Chicken Salad, and Beggar's Chicken.

Most home cooked dishes only need one cooking method, such as stir frying (e.g., Shredded Pork with Bell Peppers, Pork Slices with Garlic Paste, Beef with Oyster Sauce, Asparagus with Shrimp). But some need two steps, such as Smoked Fish (deep fried and simmered); Fish Head Casserole (deep fried and simmered); Eggplant with Ground Pork (deep fried and stir fried). A rare few need three steps, like Pork Strips with Chinese Pickled Cabbage (梅菜扣肉) (boiled, deep fried, and steamed).

I hope my readers are not just making a dish, but experiencing the taste and the history of a faraway land. To know one's culture through cooking is rather fun and interesting. With the convenience of present day travel, maybe some day you will travel to places where authentic Chinese and Taiwanese dishes are available and you will feel at home after reading through this book.

All the pronunciation in this book is Mandarin Chinese, Romanized using the Pinyin system, except for a few Taiwanese names. Some are pronounced in Taiwanese dialect where indicated.

CHAPTER 2

中菜烹飪法

Chinese Cooking Methods

Chinese Cooking Methods

A lot of people might be baffled as to how to start cooking Chinese style and what kind of ingredients to get. As a matter of fact, most of the time, I don't use any special "Chinese way," but simply stir fry with plain vegetables and a little meat for flavor plus salt. It is as simple as that. But just as if I wanted to cook in a "Western" way, I would feel baffled as to what to start with, it's as simple as macaroni with cheese. I have to gather my thoughts first before I start, so it is only a matter of practice and to remember to start from a few simple dishes and build up from there. As the saying goes, "Practice makes perfect."

Chinese food rarely uses two ingredients that are very common in Western-style cooking, namely cheese and cream, except for a few Chinese restaurant dishes: Crab Rangoon (uses cream cheese) or Tender Cabbage with Cream (uses heavy or light cream). Otherwise all the ingredients pretty much keep their original flavor without any specially made Western-style sauce.

Cutting 切菜技巧 (qie cai ji qiao)

There is a basic rule in Chinese cooking. Usually the combination is one vegetable with one meat, and most of the time, there is more vegetables and less meat. If there are more than two vegetables or a vegetable with meat, the vegetables and meat should be cut in almost the same uniform shape: if julienne, everything should be julienne (e.g. carrot, bell peppers cut into thin strips 1-2 inches long); if cut into cubes, everything should be in cubes (e.g. zucchini, carrot, cucumber, squash); if cut on a bias (cutting on the diagonal and then rolling 90 degrees and cutting again on the diagonal), everything should be in a bias cut (e.g. zucchini, eggplant, potato, cucumber); if cut into slices, everything should be in slices (e.g. zucchini, cucumber). That principal also applies to the meat.

Usually it is not right to mix cubed vegetables with leafy vegetables, not only for aesthetic reasons, but also because differently shaped vegetables will not cook through in the same amount of time. The result will be a mess.

You have to cook a few times to understand the rules of combining different vegetables into one dish. For example, zucchini will never go together with spinach; eggplant does not go with carrot. Eggplant is soft, while carrot is hard.

One time a TV cooking show about cooking Chinese was on. The woman mixed literally every vegetable on earth and then topped it with tofu cubes and sprinkled it all with soy sauce. It's hard to tell what would come out. That kind of cooking is a huge mess. It's even worse than the so-called "chop suey" 雜碎. "Chop suey" means little cubes mixed all together. "Chop" means many kinds, and "suey" is little pieces. Chop suey is more of a leftover dish that actually tastes good with the right ingredients. It is so popular that in one of Edward Hopper's painting there is a bright red neon store sign saying "Chop Suey" showing through the window.

Stir Frying 炒 (chao)

Heat up 2-3 tablespoon oil in a wok, add shallot, scallion, or garlic pieces and fry until golden to bring out the "frying aroma" (爆香). This is one major difference between Chinese and Western cooking. When a Chinese dish is cooked, you will always smell this great aroma. When shallot, garlic, or scallion turns golden brown in the oil, it will burst with this fantastic aroma, and then you add the vegetables to cook. Immediately after, add a pinch of salt to "seal" the vegetable and prevent it from turning yellow. Most of the time, water will sweat out of the vegetables, and you can use that moisture to cook the vegetable. The resulting cooked vegetable will be crunchy and not soggy.

To add flavor to the vegetable, prepare a small amount of meat, be it pork, beef, chicken, or shrimp the same way. Then the vegetable and meat are combined at the very end for only about one to two minutes. At home, I usually cook one vegetable combined with one kind of meat, or sometimes just a vegetable by itself. I like shallot the most; it is aromatic and sweet—especially the shallot grown in Taiwan.

For a stronger flavored vegetable such as spinach, green beans or eggplant, use garlic instead. You can try and see if you like shallot, scallion or garlic. There is no definite rule. The most convenient way is to open the refrigerator and see what you have and improvise.

Boiling and Blanching 燙 (tang), Keeping Vegetables Green and Crispy

Most people are very conscious about the oil they consume these days. In that case, you can boil the vegetable. However, if you just drop vegetables into water, they will turn out limp, soggy, and yellowish. Not only it does not look good, it also tastes terrible. This is the problem of most cafeteria food.

To boil vegetables, bring a pot of water to boil, add 1 teaspoon oil, a pinch of salt and then the vegetables. Bring it to another boil. Drain the vegetables and place on a large plate or immerse in icy water. In a mixing bowl, mix a pinch of salt, 1 teaspoon soy sauce, 1 teaspoon sesame oil or olive oil, one pinch of black pepper, 1 teaspoon of balsamic vinegar, stir in the blanched vegetable and toss until evenly coated and serve. You can even add some Asiago cheese or Parmesan cheese for extra flavor. (The taste of Parmesan cheese is very similar to MSG.)

Pan Frying 煎 (jian)

Pan frying is largely used for fish, meat, or pot stickers, and is accomplished without stirring the food as in "stir fry." For best results, besides using a non-stick pan, I accidentally discovered that a heavy cast iron frying pan serves this purpose well. Most of the frying pans and woks are made out of stainless steel. If the stainless steel pans are not properly heated (at least 4 minutes), be it a wok or otherwise, food tends to stick.

Deep Frying 炸 (zha)

This is one easy cooking method. In quite a few dishes, the first step is deep-frying followed by steaming to finish the dish. Two-step cooking methods which include deep frying are also very common, but three-step cooking methods are usually found in banquet dishes. There is one dish that calls for cooking "five layer pork" (五花肉) (i.e., pork belly—the cut used to make bacon). First the pork is boiled, then pan fried in medium heat to sweat out the oil, followed by steaming with pickled cabbage or black bean sauce. The end result is a pork so tender that even the fat becomes tender and soft, so it does not taste like pork fat, but tender textured meat. This dish is supposedly one of MAO Ze-Dong's favorites.

Steaming 蒸 (zhen)

For steaming, you can use a bamboo, aluminum, or stainless steel steamer; using a wok or a rice cooker with a rack in the bottom is an easy alternative. By placing a rack in the wok, it becomes a steamer. The magic about the wok is: it can stir fry, deep fry, and steam. There are two ways to steam: one is to place the food directly in the bamboo or aluminum steamer rack; the other is putting the food on a plate and then in the steamer. The method to use depends on the kind of food you are steaming.

For example, steam buns are placed directly on the steamer rack lined with only a layer of cheesecloth or parchment paper, so the steam buns will not stick to the rack when they are removed. On the other hand, for deep-fried spare ribs, the ribs usually are placed in a bowl and then in the steamer. This recipe is a two-step cooking type. By deep frying and then steaming, the spare ribs turn out tender and less greasy. Some oil will collect at the bottom of the spare rib container, which you can use in another dish.

Making Stock 高湯 (gao tang)

Most cookbooks and cooking shows have, or expect you to have, a pot of stock ready to cook up wonders. However, practically speaking, for homemade food, there is rarely a pot of stock on the side ready to be added. The best way is to get a package of bones (be it chicken or pork) and cook them in a large pot for about 1 to 1½ hours. However, these type of bones can usually only be found in a Chinatown grocery.

From a regular supermarket, you can get a package of pork chops, chicken breast with bones, chicken thigh with bones or chicken wings. Have a pot of water with 2-3 stalks of scallion, a pinch of salt, 1 teaspoon wine (optional) and a pinch of black pepper. The water should just barely cover the meat. Bring it to a boil, then reduce heat to medium low and let it cook about 1 hour. Skim the foam off the top and remove the meat. You can shred the meat and use it for a cold salad.

The stock can be added to cooking or used for Egg Flower Soup, Hot & Sour Soup or Corn Soup with Chicken. Chinese cooking rarely uses the heavy, condensed, French-type stock, which is reduced for a long time. Most Chinese soups are clear soups. Corn Soup with Chicken is an invention of combining American-style creamed corn with shredded chicken, and is not purely Chinese.

Slow Cooking 燉 (dun)

There are a few dishes which take a lot of time to cook, like beef shank and shin, pork feet and beef tendon. If they are cooked right, they are absolutely delicious. They are nicknamed "Bachelor's Dishes." They are easy and require no complicated steps. Combine beef shank, beef tendon and chicken gizzard with water, soy sauce, black pepper, wine, five-spice powder, sugar, and bring to a boil. Then let it simmer over low heat on the stove for about 1 hour. They can be served with rice and noodles. This one dish is enough to last a few days for a bachelor, hence its name.

The invention of slow cookers may shorten the cooking time; however, the end result is not the same. With the slow cooker, the soup comes out clear, and not as tasty as when it is simmered on the stove.

The aroma, the texture, and the taste of food cooked conventionally are much, much better than a slow cooker. Especially the well-known Cantonese Porridge has to be slowly simmered on the stove top for best results.

CHAPTER 3

廚房用具

Utensils

Utensils

Wok 炒鍋 (chao guo)

The English word "wok" comes from the Cantonese pronunciation. The half-moon shaped pan allows the spatula to make smooth, circular motions when stirring and mixing food inside the wok. The wok is an *all* purpose pan. It is a frying pan, a steamer, a deep fryer, and a slow cooker. As far as Chinese utensils go, the wok is of the greatest inventions only next to the automatic rice cooker, and it's safe to say virtually every family in Asia has one.

If you don't have a wok, you can use a regular frying pan to do the job. The only problem is when you stir and mix, the flat bottom does not permit a smooth, circular mixing motion. You have to be careful to apply the stirring and mixing action. There are a few versions of woks with a flat bottom available on the market; do not get those, rather get one (stainless steel is better) in a half moon shape.

However, it is not easy to get one here in the States. If you have friends going to Taiwan or Hong Kong, ask them to bring one back for you. There are many varieties of wok in Taiwan from all over the world with high quality stainless steel from Germany and the U.S.! The average price is about US$100.

Non-Stick Frying Pan 平底不沾鍋 (ping di bu zhan guo)

This is a useful modern day utensil. To fry an egg and for other purposes, this pan comes in handy.

Cast Iron Frying Pan 鑄鐵平底鍋 (zhu tie ping di guo)

This old-fashioned frying pan is the first non-stick frying pan and has no Teflon coating. For pan frying meat it is perfectly non-stick. As most woks are made out of stainless steel, if it is not handled right, the meat tends to stick to the wok easily. For stir frying a small amount of meat, this utensil is perfect. The only thing is to make sure to leave an oven mitten right next to the cast iron frying pan, otherwise one can forget and accidentally touch the heated handle and get burned.

Automatic Rice Cooker 電鍋 (dian guo)

An automatic rice cooker is an extremely useful utensil if you eat rice often. They come in different sizes. Every Asian family has one. It's one of the great inventions besides the wok. It is available in kitchenware stores, department stores with a houseware section, or can be ordered online, starting around $40. Fancy rice cookers with built-in timers and different cooking settings from Japan start from about $120.

Steamer 蒸籠 (zhen long)

Aluminum or stainless steel steamers are a complete unit, with a pot and two steaming racks. The other type is a bamboo steamer (竹蒸籠), which also comes with two steaming racks and a cover, all of which sit on top of a wok with boiling water to steam. While the metal steamers are easier to use, the bamboo steamer is good for steam ventilation, and condensation will not collect in the underside and make the food wet. If you don't have a steamer, you can also use a bowl as a steaming rack when it is placed in a large pot or wok.

Chinese Spatula 鍋鏟 (guo chan)

A Chinese spatula is a must. This spatula has a ridge around the handle end, shaped like a dustpan, so when you cook vegetables with some juices, the spatula can scoop up the vegetable and juices. It is very handy. The Western-style spatulas are just flat. They cannot pick up any juice, and the soft plastic makes it hard to press while you are cooking. It simply won't work.

Chopsticks 筷子 (kuai zi)

Chopsticks are used for serving as well as cooking. You have to learn to handle chopsticks if you want to cook Chinese food. To me it is kind of strange to use tongs to pick up food.

Chinese Cleaver 菜刀 (cai dao)

Unlike the Western-style cleaver, the Chinese-style cleaver is straight and rectangular. It is used as a knife, a chopper and a meat tenderizer. The best Chinese-style cleaver on the market here are from Japan. Normally, I use a smaller knife for cutting while I use the cleaver to chop meat with bones, like a whole chicken. Meat with bones tastes juicier and is more tender. Most of the time Chinese cooking uses meat with bones, so a cleaver is a necessary tool for the kitchen. Now we have the luxury and convenience of getting meat with or without bones.

No other special utensils are needed beyond the usual pots you should have already.

CHAPTER 4

菜肴食材

Ingredients

Ingredients

Abalone 鮑魚 (bao yu)

Abalone is an expensive item. Mexico has the best abalone under the brand name "Anchor Wheel Abalone" (車輪牌墨鮑), which costs about $40 for a 454 gram can. Although abalone is also available dried, I have never tried it myself. Like the sea cucumber, it has to be soaked for a while before using. However, canned abalone is very popular and easy to serve. Simply open the can and slice the abalone for a cold platter appetizer. It is a popular gift item. I remember after staying in the States for two years, I returned to Taiwan for the first time and I asked my mother what I should bring as a gift; she said Anchor Wheel Brand canned abalone.

Balsamic Vinegar 意大利黑醋

I discovered balsamic vinegar from watching the Japanese TV show, "Iron Chef." It is very similar to a kind of vinegar in Taiwan I remember from when I was growing up (工研黑醋). A few drops enhanced the flavor of a dish that I loved very much, Fish Paste Coated Pork Chunks in Sauce (肉羹). Balsamic vinegar is very thick and rich in flavor with a very subtle sweet taste. It is perfect for anything. I really like it. Of course, those imported from Modena, Italy—Pavarotti's hometown—are the best.

Bamboo Shoots 竹筍 (zhu sun)

Bamboo shoots are not found in traditional Western dishes. Fresh bamboo shoots are crunchy and sweet with an almost fruit-like taste, like the Chinese pear. It is very low in calories, being mostly fiber. It can be cooked in any way without changing its texture or losing its crunch. It "shoots" out of the root part of bamboo trees.

In Chinatown, there are fresh ones available. I tried them once, but they were bitter, and not as good as the ones I had had in Taiwan. The husk-like outer layers have to be removed; only the insides are edible, almost like an artichoke. Sometimes you can find frozen bamboo shoots or ones packed in plastic packages in Chinatown. These are better than the canned ones. Cut a tiny piece to taste; if it's a little bitter, boil it in a pot for about 10 minutes to get rid of the bitterness. Fresh bamboo shoots are one ingredient that I missed a lot while living in U.S.

Cellophane Noodles (Mung Bean Noodles) 綠豆粉絲 (fen si)

My kids call mung bean noodles, "see-through noodle" because of its shiny transparency when cooked. It is also called "cellophane noodles" or some food critics call it "glass noodles." They are made from the same bean used for bean sprouts. It is called "green bean" in Chinese or mung beans in English.

Mung bean noodles are a very versatile Chinese food item. It can be used in soups, in stir-fries, and even deep-fried to complement other ingredients. It is inexpensive and can be kept for a long time. It is dry like spaghetti, and usually comes in a package of ten 50-gram (1.76 oz.) bundles. They are also widely used in Southeast Asia cooking, such as Thai cuisine.

Chinese Black Mushrooms 香菇 (xiang gu)

Dried black mushrooms have a very distinctive aroma. They are not cheap, but you can find inexpensive ones imported from mainland China. The ones from Japan are pricey, but plump and aromatic and safer to consume.

Before using, dried black mushrooms have to soak in hot water for about one hour. When soft, remove the stem, which is too hard to use, and cut into thin strips. They are very aromatic. I like them a lot. Especially for Taiwanese Glutinous Fried Rice and vegetarian dishes, it is an absolute necessity. There is no substitute for Chinese black mushrooms. My mother used black mushrooms only on special occasions. Because it was such a pricey item, she would use only three to four mushrooms in one dish.

Cloves 丁香 (ding xiang)

A very aromatic spice, cloves are good for browning big chunks of meat, like beef shin or shank. It is also good for making clear aromatic soup like beef soup or the Vietnamese *pho* beef noodle soup.

Cooking Oil 油 (you)

Traditionally, Chinese cooks use peanut oil, because I guess, it was readily available. There were only peanut oil and vegetable seed oils when I was growing up in Taiwan. In that peanut oil, you could really smell the fresh roasted peanut aroma. I think it was because of the way the peanut oil was manufactured. No machine was sophisticated enough to remove any original peanut flavor in the old days, so the peanut oil was really aromatic. Now most oils are completely tasteless with no aroma—with the exception of very good olive oil. Any kind of cooking oil you like should be fine.

Cooking Wine 料酒 (liao jiuo)

I usually use Cognac or Savignon Blanc for their aroma. You can use any kind of wine you like. Cooking wine on the supermarket shelf usually is not as good. The wine both adds to the aroma of the food and acts as a meat tenderizer. Use the wine for cooking like the French and you will never go wrong. The French marinate meat with wine for a few hours before cooking; it is an excellent way to cook meat.

Cornstarch or Sweet Potato Starch 太白粉/蕃薯粉 (tai bai fen/fan shu fen)

Most meat is marinated with soy sauce, wine, and cornstarch (or egg white) before cooking so that it will come out tender and juicy. This marinating is a big difference between Chinese cooking and other cuisines. Chinese meatballs will be mixed with wine, soy sauce, eggs, and cornstarch before frying, resulting in juicy and tender meatballs. In Taiwan we use a lot of sweet potato starch. It is coarser and grainier than cornstarch.

Dried Scallops 干貝 (gan bei)

This is an exotic item—even for the Chinese—that ranks up there with shark fin and swallow's nest.

It is expensive, between $90 and $140 per pound. These days there are smaller dried scallops which are a little more affordable, but of course, the taste is not the same. The regular fancy dried scallop is about ¾" in diameter and ½" thick. If it is steamed with just clear water, it creates a chicken soup-like flavor, but without the grease and fowl taste. The original taste of scallop is the ultimate taste in Chinese food. It is soaked first, and then pulled apart into stringy bits before it is cooked with other ingredients. The water used to reconstitute the dried scallop is very tasty and should be saved to cook with something else later.

Fermented Bean Paste 豆瓣醬 (do ban jiang)

There are several kinds of fermented bean paste. They are made from fermented beans, black beans, or soy beans. Examples include Sichuan bean paste, spicy Sichuan bean paste, black bean sauce, and hoisin sauce. After the beans are fermented, they become very soft and can be crushed into a paste.

Most bean pastes are very salty. Do not start with more than 1 teaspoon. The sweetest one is Cantonese-style hoisin sauce (海鮮醬) meaning "ocean fresh sauce." It can be used in cooking, dipping, barbecue, or brushed on the pancake used to wrap up Peking Duck or to make fresh egg rolls. Every Westerner loves hoisin sauce, which is available at the Chinese market and supermarkets. Check it out.

Japanese-style bean paste, *miso,* is good for miso soup, cooking with fish, or making salad dressing that is served in Japanese restaurants. They usually come in a yellowish, beige or dark brown color, but the taste is very similar. They are very salty, too.

Fish Maw 花膠/魚肚 (hua jiao)

The texture is similar to fried pork rind that is very popular in the South of the U.S. It is pale yellow and puffy-looking but hard in texture. Crinkly shaped pieces about 10 x 12-inches are packed in large plastic bags. After it is soaked in hot water for 30-60 minutes, it can be cut up into one-inch pieces and cooked in soup or added to stir fry.

Five Spice Powder 五香粉 (wu xiang fen)

This brown spice with a very distinctive aroma is sold in four-ounce packets in Chinatown. It is usually added to braises with a large chunk of beef shank or shin cooked with soy sauce, as in Bachelor's Pot or "red cooked dishes[3]," which look like Hungarian goulash. Most Chinese never bother finding out what those five spices are, but they are Sichuan peppercorn (四川花椒), star anise (八角), clove (丁香), cinnamon (肉桂皮), and fennel seeds (茴香).

Ginger 老薑/嫩薑 (lao jiang/nen jiang)

Only fresh ginger should be used in cooking. My husband has discovered that you can keep fresh ginger almost indefinitely by soaking it in any kind of white wine. Ginger is cooked but rarely eaten except for fresh young ginger, which is a very pale yellow with a very thin skin. It is in season during the summer. Sometimes you can find it in Chinatown grocery stores. The fresh young ginger is usually

---

3 "Red cooked" (紅燒) refers to anything, usually large pieces of meat, that is slow cooked with soy sauce and five spice powder. So when it's finished, the meat will be brown with a distinctive flavor. Red cooked hard boiled eggs is another dish using this type of cooking method.

cut julienne and mixed with rice vinegar and light soy sauce to use as dipping sauce. The regular ginger usually available in the market is what the Chinese call "old ginger." There is a saying in Chinese that describes a shrewd old person, as an "old ginger"— "The old ginger is spicier than the young ginger." (薑是老的辣)

Ginger is often used with fish to get rid of the fishy smell. It is sautéed until golden brown, and discarded before the seafood is added to the wok. Ginger is used where a Western chef would use lemon to get rid of the fishy odor of seafood.

When sautéed, fresh ginger produces a distinctive aroma. If you cannot find fresh ginger, use garlic or shallot as a substitute, but NOT ginger powder.

Ginseng 人參 (ren shen)

In Chinese, the *gin* of ginseng, means "person," and *seng* means "root." A good grade of whole ginseng root is shaped like a person, with head, body, and arms.

There are two kinds of ginseng. One is red (高麗參), traditionally called "Korean Ginseng" because it was originally produced in Korea. The other kind is white, called "Stars and Stripes Ginseng," an American ginseng (花旗參) produced in Wisconsin. The red ginseng is good for people with a "cool body" (寒)—that is, someone who always has cold feet at night. White ginseng is good for people with a "hot body" (熱)—that is, someone who gets nosebleeds frequently.

It takes five years to produce a ginseng root. There are wild ginseng and cultured ginseng. For wild ginseng, the sky is the limit when it comes to price. If it has been grown deep in the mountains for many years it is called 『深山老參』.

In the old days, only rich people or royal families could afford wild ginseng. Even today wild ginseng is quite expensive. (I have seen 2 ounces sell for $485.) Ginseng is the ultimate root that the Chinese believe will strengthen one's body and health, prolong one's life, and maintain a youthful body. I remember my mother used to steam ginseng with chicken for me whenever I kept catching colds. It is also good for woman as nourishment after childbirth, and old folks to regain their strength after an illness.

Red Korean ginseng is quite expensive; one pound costs over $100. White Stars and Stripes ginseng costs about $35 for an 8 oz. pack. You can order it online through a Taiwan merchant Mr. Hsu who has cultivated a very successful ginseng farm in Wisconsin. His website is ***www.hsuginseng.com***.

Meat 肉 (ro)

Most of the time, pork is used in this recipe book. My mother had never cooked with beef and lamb. First of all beef was very scarce at the time I was growing up; only a handful of people ate beef at that time. It was expensive, and not popular with Taiwanese during the 1950s. Taiwan was an island dependent on agriculture to survive, and cows were the primary source of labor for farmers. The Taiwanese believed that it was too cruel to kill a cow for its meat after it had worked so hard all its life for the farmers.

However, if you like beef, you can substitute beef for pork. It is very important to use the correct part for each dish. Beef shin or shank can only be used for long and slow cooking because they tend to be tough. For most Chinese stir fry dishes, use rib eye, tenderloin, or London broil—or even better, filet mignon.

I am partial to pork; it is more tender and easy to cook, especially quick with a stir fry dish. As for lamb I have never tried it as my mother used to say it had an unpleasant odor. So I have never touched it. Chicken is also easy to use. Since boneless chicken is readily available, it is a good source of stir fry meat.

Most of the time before cooking, the meat (including ground meat) is marinated with soy sauce, cornstarch, egg whites (optional), and pepper, for at least 10 minutes. Using this method, the meat will come out tender and not dry. After watching a variety of cooking shows on TV, I think a main difference in cooking Chinese and Western food is the marinating.

MSG 味精 (wei jing)

MSG is sold as "Accent" in the U.S. or under the Japanese commercial brand "Ajinomoto."

In the old days, as meat on the dining table was scarce because of the price, to make any dish tasty, most housewives and even cooks would add a pinch of MSG to any vegetable dish to make it tasty. It's not surprising that a lot of restaurants rely heavily on MSG to make their food taste good. In Taiwan, there was an MSG commercial with the jingle "To make everything tastes as good as chicken soup."

MSG has become a controversial ingredient in Chinese cooking. Some claim that it gives them an allergic reaction or some sort of hot flash. I once had a hot flash effect after I ate at a Chinese restaurant; however, in home cooking I have never had any problems using MSG, and I have used it for as long as I can remember. It is almost universally used in canned soups sold in supermarkets.

Oyster Sauce 蠔油 (hao you)

Oyster sauce is a Cantonese-style sauce. It is supposed to be an extract from the oyster, but with modern techniques it is likely to have some preservatives and taste enhancers. It has a distinctive fishy taste and is quite salty. I don't use it too often. If you like the Beef with Oyster Sauce in Chinese restaurants, buy a small bottle to start with. Don't add any salt if you have added the oyster sauce already. After opening, the bottle needs to be refrigerated although the bottle may not say so.

Rice 米飯 (mi fan)

Most Chinese people from the southern part of China eat rice. However, in the northern part of China, including Beijing and the northeast, people eat flour-based staples more than rice, like steamed buns.

Rice comes in long grain and short grain varieties. Chinese restaurants across the U.S. serve long grain rice because many early Chinese restaurants were established by immigrants from Canton. Canton and other parts of China eat long grain rice as a staple, except for the northeast which was occupied by the Japanese during World War II. Following the Japanese tradition, they eat short grain rice.

Long grain is drier and harder. I grew up eating short grain rice that is more moist, chewy, and fluffy in texture. I am particularly partial to the short grain rice grown in California, called Kokuho Rice. (The

Japanese brand name, 國寶米, means "national treasure.")

Short grain rice can be found in Japanese restaurants, for both regular rice and sushi rice. Rice preference is very personal, but the cooking methods are about the same. To tell you the truth, I have never cooked rice using a regular pot for as long as I can remember. The rice cooker was invented in the 1950s. To use a rice cooker, you simply push a button. Rice cookers are readily available from kitchenware stores now, so you don't have to venture into Chinatown to get one.

Rice Sticks 米粉 (mi fen)

Rice noodles comes in many forms, some are thin, like white hair in bundles. Some are a little heavier, like the Vietnamese *pho* in straight long sticks. They are all made from rice. It is very popular in Taiwan, Singapore—which has the well-known Singapore Curry Rice Noodle—and the southern part of China in Fujian Province. It is one of my favorites, even more so than Italian spaghetti. However, it is one ingredient that is not easy to handle. If they are not prepared correctly, they come out either too hard or the rice sticks break into tiny shreds. In Taiwan, there are stores that only specialize in stir-fried rice sticks. I often dream of those eateries back home in Taiwan. Because it is made from rice, it is not as filling as spaghetti made from wheat.

Rice Vinegar 米醋 (mi cu)

When selecting a rice vinegar get a Japanese brand. They are light, and especially good as dipping sauce when mixed with soy sauce. The vinegar from Shan-Xi, China (山西醋) is supposed to be the best; another well-known brand is from Zhen-Jiang, China (鎮江醋). White vinegar from the supermarket is also good, but it is stronger and the flavor is not as subtle.

Sea Cucumber 海參 (hai shen)

Dried sea cucumber looks like a small black pickle. I have never seen a fresh sea cucumber. It is gelatinous and very low in calories. Because of the health benefits of eating sea cucumber, it's called "sea ginseng" (海參) in Chinese.

The average sea cucumber weighs about 2 ounces and is about 5 inches long, but they come in different sizes. The price is rather high. A large one could cost about $15. A package of ten small ones weighing 2 oz. each costs $26. It takes quite a while to reconstitute in water, 7 days to be exact.

The Fu Yuan Restaurant on Lin Yi Street in Taipei (台北市臨沂街馥園餐廳) is well known for its Scallion-Flavored Sea Cucumbers (蔥燒海參). They have two employees whose full time job is to take care of the sea cucumber soaking process.[4] Sea cucumber is soft and chewy when it is cooked right. There is a slimy flaky substance on the skin. Use a sponge to clean it off. The sea cucumber itself does not have too much taste, much like shark fin. It is the texture that is interesting. After cooking a long time with meat, sea cucumber's soft but chewy texture comes out, satisfying one's palate. Sea cucumber is one of my favorite dishes.

There is also frozen sea cucumber available in Chinatown grocery stores already soaked through and

---

4   *100 Best Restaurant Dish Guide in Taiwan* by LEE Ze-Zhi, 1995, Eating All Chinese Publisher, Taipei. "台灣100種 最美味的佳肴"，李澤治著，1995， 台北吃遍中國出版社).

ready to cook. One time my friend Grace Lee (李懿真), who was working for the Taipei Economic and Cultural Office, took me to a restaurant located in Manhattan, Tong's Pavilion (山王飯店). She ordered a Red Cooked Sea Cucumber (紅燒海參) dish. That was the most gorgeous and tasty sea cucumber dish I have ever had. The whole sea cucumber was gleaming with brown sauce. Grace told me that the restaurant was opened by the chef who used to cook for CHIANG Kai-Shek.

Sesame Oil 麻油 (ma you)

Sesame oil is made from black sesame seeds. It has a very distinctive aroma. The best kind is a dark amber color. In Chinese medicine, it is considered a very "hot" (熱) food.

People are assessed in Chinese medicine as having "hot" (熱) or "cool" (寒) bodies. People who get nosebleeds are "hot"; people who get cold feet at night are usually "cool." The sesame oil is "hot," or when cooked with meat and mixed with wine will give a body a "hot" effect, which is why it is considered especially good for women after childbirth as it gives nourishment to their bodies.

Sesame oil has become synonymous with Chinese food. It is especially good to enhance the aroma of meat or vegetable dishes. It is used in a manner similar to extra virgin olive oil in Italian cooking. It is a matter of tradition. A few houses from my home in Taiwan, there was a sesame oil press store. They used the old fashioned way, and literally pressed out the sesame oil. My mother always sent me out with an empty bottle to get their first press sesame oil. It was dark and aromatic, the real sesame oil. The sesame oil nowadays is lighter. The darker kind of sesame oil still can be found in Taiwan.

Sesame Paste 芝麻醬 (zhi ma jiang)

Sesame paste is made from sesame seeds. It is beige in color, and is usually mixed with bean paste and other condiments to make a flavorful topping sauce on cold noodles or cold chicken. It is very aromatic.

Sha Cha Barbecue Sauce 沙茶醬 (sha cha jiang)

This sauce is made out of peanuts, soy beans, shallots, garlic, soy sauce, chili oil, five spice powder, dried shrimp, dried small fish, and more. It is very versatile, and can be used for stir fry with meat, like Beef with Sha Cha Sauce. It can also be used for hot pot sauce, and mixed into egg and soy sauce into which the diner dips meat and vegetables cooked in the hot pot. There is also a vegetarian Sha Cha Sauce. The best brand is one from Taiwan called "Bull Head Barbecue Sauce" (牛頭牌沙茶醬).

Shark Fin 魚翅 (yu chi)

Shark fin is a status symbol in Chinese food. It is an extremely high priced item; one pound costs between $210 to $350, depending on the size of the fin. Some restaurants in Taipei display a huge shark fin in the lobby window to attract the attention of customers walking in. At wedding banquets, even if it is held in a fancy restaurant, if there is no shark fin, the host will be labeled "cheap."

However when the former Taiwan President Mr. CHEN Shui-Bian (陳水扁), a native Taiwanese was elected the President of Taiwan, his official banquets for foreign dignitaries did not include shark fin any more. Mr. Chen came from a humble background; his father was a tenant farmer who struggled all his life to provide the family with a decent living. When Mr. Chen was a child, he asked his mother why they only picked yams (Taiwanese potato) after there were none left in the fields. He didn't know that they were picking the leavings from after the regular harvest had finished. For national banquets, he was known for serving popular, local food items that were affordable even to the poor.

Soy Sauce 醬油 (jiang you)

Soy sauce is one ingredient that you must have to cook any Chinese dish. Unlike salt, the combination of soy sauce with food, particularly meat, produces a special aroma that distinguishes Chinese food from any other kind of food. Use the regular kind of soy sauce or light soy sauce. If you venture into Chinatown, there are many kinds of soy sauce: dark, regular, light, or a thick sauce-like soy sauce used for dipping.

Naturally brewed soy sauce (aged 18-24 months) that is made in Japan is good for everything. It has a true soy sauce flavor, which is worth getting even though it may cost a little bit more. You will have to go to a Japanese market to find it. In supermarkets, there is Japanese-made Kikkoman soy sauce available. The worst soy sauce I have ever tasted is the small plastic packets of soy sauce which come with Chinese restaurant takeout. Just throw them away; it is not soy sauce. It tastes like water with salt and food coloring.

Sweet Rice (a.k.a. Sticky Rice or Glutinous Rice) 糯米 (no mi)

Sweet rice is mostly prepared for special occasions, like a baby's first birthday or it is made into a sweet, such as Eight Treasure Rice (八寶飯). It has to be cooked and steamed in two steps to come out right. Glutinous Fried Rice (油飯) is a speciality of the Taiwanese. Whenever my eldest daughter Tina comes home from abroad, that is the one dish she wants to eat.

Taro Root 芋頭 (shan yu)

Taro root is very similar to Malanga Coco, but the latter has a blander flavor. When peeling a taro root, there is a slimy substance under the skin which some people are allergic to, so wear gloves when peeling. The other way is to boil the whole taro root for 3-4 minutes, and then remove the skin. Alternatively, rinse clean the whole taro root, cut it into four wedges, and place on a plate and steam for 10 minutes. Remove the skin and steam again if it does not steam through the first time.

A good taro root tastes very fluffy and good. Taro root, like potatoes, can be deep fried. It is usually steamed and served with soy sauce. A lot of time it is mixed with rice powder to make a taro root rice cake.

Thousand Year Egg (Preserved Duck Egg) 皮蛋 (pi dan)

This is one of the strangest Chinese foods. For people unfamiliar with the egg, it smells stinky. When I was little, people used to tell me the thousand year egg was soaked in horse urine. The egg used to be coated with mud and rice hulls to cushion the egg against breakage.

In the old days, it was coated with a mixture of salt, hay, pine needle ashes, lime, tea leaves, red sticky mud, and rice hull and kept in a large ceramic pot at room temperature for a couple of months. The natural alkali from the lime, hay, and pine needle ashes contains potassium carbonate and sodium carbonate that create the chemical reaction in the egg and changes its texture and color entirely.

Crack the mud outside and remove the shell. Inside, the egg white becomes a translucent, black hard jelly consistency; while the egg yolk becomes a gooey dark green. It can be served as is with a little soy sauce for dipping. No need to cook! Somehow the chemical reaction cooks the egg. Nowadays, the egg is packed inside a styrofoam container and individually wrapped with plastic. An easy way to serve it is to chop a thousand year egg and sprinkle over a square of tofu, then sprinkle with soy sauce. There is a well-known Cantonese porridge that mixes thousand year egg with ground pork.

Tiger Lilies 金針 (jin zhen)

In New England, you often find tiger lilies blooming in gardens, but I am not sure if they are the same as the dried tiger lilies used in Chinese cooking. Dried tiger lilies are an important ingredient in vegetarian Chinese food. To prepare them, soak 10 minutes in hot water, then pluck off the tough stem end of the tiger lilies, and tie the lily into a knot, so it does not fall apart into thin pieces while cooking. Of course you don't have to knot them if it is troublesome for you, but it's easier to find the tiger lilies in the dish if they've been knotted. Most of the time, tiger lilies are used with a mix of vegetables as in egg rolls, hot and sour soup, or some vegetarian dishes like Buddha's Delight (羅漢齋). The texture is crunchy with a distinctive tiger lily aroma.

Tofu or Bean Curd 豆腐 (do fu or to fu)

Tofu is the least expensive staple for the Chinese. It is "poor people's steak," a hugely versatile product. Everyone can afford it. Yet it can be prepared into exotic dishes or as part of daily meals. There are many forms of tofu, but the one most people are familiar with is white tofu. Supermarkets carry three kinds: silken, soft, and hard.

An array of flavored tofu is also available for the Western palate with names like French Country style tofu—although I guess the French are not well-known for tofu products, but in the U.S. everything labeled "French" seems to indicate a fancy or delicious product. Unless you have tried those flavored tofu, and like them, I don't recommend them at all.

Traditional types of tofu found in the Chinese market are fried tofu, brown five-spiced tofu, tofu noodles, and "bean flower" (豆花), which is a tofu with a yogurt-like texture. Tofu itself has no strong flavor, unlike cheese. It is the combination of other ingredients that give tofu its taste, and its texture that makes it an extraordinary ingredient.

Tofu is made from soy bean milk. To make tofu, soak soy beans in water overnight; puree with water and squeeze out the liquid (soy bean milk); cook the soy bean milk; add calcium and magnesium chloride (found in drug stores) to coagulate. When the soy milk is still hot and after the curds have formed, drain the liquid in a tofu mold lined with cheesecloth. After the liquid has drained, the tofu is shaped into slabs.

You can find really soft, white, Japanese-style tofu at Japanese markets, or the firmer regular kind at Chinese markets or supermarkets. The "silken" kind sold at supermarkets is pretty good, but it is too soft for cooking. The very soft kind can be simply served cut into small cubes, and sprinkled with soy sauce and cilantro. The soft and firm tofu from the supermarket are generally too coarse, but if you cannot find the real thing, they are acceptable.

You can judge the quality of tofu by looking at the formation of the curd. My home town Sing Zhuang (新莊) was well known for tofu products. During my elementary school years, there was a tofu shop right across the street from my house, an old hunchbacked lady took care of the tofu making. The art was in coagulating the soy milk. She was so well known that people came from other towns just to buy her tofu, which had a tender and smooth curd.

Because tofu is easy to eat, white and soft, almost like the skin of a young girl, there is a Chinese saying "Eat tofu" (吃豆腐 chi dou fu) which refers to a guy flirting with a girl.

Tofu Products 豆腐類 (do fu lei)

Tofu comes in several forms other than the white tofu available on the market. There is five spice tofu (五香豆腐干), fried tofu (油豆腐), fermented tofu (豆腐乳)—served with rice porridge—and one called "stinky tofu"(臭豆腐).

The "stinky" aroma of eateries selling stinky tofu can be smelled miles away. They don't need any sign to promote their product. People who like it are crazy about this special kind of tofu. Stinky tofu is usually deep fried and dipped in spicy chili sauce mixed with soy sauce.

There are also several varieties of dried tofu: tofu threads (豆干絲), tofu sheets (豆腐皮), tofu sheet sticks (腐竹), and tofu sheet knots (腐竹卷). Drying is an ingenious way to preserve tofu for an indefinite period of time. Tofu sheets can be used as a wrapper like an egg roll skin, but it is lighter and less doughy. It can also be used in stir fry or added to soup. If you see wrinkly, large yellow sheets displayed in a Chinatown grocery, that is tofu sheets. Tofu sticks need to be softened by soaking in hot water for about 30 minutes or simmered in soup for at least 15 minutes until it is soft and edible.

Tofu products are the main staple of Chinese vegetarians. In a fancy vegetarian banquet, the tofu sheet is used like papier-mâché to create the shape of a chicken, duck or fish. In the old days, tofu took the place of meat for those who could not afford the luxury of buying meat. Tofu is inexpensive enough for everyone to eat.

Tree Ears/Cloud Ears 木耳/雲耳 (mu er/yun er)

Tree ears are a fungus which grows on trees, similar to mushrooms growing on wood. Tree ears are an important ingredient in Chinese vegetarian cooking. They are black, and have a crunchy texture, but without much flavor. Recently it's been said that tree ears are good for fighting high cholesterol. There is no equivalent among Western ingredients. When it is mixed with other ingredients, tree ears enhance the foods, adding interesting texture to it.

Whenever I feel that a one-vegetable dish is too boring, I will add tree ears to it. They are sold dried, and must first be reconstituted by soaking at least 30 minutes in hot water. They will expand a lot. A half cup of dried tree ears goes a long way.

The summer of 2000, I was back in Taiwan to see my second sister Shu-Ying (淑英) who was recuperating from surgery. For the first time I saw fresh tree ears at the market. They were as big as my palm and delicious like nothing else. I helped my sister cook, and I was so delighted with the newly found product that I made fresh tree ears almost everyday.

My mother had a superstition about tree ears. She used to say not to cook them for dinner—specifically after dark—but she had never told us why. My sister said that maybe tree ears are hard to digest, being crunchy in texture, so my mother did not want to cook them for dinner. Or, perhaps because tree ears are black, it indicates they are for the after world. Nobody really knows, but it makes an interesting anecdote about tree ears.

Water Chestnuts荸薺 (bi qi)

Water chestnuts are shaped like a chestnut, except the outer skin is very thin. Fresh ones are normally only found in Chinatown. As they are very perishable, squeeze them and select only the ones which are firm all over; often parts of it will be rotten.

Use a knife to cut off the top and bottom, and then peel off the skin. Pare off any yellowish parts. A good water chestnut is white all over. Put the peeled chestnuts in a pot of cold water with a pinch of salt, to prevent discoloration. The water chestnut is best when it is crushed and mixed with ground meat to use as filling for dumplings. Place inside a large plastic bag to prevent splattering, smash them with the flat side of a cleaver or mix it in a food processor with other ingredients. If you cannot find fresh ones, canned ones can be substituted, but the flavor is not as good. For the sweetness of fresh water chestnuts, it is worth the hard work of peeling.

CHAPTER 5

上菜禮儀

About Chinese Dining Culture

About Chinese Dining Culture

Serving Portions in Chinese Food 上菜份量 (shang cai fen liang)

Chinese food is rarely served in individual portions as in the Western serving tradition. Instead, it is served in a single plate that is shared by everyone. The most common family meal presentation is "three dishes and one soup" (三菜一湯) for a family of four to five people, or "four dishes and one soup" (四菜一湯) served to a group of six male college students at their mandatory summer army camp in Cheng Gong Hill, Taichung (台中成功嶺).

During the 1960s every male college student in Taiwan had to report for three summers of basic army training at Cheng Gong Hill. For a group of about six people, there was always at least three or four different dishes for variety. When we are ordering dishes in a restaurant, the same dishes are never ordered for different people. Sharing food is an essential part of eating Chinese food.

That is also one way to explain the lifestyle of Chinese vs. Westerners. Chinese always treat a family as a single unit. However the Westerner sees one individual as a single unit. There was a research group, which looked at one order of Kun Pao Chicken (宮保雞丁) from a Chinese restaurant, assuming it was for one person to eat, and concluded that Chinese food contains too many calories for a person. One order of Kun Pao Chicken is usually sufficient to feed three to four people. How could that kind of research be accurate? The researchers didn't even know how the Chinese serve food.

I have a friend who told me that one time she saw four Westerners order the same Ma Po Do Fu (麻婆豆腐) at a Chinese restaurant. She could not bear to look. The Chinese and Western customs are entirely different as far as serving food goes.

A distinctive difference between a typical American meal and Chinese meal is, dessert was not an important part of the daily meal in my house. I don't remember our family ever having any dessert at the end of a meal. We ate dessert-like dishes for special occasions. We made offerings to Buddha with rice cakes filled with sweet red bean paste stamped with a wooden mold that had the design of a turtle shell, signifying long life. For weddings or the birth of a baby, we made glutinous rice cakes with or without fillings or sweet soup with small glutinous rice balls.

Most kitchens in Taiwan were and still are not equipped with an oven, so it is not easy to bake something. Not surprisingly, most Chinese restaurants do not offer dessert, although sweet tapioca red bean soup might appear at the end of a banquet in some restaurants nowadays.

Dessert 甜點

Of course, there were elaborate desserts in Chinese cuisine in the era of royal family dynasties, as described in a novel by Qing dynasty (清朝) writer CAO Xue-Qing (曹雪芹) in *The Dream of the Red Chamber* (紅樓夢). The author came from a wealthy family. His great grandfather was a court-appointed fabric merchant (江寧織造) for the royal family of the Qing Dynasty in the Forbidden City (紫禁城). An incident caused the family to lose their fortune when his father was the head of the family. The author had to struggle to finish this book. *The Dream of the Red Chamber* has been translated into English. It is one of the most famous Chinese classics. You can read it to get a glimpse of family life for the highest upper crust of China during the Qing Dynasty around the 18th century: how they ate, how they played, and how they loved. To the author, it was only a dream. In the end the main character JIA Bao-Yu (賈寶玉) leaves home and to become a monk after a lifetime of privilege.

CHAPTER 6

Soups

Soups

Soup is a very important part of Taiwanese cuisine. As Taiwan is sub-tropical for almost half a year, from May through mid-October, the temperature hovers between 80° to 95° F and sometimes goes over 100° with unbearable humidity. So at a typical Taiwanese banquet, out of 10 to 12 dishes, nearly half of those dishes will be soup—especially in the old days before 1960 when there was only a handful of air conditioned facilities available.

A very typical Taiwanese banquet dish is as follows: the chef steams dishes neatly lined with pieces of spareribs, duck, or chicken in a big bowl, topped with fried taro or potato chunks as filler. When it is fully cooked, the chef will get an even bigger bowl, to cover the steamed bowl and flip the food of the steamed bowl into the bigger bowl. The big bowl will display the intricately arranged food in a dome. Some have pretty elaborate patterns. Then a clear stock soup is poured into the bigger bowl before serving to guests. With this kind of operation, the chef can prepare quite a few dishes (steamed in a huge steamer) ahead of time. At serving time, the chef just ladles in the piping hot soup.

Fish Chowder 魚片濃湯
(Yu pian nong tang) **

This is a variation of New England Fish or Clam Chowder. This dish is simple and delicious. It is a quick, last-minute dish to feed even a large group of people. With some toasted French bread it is a perfect meal for a cold, snowy evening.

Yield: 6-8 servings

- ½ to ¾ lbs. haddock
- ½ to ¾ lbs. cod or sole (*Use two kinds of fish of your choice. Haddock, cod, or sole go well together.*)
- 2 medium-sized Russet potatoes
- 1 medium-sized yellow onion (*I don't recommend the white onion. Vidalia onions are especially nice. They cook into a soft and sweet mass.*)
- 2 Tbsp. canola oil
- ½ cup heavy cream (or light cream)
- 1 to 2 tsp. balsamic vinegar
- Salt to taste
- Black or white pepper

1 Peel and cut the potatoes into ½-inch cubes. Bring them to a boil in 2½ cups water, then turn to medium heat and let cook another 5-8 minutes or until the potato can be pierced easily with a fork, but is not falling apart. Set the whole pot aside with the potato and the liquid.

2 Peel the onion, discarding any dried or damaged layers. Cut into four wedges and soak in cold water (to prevent your eyes from tearing up when you cut them.) Slice the onions thinly.

3 Heat 2 Tbsp. canola oil in a frying pan over medium heat; add the onion and a dash of salt. Sauté the onion until it caramelizes to a light brown (about 10-15 minutes). Add the cooked onion to the potato pot.

4 Put the haddock on the cutting board, skin-side down and use a knife to pull off the haddock skin. From one end separate about ½ inch of the skin from the fish meat so you can hold the skin .While pressing the knife blade against the skin, slowly cut between the skin and the fish meat to remove the skin. (This is not easy to do; you can have a fishmonger remove the skin for you.)

Uses for Fish Skin:

For a tasty appetizer or a crunchy sprinkle over salad, cut the fish skin into strips about ½-inch wide and 2 inches in length, dredge in some flour and deep fry. Haddock and salmon skin are especially good, served with rice wrapped in a piece of seaweed, like a hand roll in a Japanese restaurant.

5 Cut the fish into ½ inch cubes and rub all over with a little salt, and then add it to the onion and potatoes. Mix well and bring the whole pot to a gentle boil over medium heat (do not turn the heat too high otherwise it will burn) or until the fish has changed color and thoroughly cooked, about 7-10 minutes. Add ½ cup heavy cream (or light cream) and 1-2 tsp. balsamic vinegar. Mix well and salt to taste. Sprinkle with black or white pepper and serve hot.

Onion can be added directly with the potato without first sautéing. However sautéed onion tastes a lot sweeter and will "melt" into the soup with striking results. Balsamic vinegar adds a natural sweetness; use the one from Modena, Italy—the hometown of my favorite opera singer, Luciano Pavarotti—for best results. Other types of vinegar tend to be too sour.

Mahogany Clam Soup 蛤蜊湯 (ge li tang) *

There are many kinds of clams in the fish market. Any type of clam will work for this recipe, but Mahogany clams are inexpensive, a good size and look pretty in the soup. This type of soup is often found in Japanese restaurant menus.

Yield: 3-4 servings

 1 lb. mahogany clams

 2 to 2½ cups water

 4 to 5 slices fresh ginger (Do not substitute with ginger powder. It is bitter.)

 Salt and black pepper to taste

1 Soak the clams in a pot of cold water with a dash of salt for 2-3 hours to allow the clams to spit out the sand inside. (Do not skip this step, otherwise the clams will add sand to the soup.)

2 Rinse the clams clean; wipe the shell with a sponge; and place in a large pot with 2-2½ cups water. Too much water will dilute the taste.

3 Add the ginger slices. Bring to a boil, and cook for 5 minutes or until the clams open. It usually does not take too long to cook. Discard any unopened clams. Salt to taste and sprinkle with black pepper and serve hot.

After cooking, the unopened clams are the ones that were not alive. Don't eat them.

Corn Soup with Chicken

雞茸玉米湯 (ji rong yu mi tang) *

This soup takes advantage of canned creamed corn available here in the States. It is a very popular dish in Chinese restaurants, and is also very easy to make.

Yield: 3-4 servings

- 1 can (14¾ oz. or 418 g) creamed sweet corn (Green Giant is the best brand.)
- 1 can water (Use the creamed corn can to measure.)
- 4 to 6 oz. chopped chicken breast or ground chicken

Chicken Marinade:

- 1 egg white (Reserve the egg yolk to mix with the 2 eggs later in the recipe.)
- 1 tsp. cornstarch
- A pinch of salt
- 1 Tbsp. cornstarch
- ½ cup water
- 2 eggs
- 1 tsp. water

1 Marinate the chicken in egg white, salt, and cornstarch and set aside.

2 Mix one can of creamed corn with one can of water in a pot. Mix thoroughly and bring to a boil. Reduce to medium heat. Break the marinated chicken into smaller lumps as you add it to the mixture gradually. Mix well. Bring to another boil and reduce heat to medium low. In a separate bowl, mix 1 Tbsp. cornstarch with ½ cup water. Gradually add the starch water to the corn/chicken mixture. Gently mix well. Turn off the heat, but leave the pot on the stove.

3 Beat two eggs plus reserved egg yolk with 1 tsp. water. While mixing the soup in a slow circular motion, slowly pour the egg in a thin, steady stream. Salt to taste. Serve hot.

This dish can be prepared ahead of time and heated up at serving time.

The Best Shark Fin Soup — Taiwanese-Style 台式魚翅湯 (tai shi yu chi tang) *****

Shark Fin Soup is the ultimate in Taiwanese cooking. My mother made the most memorable shark fin soup that I have ever tasted. We only had shark fin soup when there were special occasions for a banquet for special guests or on Chinese New Year.

I was in Taiwan in the 1990s at a time when every restaurant was promoting their best version of shark fin soup. My husband's sister took me to the most famous one, the "Seafood King" Restaurant (海霸王) in Taipei. It was bland and with only a small quantity of shark fin displayed on top of a small dish and had no real flavor. Like tofu, cellophane noodle and sea cucumber, shark fin does not have a taste of its own, but the texture makes it interesting.

When it is cooked right with other ingredients, it is a dream dish for anyone. Nowadays, shark fin is pre-processed and easy to use. In the old days, shark fin had to be soaked for a long time to separate the fin from the skin, and then cooked for a long time to soften. I have since cooked it a few times to satisfy my cravings. The ingredients are readily available.

The price of ready-to-cook shark fin is not cheap. One 5 oz. package for $45 can be used to make two dishes, but one pot of soup will serve 6 people or more.

The original dried shark fin costs between $210 to $350 per pound. It takes quite a while to soak it through before it is ready to cook. Some fancy restaurants in Taipei often display a huge piece of dried shark fin in their display window. A small bowl of shark fin soup at a Chinese restaurant in Boston is easily $20, and only available by special order.

It is not practical to cook a small quantity of shark fin soup. It takes at least three hours to make—not including the soaking time. The following is a version that I adapted from the memory of how my mother used to make it.

The presence of shark fin soup at a banquet is an indicator of how luxurious the banquet is. It brings satisfaction to every guest. It's like seeing caviar in French cuisine. I was in Taiwan in late 2004, and every wedding banquet I attended had one or two dishes with shark fin.

Yield: 8-10 servings

For Shark Fin Preparation

Half of a 5 oz. package of shark fin
(*It looks like yellowish, shiny, translucent, thin spaghetti. It is available only in Chinatown grocery stores for about $45. In Boston Chinatown, they carry the Diamond brand; ask for it at the counter.*)

3 stalks scallions

3 slices fresh ginger

1 Tbsp. Cognac or Sauvignon Blanc

For Chicken Stock Preparation

One game hen or ½ of a chicken breast with bones (*Do not use boneless chicken as it will not produce a savory chicken stock.*)

3 to 6 stalks scallions (*More scallion is better.*)

1 Tbsp. Cognac or Sauvignon Blanc

Black pepper to taste

Salt to taste

For Egg Preparation:

¼ to ½ cup canola oil

2 eggs, beaten

For Chinese Napa Cabbage Preparation:

5 to 6 cloves shallot (*More is better.*)

1½ lbs. Chinese Napa cabbage (*roughly one medium cabbage.*)

Salt to taste

½ cup water

1 Tbsp. balsamic vinegar or Chinese black vinegar

Black pepper

Salt to taste

1 *Shark Fin Preparation:* Cut off the tops of the scallions, peel off the outer layer and cut off the damaged ends of the scallion, and then cut into 2 inch lengths. Gently break off about half from the shark fin package and save the rest for next time. It is pretty crumbly, so quite easy to break off. It is too decadent to use the whole package for one dish. Soak in cold water for one hour. Drain the water and put the reconstituted shark fin in a pot with enough cold water to cover the shark fin (at least 2 inches of water over the shark fin). Add the scallions, fresh ginger, and Cognac. Bring to a boil and then reduce heat to medium low to simmer for 30 minutes. Drain the water. Discard the ginger slices.

2 *Chicken Pre-Preparation:* Remove the paper package inside the game hen with the giblets, neck, liver, gizzard, and heart, and rinse them clean. Rub the game hen with some salt, and rinse clean. Bring a pot of water to boil, and pour the boiling water over the whole body of the game hen inside and out, and drain. The boiling water removes the game hen's raw smell.

3 *Chicken Stock Preparation:* Place the whole game hen in a large pot. Add water until it covers the whole hen well. Cut off the tops of the scallions and any damaged ends. Use the side of a knife, to pound the scallions flat and cut into about 3 inches length Add the pounded scallion, 1 Tbsp. Cognac, and sprinkle with a pinch of salt and a pinch of black pepper. Bring to a boil then reduce heat to low, and let simmer covered for about 30-40 minutes or more until the meat is tender. Remove the game hen from the pot. Skim off the foam floating on top. When the game hen cools down, remove the skin and separate the meat from the bone. Shred the meat into strings with your hands. Set aside the shredded meat. Reserve the chicken broth.

4 *Egg Preparation:* Heat up ¼ to ½ cup canola oil over medium heat for about 3 minutes. Beat two eggs well. Drop a little bit of egg into the oil to see if it is hot enough. If it sizzles, it is hot enough. Circling around the wok as you go, slowly pour the egg in a thin stream into the oil. Stop pouring when one layer of egg covers the surface. The egg mixture will puff up. Remove with a spatula or a sieve and let the oil drain. Repeat the process until the eggs are all fried. It is important to have enough oil, so that when the egg is fried, it will float. If too much egg is poured in all at once, the fried egg will be too thick. The idea is to fry the egg so it will come out very stringy and light. Actually it is better to pour the egg over a sieve as you move the sieve around over the oil, but once one layer of egg is completed, stop, remove the fried egg, and start another batch.

5 ***Chinese Napa Cabbage Preparation:*** Peel the leaves off the Napa cabbage and wash well. Then shred by stacking the leaves and cutting crosswise. Peel the shallot and thinly slice. Heat up 2-3 tablespoon canola oil in a wok, add shallot slices and stir fry until golden brown, but not too brown, otherwise it will burn. Add shredded cabbage, sprinkle with a little salt. Stir well and cover. Turn heat to medium and let it cook for about 5 minutes. Uncover and add ½ cup water and stir well. Reduce heat to low. Cover again for another 20 minutes or until the cabbage turns translucent and limp, but occasionally stir the cabbage. Set aside the cooked cabbage.

6 Add the cooked shark fin to the chicken stock pot. Add 1 cup water and bring the whole pot to a boil and reduce heat to low. Cover and cook for 2 hours.

7 Add cabbage, eggs and shredded chicken to the shark fin soup and let simmer over low heat for 30 minutes to 1 hour. (Longer is better, for the flavors to blend well.) Add 1 tablespoon balsamic vinegar or Chinese black vinegar and mix well. Salt to taste, and sprinkle with some white or black pepper. Serve hot.

Hot and Sour Soup 酸辣湯
(suan la tang) ***

Hot and Sour Soup is immensely popular at Chinese restaurants. Its origins are as a home-style soup from Sichuan Province, well-known for its spicy food. The original recipe calls for chicken, pork (or ham), sea cucumber, squid, bamboo shoots, tofu, and egg. Here in the States, most Chinese restaurants use pork, tree ears, and tiger lilies.

Every Chinese family has their own version of Hot and Sour Soup. This is one soup where more ingredients are better than fewer. You can adjust the seasonings and ingredients to your own taste, just do not use any leafy vegetables as they will become yellow and look unappetizing.

Hot and Sour Soup pairs well with jiao zi *(called Chinese ravioli or Pot Stickers). In Taiwan it is also very common to add "coagulated pork blood" to this dish. It comes in a large chunk, like tofu slabs. The texture is like tofu, silky and smooth and a dull coffee color, with not much taste. It sounds awful to people who have never heard of it. I mention it here so you will know what it is if you have the opportunity to try it, on a trip to Taiwan, Hong Kong, or China, where it is a very common ingredient. Historically, because of the shortage of food, every part of the slaughtered animal found its way into meals.*

Yield: 5-6 servings

　　1 lb. chicken wings *(for soup stock)*

　　6 to 8 oz. pork loin, cut into thin strips

　　Pork Marinade:

　　1 to 2 tsp. Sauvignon Blanc or your favorite wine

　　1 tsp. soy sauce

　　1 to 2 tsp. cornstarch

　　½ cup dried tree ears

　　One flat can bamboo shoots

　　One square of "soft" tofu cut into thin strips

　　1 carrot

　　3 to 4 slices fresh ginger *(Buy the pale yellow, young ginger if you can. It is usually available in Chinatown during the summer.)*

2 to 3 stalks scallion

1 to 2 tsp. soy sauce

1 tsp. Balsamic vinegar or rice vinegar

A pinch of black pepper

Chili paste or Tabasco™

½ cup water

1 to 2 Tbsp. cornstarch

1 to 2 eggs, beaten

Fresh coriander (optional)

Optional for Frying Chicken Wings Used to Make Stock:

2 tsp. soy sauce

½ cup cornstarch or flour

2 cup canola oil for frying

1 Combine pork strips with marinade and set aside.

2 Soak the dried tree ears in hot water for one hour, and then briskly rub them with both hands in a pot of water. Pick out the tree ears instead of pouring out the water, since the bottom of the pot will have sand. Discard the water. Check each tree ear for a little stem-like piece—where the tree ear attached to the tree. Cut off that tough bit with a small knife and discard. Place tree ears back in a pot of water and repeat the same cleaning procedure two more times. Let the tree ears soak in clean water until ready to cook. Cut into thin strips.

3 Feel the bottom of each bamboo shoot. If the wide bottom feels coarse, that part is very tough. Slice off the bottom until it feels smooth to the touch. Cut the bamboo shoots into thin strips.

4 Peel the carrot and julienne into thin strips, or use a box grater with larger holes to shred.

5 Rub off the ginger skin with the back of a small knife. Cut 3-4 slices of fresh ginger, stack the slices together and cut into very thin strips.

6 Wash the scallions; cut off the tops and any damaged ends; and then cut into 2-inch lengths. Cut lengthwise into thin strips.

7 Bring 4-5 cups water to a boil in a large pot. Rinse chicken wings, add to the boiling water, add a pinch of salt and bring to another boil. Reduce heat to medium low, and cover, simmering 30 minutes. Skim off any foam floating on top of the soup. Reserve the broth.

For Serving Chicken Wings from Broth Making as a Separate Dish:

Take out the chicken wings and sprinkle with 2 tsp. soy sauce, ½ cup cornstarch (or flour), mix well and shake off the excess cornstarch or flour. Deep fry chicken wings and serve. Chicken wings will be very tender, a delicious bonus to making Hot and Sour Soup.

9 Add tree ears, tofu, bamboo shoots, and carrots to the chicken stock. Bring to a boil. Try to separate the marinated pork strips into small lumps, and add to the stock. Bring to another boil, mix well, and reduce heat to medium and cook for another 10-15 minutes.

10 Reduce heat to low, add 1-2 tsp soy sauce, vinegar, black pepper, and chili paste or Tabasco. Adjust seasonings to taste. Mix ½ cup water with 1-2 Tbsp. cornstarch and add to the soup mixture stirring well. Add beaten egg in a steady thin stream while simultaneously stirring in one direction so the egg becomes a feather-like texture. Egg flower soup uses this technique. Turn off the heat, and garnish with thin strips of fresh ginger or fresh coriander. Remove the soup from heat and serve hot.

Fresh Shell Pasta Soup

貓耳朵/麵疙瘩

(mao er duo/mian ge da) ***

The "pasta" used here resembles Italian gnocchi. One restaurant in China asks customers to break dough for their pasta into bits, which the waiter then takes into the kitchen. The chef pours piping hot soup with meat and vegetable over the bowl of customer-created pasta, which is served to the customers. It is a rather interesting way of serving. Here I use dried pasta shells to replace the fresh dough.

Besides pasta shells, any other kind of short pasta like tortellini and capelletti can be substituted. The ingredients can be replaced with whatever is available. Just make sure the ingredients are cut into similar sized shapes. The fresh dough recipe is also included.

Yield: 5-6 servings

3½ cups chicken stock

4 oz. pork loin

Pork Marinade:

1 tsp. soy sauce

1 tsp. Sauvignon Blanc

A pinch of black pepper

1 tsp. cornstarch

4 oz boneless chicken

Chicken Marinade:

1 tsp. Sauvignon Blanc

Pinch of black pepper

Pinch of salt

1 tsp. cornstarch

1 cup small pasta shells

6 to 8 oz. celery hearts

1 medium carrot

1 Tbsp. soy sauce

4 dried Chinese black mushrooms, soak in hot water for 1 hour or longer, remove the center tough stem, and slice into thin strips

4 oz. fresh mushrooms, sliced

½ tsp. balsamic vinegar

2 slices ham, cut into thin strips

1 Using the back of the cleaver, pound both sides of the pork to tenderize it and then cut into thin strips. Combine with pork marinade ingredients, mixing well, and set aside.

2 Cut the chicken into thin strips and then mix well with chicken marinade ingredients and set aside.

3 Bring a pot of water to a boil and add the shell pasta. Cook until *al dente*, following the directions on the package. When done, drain and rinse in cold water, and set aside.

4 Peel the strings from the celery and cut into 2-inch lengths and then lengthwise into strips.

5 Peel the carrot and julienne or shred using the large holes of a box grater.

6 Bring 3½ cups chicken stock (or water) to boil. Add pork and chicken and add 1 Tbsp. soy sauce, stir and let the pork and chicken all cook. Skim off the foam if there is any. Reduce heat to medium high, add carrots, celery heart, Chinese black mushrooms, fresh mushrooms, and ham slices. Mix well, and cook 3 more minutes.

7 Add the cooked shell pasta, ½ tsp. of balsamic vinegar or less to your taste, and stir well. Salt to taste. Serve hot.

Fresh dough alternative

Replace step **3** above with the following for fresh "cat's ear pasta."

3 cups all purpose flour

1⅓ cup water

1 Mix the flour and water and knead until smooth. Cover with plastic wrap and let sit at room temperature for 30 minutes to relax the dough.

2 Prepare a bowl of cold water on the side. Heat a pot of water. When you see it bubble but not vigorously

boil, break off a bite-size piece of dough. Try to make it thin like a cat's ear not as thick as gnocchi. Press the little piece of dough using a fork to make a little pattern. Drop each piece into the water one at a time and stir gently. If the water starts to boil, add some more cold water about ¼ cup to bring down the boiling. When the "cat's ears" start to float on the surface, they are done. Do not add too many and crowd the pot. Scoop them out with a sieve or a slotted spoon and drop into a bowl of cold water. Use the same pot of water to finish cooking all the "ears." Drain the water.

3 Alternatively, press the bite-size dough with your thumb or a fork to get the dough to "curl" like gnocchi, and drop it directly into the soup in step **7** above.

Fried Wontons or Wonton Soup 雲吞/雲吞湯 (hun tun/hun tun tang) **

Wontons are one of the most popular dishes in Chinese restaurants. Wonton skins are readily available at supermarkets, but if you venture into Chinatown you will find many types of wonton skins: round, square, thin, and thick. Get the kind labeled Hong Kong-style. It is thinner and usually comes in squares.

The filling can be anything you like. Usually it is pork; pork with American chives or Chinese chives (either green or white 韭菜); or pork mixed with shrimp, or just shrimp. For vegetarians, mix two or more kinds of pre-blanched mushrooms (to reduce the volume) with some chopped celery heart. Sichuan type wontons use a very spicy red chili oil sauce and are called Hon You Chao Shou (紅油抄手), literally meaning "red oil wonton." However, the Chinese do not use cheese for fillings except for the Chinese restaurant appetizer called "Crab Rangoon" that is filled with cream cheese.

Unlike the Italian who "stamp" raviolis, wonton have to be individually wrapped. The skin is much thinner than the ravioli skin. Depending on the shape of the wrapper, the wonton will look different.

Yield: 32 wontons

1 package (16 oz) round or square wonton skin
—Get the thinner Hong Kong style, if possible

Wonton Filling:

10 to 12 oz. coarsely ground pork or a piece of pork loin, chopped

6 to 8 fresh water chestnuts, or canned if fresh ones are not available. If you cannot get water chestnuts, substitute with 2 to 3 stalks of chopped celery—string the celery.

1 Tbsp. light or regular soy sauce (prefer Japanese made brands)

½ tsp. Cognac

1 Tbsp. cornstarch

1 egg

A pinch of salt

A pinch of black pepper

A few drops sesame oil

For Fried Wontons:

2 cups canola oil

Dipping Sauce for Boiled Wontons:

1 part soy sauce

1 part vinegar

Chili oil (optional)

Simple Soup for Wontons:

3 cups chicken stock or canned chicken soup

2 stalks scallions, tops and damaged ends chopped off and then finely chopped

A few drops sesame oil

1 If using fresh water chestnuts, cut off the top and bottom of the water chestnut, then peel the rest of the skin with a knife or peeler. Cut off any yellowish or rotten parts until the chestnut is all white. If using canned water chestnuts, or once you have peeled and washed the fresh ones, use the flat side of a cleaver to crush the water chestnut into smaller pieces. To prevent splattering, you can do this inside a plastic bag. Water chestnut is especially good in wontons or *jiao zi* (dumplings).

2 Mix the ground pork with the crushed water chestnut and the rest of the filling ingredients. Adjust salt, pepper and soy sauce to taste. Use one finger to touch the raw meat and taste your finger to taste for seasonings. Put the meat in the fridge for about 30 minutes. The cold makes the pork mixture stick together so it will be easier to do the wrapping later. If you don't have time, you can skip refrigerating the meat mixture.

3 To prepare for making wontons, line a large plate with a piece of plastic wrap to prevent the wontons from sticking to the plate. Also prepare a small bowl of water for dipping your finger in.

4 Place a piece of wonton skin on a small plate, spoon about 1 tsp. pork filling in the center of the skin, dip a finger in a bowl of water and wet the edges of the skin with your finger. Fold the skin in half over the filling to form a triangle and press the edges together. Press the two bottom corners

(along the longest edge of the triangle) together with a dab of water. The result should look like a "flying nun's hat" or a big tortellini.

Fried Wontons

1 To fry wontons, heat up 2 cups of canola oil in the wok over medium high heat for about 3 minutes. Reduce the heat to medium. Drop one wonton in. If it sizzles, it is hot enough. Place wontons slowly into the oil and deep fry for about 3 minutes until wontons turned golden brown and float. Remove, drain, and serve hot.

Wonton Soup

1 Bring a pot of water to a vigorous boil. NEVER put wontons into cold water, as they will fall apart. Put in the wontons one at a time and cook until they float. Remove the floating wontons, drain, and serve hot.

2 Mix equal parts soy sauce and vinegar, plus a little chili sauce (optional) to make a dipping sauce for the boiled wontons.

3 Or, simply add wontons to soup for wonton soup.

4 *Wonton soup:* Bring chicken stock to a boil, add uncooked wontons. When they float, turn off the heat and sprinkle with finely chopped scallions and a few drops of sesame oil.

Finely chopped scallion is also good in ground pork fillings. If you have leftover wonton skins, cut them into noodles and separate into separate strands. Deep fry them and use them as the crunchy noodle served by Chinese restaurants as an appetizer called "chow mein."

Leftover Wontons

The uncooked leftover wontons can be frozen. Place wontons on a plate lined with a piece of plastic wrap, make sure the wontons do not touch each other. Put them with the plate in the freezer until frozen, about 1 hour. Remove the wontons and store in a plastic bag in the freezer.

To cook frozen wontons, bring a pot of water to boil, place the wontons in the boiling water and bring to another boil. Add about ¼ cup water to stop boiling. Bring the pot to a second boil, and add more water to stop the boiling. When it boils a third time, remove the wontons and serve. With the alternating hot and cold water effect, the wontons will cook without becoming too soft and mushy.

West Lake Beef Soup
西湖牛肉羹 (xi hu niu ro geng) **

West Lake Beef Soup is a very popular velvety soup in Chinese restaurants. The original recipe calls for crab meat and straw mushrooms (only available canned in the U.S.) which can be substituted with your favorite fresh mushrooms. Here I list all the ingredients from the original recipes, but you can reduce the ingredient list to those that are available to you.

This soup should come out velvety and smooth. Most of the ground beef sold in supermarkets is very lean, making for a very dry texture. Instead of buying ground beef, you can buy a piece of rib-eye steak and ask the butcher to grind it up for you.

Yield: 3-4 servings

- 3½ to 4 cups homemade or canned chicken stock
- 1 small bunch of coriander (also called Chinese parsley or cilantro)
- 6 to 8 oz. ground beef (Get the kind with more fat content, about 85% lean. The leaner ground beef tastes like cardboard, and is too dry.)

  Ground Beef Marinade:
  - 1 tsp. soy sauce
  - 1 tsp. Sauvignon Blanc
  - 1 Tbsp. cornstarch
  - ¼ tsp. sugar
  - A pinch of black pepper
  - 6 Tbsp. water (The water makes the beef mixture less dense and easier to break up in the soup.)
  - ½ tsp. canola oil (optional, to make the beef smooth and tender)
  - 1 egg white (optional)

- 6 white mushrooms or your favorite fresh mushrooms, washed and thinly sliced
- 2 oz. crab meat (optional)
- 1 Tbsp. cornstarch mixed with ½ cup water
- 1 tsp. balsamic vinegar or Chinese black vinegar
- 1 egg white, beaten
- 2 slices fresh ginger julienned (Use young ginger if you can find it.)

1 *To make homemade chicken stock:* Put about half a carcass of chicken bones in a large pot with just enough water to barely cover the bones. Bring to a boil, cover, and reduce heat to low and simmer for 30-40 minutes.

2 Cut off the roots of the coriander and then place the coriander in a large pot of cold water and briskly stir them inside the water to shake off the sand. Pick out the coriander and repeat two more times. Leave in a pot of cold water for 30 minutes, and then coarsely chop stems and leaves.

3 Bring chicken stock to a boil; add marinated ground beef; and using chopsticks or a spoon, chunk up the beef. Skim off the foam that will appear on the surface.

4 Add mushrooms and cook for 2 minutes. Add crab meat and stir well. Turn heat to medium low and add the cornstarch and water mixture (1 Tbsp. cornstarch mixed with ½ cup water). Stir well and salt to taste; add 1 tsp balsamic vinegar or Chinese black vinegar. Turn off the heat.

5 Add beaten egg white (or one whole egg is fine) slowly in a thin stream, while simultaneously mixing the soup in a circular motion with a pair of chopsticks or a long handled spoon. Salt to taste. Garnish with coarsely chopped coriander and julienned fresh ginger. Serve hot.

Beef Noodle Soup 牛肉麵
(niu ro mian) ****

This is the most popular noodle soup in Taiwan. It brings back a lot of memories for me. In 2001, I was in Taipei window shopping around the area where I passed by every day as a high school student. I was looking for the familiar beef noodle soup, but it was nowhere to be found. The main streets were packed with Western chain restaurants like McDonald's, Kentucky Fried Chicken, Friday's, etc.

Finally I asked a store sales girl, who pointed me to a beef noodle soup eatery in a street off Heng Yang Road (衡陽路). The shop was packed full. Every seat was taken. On the table there was the familiar sight of bowls of the sour pickled cabbage (酸菜) that accompany beef noodle soup, for the customers to add to their soup. After a 10-minute wait, I got a seat and tasted that most familiar taste that I have dreamed of all these years. And, this place had no store sign at all, like the No Name Restaurant in Boston!

Yield: 4-5 servings

> 3 or more pork bones and a chicken carcass for stock (*A variety of bones make a wonderfully tasty soup. It's not easy to get just bones at the supermarket, so you can use any meat that has more bones than meat.*)

> 4½ cups water

> **Soup Ingredients:**

> 1¼ lbs. beef shin or shank, cut into 4 large chunks

> 1 onion, peel off the skin, cut into 4 wedges (soak in water)

> 3 Tbsp. soy sauce

> 1 tsp. sugar

> 1 Tbsp. Sauvignon Blanc or your favorite wine

> 2 star anise

> ¼ tsp. five spice powder

> ½ tsp. balsamic vinegar from Modena, Italy or Chinese black vinegar

> A pinch of black pepper

A pinch of Accent

A pinch of salt

4½ cups water

2 medium size tomatoes, cut into 8 wedges or big chunks

2 carrots

1 lb. dried spaghetti

1 Tbsp. sesame oil or canola oil

Garnish:

2 Tbsp. canola oil

Sour mustard greens (酸菜) *These come packed in a 10 oz. plastic bag. It's made in Thailand and sold in Chinatown.*

2 fresh chili peppers

1 ***Making chicken or pork stock:*** If you can get more than just 3 pork bones and a chicken carcass, the more the better. Boil them in a pot of water with 4½ cups water. Bring the water to a boil and simmer for 50-60 minutes. Discard the bones. (If there is meat, save it.)

2 Peel the onion and cut into four wedges, and then soak in water.

3 Peel the carrots, and cut on a bias into approximately ½-inch pieces. For a bias cut, make the first cut on the diagonal, then roll the carrot 90 degrees and make a second diagonal cut, approximately bisecting the edge of the previous cut closest to you and repeat the rolling and cutting.

4 Slice the sour mustard greens into thin slices, just enough for an accompaniment to the soup.

5 Thinly slice the fresh chili peppers crosswise into rings. Remove the seeds as they are very spicy. Don't rub your eyes with your hands after handling the chili peppers. Wash your hands with soap after handling the spicy chili pepper.

6 In a large pot with stock from the bones, add beef and all the soup ingredients except the carrots. Bring to a boil; skim off the foam; cover; and reduce heat to low. Simmer for 1 to 1½ hours if

you use the shin or shank. If you use other beef cuts like rib eye steak, 60 minutes is enough.

7 Adjust salt and pepper to taste, and add the carrots. Cover and continue to simmer for 15 more minutes.

8 Cook enough pasta for four people (1 lb package dried spaghetti) following instructions on the package. Drain the water and toss thoroughly with 1 Tbsp. sesame oil or canola oil so the spaghetti will not stick together.

9 Heat up the wok over medium heat, and add 2 Tbsp. oil, sour mustard green, and the sliced fresh chili pepper. Stir for 3-4 minutes. Add ½-1 tsp. sugar if you like it a little sweet.

10 Cut beef shin or shank into one-inch cubes. In a large bowl, place one serving of spaghetti, a few cubes of beef and carrots, and ladle over with soup. Top with sour mustard greens. Mix and serve individually. The sour mustard greens enhance the noodle soup flavor tremendously.

Most of the beef noodle soup sold in Taiwan contains many kinds of Chinese herbs as each restaurant's "secret ingredients." "Dried sweet grass" (Glycyrrhiza uralensis 甘草) is popular. It is a natural sweetener used in Chinese herbal medicine to counteract the bitterness of brewed Chinese herbs. If you go to a Chinese herbal medicine store in Taiwan, they will sell a pouch of Chinese herbs for cooking beef noodle soup. Some beef noodle soup sellers boast that their soup is cooked with more than 10 kinds of Chinese herbs.

Sichuan Pickled Mustard Green Soup with Pork
榨菜肉絲湯 (zha cai rou si tang) *

This is a very tasty and appetizing soup. It is easy and can be prepared in no time. All you need is a small chunk of pork and a small piece of Sichuan pickled mustard green. This is my favorite dish and also is one of the most popular, well-known soups among the Chinese. It can be found in most Chinese restaurants.

There is no freshly made Sichuan pickled mustard green available here in the States, but the one imported from Taiwan in a plastic bag is quite good. The mustard green is salty, so no additional salt is necessary.

Yield: 3-4 servings

4 cups chicken stock or water

8-10 oz. pork loin

> **Pork Marinade:**
>
> 1 tsp. soy sauce
>
> 1 Tbsp. cornstarch
>
> 1 tsp. Sauvignon Blanc or your favorite wine
>
> A pinch of black pepper
>
> 1 Tbsp. cornstarch

½ cup shredded Sichuan pickled mustard green (You can choose to not wash it to retain the original spiciness. Get the one sold whole. Don't get the pre-shredded type. They tend to have tough, coarse parts mixed in. With the whole mustard green, you can check to see if any part is tough, and simply cut it off.)

1 Tenderize the pork using the backside of a cleaver to pound both sides. Cut into thin strips. Mix pork well with the marinade ingredients and set aside.

2 Bring the chicken stock or water to boil in a pot with the shredded pickled mustard green.

3 Add the marinated pork and turn heat to low and simmer for 10 minutes. Skim the foam on the soup surface. Serve hot.

Ginseng Steamed with Chicken
人參燉雞 (ren sen dun ji) *

The Chinese frequently cook dishes with medicinal herbs (mostly dried) to sustain and improve one's health especially when the weather turns cold. These dishes are known as "food cure" (食療). I remember my mother always steamed chicken with ginseng and sometimes, added a few other herbal ingredients in order to boost our energy. The taste of ginseng is actually quite bland.

There are two types of ginseng: Korean Ginseng (red) (高麗參) and white ginseng, the so-called American "Stars and Stripes" Ginseng (花旗參). The American ginseng grows in the cold weather of Wisconsin. It takes up to five years to grow a ginseng root, which is then sold in dried form and is quite expensive. For an 8 oz. package, American ginseng costs around $30 (Boston Chinatown price). The price of Korean ginseng is even higher, but a little goes a long way. When you buy the dried American ginseng root, it is about 3½ inches in length and very hard. Ask the store to slice it for you.

A few years ago, I had surgery to remove my gall bladder. After the operation, I experienced diarrhea any time I had food with some oil. The doctor gave me a few prescriptions to stop the reaction without any success. Out of frustration, I tried taking American ginseng, and it has helped me to lead a normal life ever since.

Every day I place about 2 tablespoon (or 50 slices) of American ginseng in a cup and pour boiling water over it and let it steep covered for about 30 minutes to 1 hour before drinking it. I can steep the same ginseng slices again once or twice before restarting with fresh slices.

*You can eat the softened ginseng, but it does not have much taste. Most of the American ginseng is sold in Chinese herbal medicine stores in Chinatown or through the Internet. A Taiwanese, Mr. Hsu, has successfully grown ginseng in Wisconsin. From his website (**www.hsuginseng.com**) you can buy a 4 or 8 oz. package with different size ginseng root; the larger one costs more. You can buy whole roots or pre-sliced ones. Buy the sliced ones, as the dried root is too hard to slice yourself. If you have a ginseng root and no one can cut it for you, you can steam the ginseng until it softens, then cut it.*

Yield: 2-3 servings

- 2 Tbsp. "Stars & Stripes" American white ginseng slices (花旗參) (50-60 slices)

- 2 chicken thighs or drum sticks *(The soup tastes better using chicken with bones.)*

Equipment:

A steamer or a rack to be placed inside the wok

1 Boil the water for the steamer. Make sure there is enough water to steam for 1 hour. In a large bowl, place chicken thighs or drum sticks with the ginseng slices on top. Add some water so the chicken is totally immersed in water and cover the bowl with a piece of parchment paper. If the paper does not stay, place a small dipping dish to weigh it down. Reduce heat and place the bowl on the steaming rack. Turn heat to medium.

2 Cover the steamer and steam over medium heat for about 1 hour. Set the timer, and after 30 minutes, check the water level. Add some more water if necessary.

Chicken thighs usually come packaged in fours. Steam two at a time and do not reuse the ginseng. Use a fresh 50 slices for every two thighs. No salt is added to this dish. I don't know why, but my mother never added any salt to chicken steamed with ginseng, same as when brewing Chinese herbal medicines. There are a lot of theories on serving Chinese medicinal herbs (including ginseng): some kinds of vegetables not supposed to be served with the Chinese herbal medicine one is taking, especially the turnip and Napa Chinese cabbage. Those vegetables are considered "cold" and can cancel the effect of taking ginseng or Chinese herbal medicine.

CHAPTER 7

豬肉主菜

Pork Entrees

Pork Entrees

Pork is the *main* meat used in Taiwanese cuisine. In the old days, no one sold chicken meat. Chicken meat came from one's household. Each family raised chickens and when it was time to celebrate a festival or a special occasion, the chicken was killed to create a gourmet dish for family members or guests.

That beef is not a popular meat in Taiwan is a remnant of Taiwan's agrarian roots. Up until the 1960s, the Taiwanese still relied on agricultural to survive, and before machines were used to till farm land, oxen were the muscle of labor-intensive agriculture. Even now it is still true. Since the cow helped the farmer work for its entire life, it was considered inhumane to slaughter the animal for meat. Although cows were not considered sacred as they are in India, its status was close to that concept, so people just didn't touch beef. The idea was passed on from generation to generation, so it is natural that there are a lot of people in Taiwan who still don't eat beef, such as my eldest sister.

There is a custom in Taiwan still kept in the countryside where for Buddha's birthday a group of neighboring families will sponsor a sacrificial pig to ask for peace and prosperity in the coming year. The sacrificial pig will be put on display with other offerings on a table in the street to worship the "walking gods" parade. An almost life-size mannequin of a god is built on a frame that sits on the shoulders of a person hidden inside. The person wearing the god frame joins the celebration parade, walking through the streets to accept the offerings alongside the road. (There are a few "walking gods" who join the parade, and there are quite a few pigs. As the celebration goes on, a prize is given to the biggest pig.)

After the ceremony, the whole pig is divided into portions and distributed to the families that sponsored the pig. In the old days there was no refrigeration, so each family had to think of a way to cook the meat. The most common one is cutting pork into chunks and cooking with soy sauce and spices — like five-spice powder — in a large pot. With the saltiness, it does not spoil easily. This dish has become one of the most popular in Taiwanese cuisine, Taiwanese Stewed Fatty Pork Sauce (滷肉). Nowadays you can find this dish sold at every street corner or restaurant in Taiwan.

Yu Xiang Eggplant 魚香茄子
(yu xiang qie zi) ***

Eggplant tastes best when boiled, grilled, or deep fried before being added to a stir fry. If it is added raw and stir-fried, the eggplant does not readily soften and sometimes remains hard. The eggplant shrinks a lot in this recipe. The "yu xiang" (fish aroma 魚香) refers to a sauce used for fish in Sichuan cooking. There are many dishes using this sauce, so you will see "Yu Xiang Eggplant," "Yu Xiang Pork" (魚香肉絲) and other "Yu Xiang" dishes in Chinese restaurant menus.

Yield: 6 servings/One plate presentation

- 5-6 Chinese or Japanese eggplant, which are longer and skinnier than the usual ball-shaped Western eggplant

- 8 oz. ground pork *(Buy a piece of pork tenderloin and chop it coarsely. It's a lot juicier than the pre-ground pork. If you buy ground pork, buy one with higher fat content.)*

- 1 large shallot, peeled and sliced thinly

  ### Pork Marinade:

  2 Tbsp. soy sauce

  1 tsp. sugar

  Black pepper to taste

  ½ tsp. Sauvignon Blanc or your favorite white wine

  1 tsp. sesame oil (optional)

  1 tsp. cornstarch

  2 Tbsp. water

- 1 cup vegetable oil

  ### Sauce Mixture:

  2 Tbsp. soy sauce

  1 tsp. cornstarch

  1 tsp. sugar

  1 tsp. sesame oil

  1 tsp. Sauvignon Blanc or your favorite white wine

  ½ tsp. balsamic vinegar (or black vinegar)

  Salt and black pepper to taste

1 Marinate the ground pork in the marinade ingredients listed above.

2 Prepare the eggplant as follo Trim off the stem of the eggplant. About 1 inch from the top, cut the eggplant lengthwise into skinny strips held together by the uncut 1-inch at the top. It makes the eggplant look like a lantern.

3 (Go to step **4** for a lower fat alternative.) Heat up 1 cup vegetable oil in the wok until a little piece of eggplant in the oil sizzles. Pat dry the eggplant. Then over the sink, sprinkle the eggplant with some cornstarch and shake off any excess. Slide the pieces one by one into the oil. Rotate the pieces around the wok so they cook evenly. Remove the pieces when the eggplant turns soft and wrinkly (about 5 minutes). For cleanup, drain the oil in a hand-held strai (Go to step **5**.)

4 *Low-fat eggplant preparation:* If deep frying sounds too greasy, boil the eggplants whole in boiling water for about 5 minutes. Boil until the eggplant is soft and limp. The eggplant will become a faded dull purple. Remove the eggplant and drain the water. Let it cool down and cut into long strips starting 1 inch from the top. Do not cut through the top.

5 Heat up 3 Tbsp. oil in the wok over medium high heat. Add shallot slices and stir fry until golden but not brown. Add marinated ground pork, break up the clumps and stir constantly until the color changes to pale pink. If the meat sticks to the bottom of the wok, it's OK. The caramelizing of the meat adds to the flavor of the dish.

6 Reduce heat to medium and add eggplants (f Step **3** or **4**) to the meat, and mix well. Scrape the bottom and sides of the wok regularly. Add the sauce mixture and mix well. This dish tastes better if it's a little on the salty side. Serve hot with rice. After it's cooked, the eggplant will look like a soft mass, but even if the presentation is not that attractive, it tastes really good, even though I'm not too crazy about eggplant.

This dish can be prepared ahead of time. It is very good even as leftovers. Do not substitute with other kinds of meat. This recipe is best with pork.

Red Cooked Pig Feet/Pork Butt

紅燒豬蹄/蹄膀

(hon shao zhu ti/ti pang) ***

"Red cooking" is a popular method of Chinese cooking. The soy sauce added gives the sauce a deliciously brown color–hence the name "red cooked" (紅燒). The Cantonese call the front feet of a pig, "pig hands" (豬手), and the rear feet, "pig feet." It is hard for the ordinary person to distinguish between the front and the rear pig feet. Some butchers know the difference. The pig hands are supposed to have more meat and be bigger, while the rear pig feet are skinnier with more bone and tendon.

There are many ways to "red cook" pig feet. Here are three simple ways to cook them without creating too much fuss. You can use the same method to cook beef shank and beef tendon. The only difference is the cooking time.

There is a town in southern Taiwan called Wan Luan in Pin Dong County (屏東縣萬巒鄉) well known for their pig feet, called Wan Luan Pig Feet (萬巒豬腳).

Yield: 5-6 servings

Recipe Variation A:

- 2 pig feet or about 3 lbs. of pork butt. *Ask the butcher to chop the pig feet into approximately 2-inch cubes, if it comes in one piece. If using pork butt, ask to have it cut into 2-3 pieces for you.*

- 3 Tbsp. canola oil

- 1 Tbsp. sugar (or rock sugar) *Rock sugar brings a shine to the pig feet after it's cooked.*

- 4-5 cloves shallots (more is better)

- 1-1½ cup Sauvignon Blanc or other favorite wine

- 5-6 Tbsp. soy sauce

- ¼ tsp salt

- ¼ tsp. black pepper

- ¼-1 tsp. five spice powder (五香粉) (optional)

- 2-3 cloves (茴香)

1 Remove the outer skin of the shallot and slice thinly.

2 Heat up 3 Tbsp. canola oil in the wok over medium high heat. Add the shallots and stir fry until golden. Pat dry pig feet chunks with paper towel and add to the wok. Be careful, as it will splatter. Stir and cover for 5 minutes. Remove the cover, and stir well.

You can skip the initial frying of shallots and the pig feet and just put everything into the pot, but pre-stir frying gives the dish aroma. Alternatively, you can just deep fry a few cloves of shallot and add i the pot in step **3** below.

3 Add 2 Tbsp. soy sauce, 1 Tbsp. sugar, 1 cup Sauvignon Blanc, a pinch of black pepper, a pinch of five spice powder and the cloves. Stir and mix well.

4 Transfer the mixture to a large pot with a cover. Add water so it barely covers the pig feet. Bring to a boil, turn heat to low, and let it simmer covered for 30 minutes.

5 Check the pot and if it looks dry, add ½ cup more wine (or water), and stir well. Simmer covered for another 30 minutes. Mix and stir well. Repeat the same procedure for a total cooking time of 2½ hours. If it becomes too dry at any time, add a little more wine or water and continue to simmer. Try one little piece of meat to see if it is tender.

6 When the meat is tender, remove and serve warm or at room temperature. The brown sauce at the bottom of the pot is good for anything, especially served with piping hot rice.

I learned the following method, Recipe Variation B, from a taxi driver in Taipei. It's a Taiwanese custom that after childbirth, the mother is treated to especially nourishing food for one month so that she may regain her strength and at the same time produce more milk to breastfeed the baby.

One of these special post-delivery dishes is pig feet cooked with freshly shelled raw peanuts. The taxi driver and his wife have five kids. He loves this dish himself and with five times practice, he is good at making it. He told me to cook the pig feet and the peanuts in a rice cooker with water. "Cook" once in the rice cooker. When done, cool the contents for 30 minutes, add more water, and push down the "cook" button again. Voilà, the pig feet are done.

Recipe Variation B: (Cook in an automatic rice cooker, direct heat type)

- 2 pig feet (2 lbs) or pork butt (*Ask your butcher to chop it into chunks*)

- 4-5 cloves shallot

- 1 medium size onion, peeled, cut into 4 wedges, and then sliced

- 5-6 Tbsp. soy sauce

- 1 Tbsp. rice wine or Sauvignon Blanc

- 1 tsp. balsamic vinegar (optional)

- 1 tsp. sugar

- ¼ tsp. salt

- 1 tsp five spice powder

- ½ tsp black pepper

- 1 Tbsp. sesame oil (optional)

1 Peel the shallots and slice thinly. If using, peel the onion and cut into 4 wedges and slice. The onion adds a natural sweetness to the dish.

2 Brown the shallots in oil until golden brown, then remove and set aside.

3 Bring a large pot of water to boil. Add pork feet and butt to the boiling water and cook for 3-5 minutes. Remove the pork feet and butt and rinse clean with cold water. Discard the water from the pot. This step is to remove the raw smell from the pork.

4 Place the pig feet chunks in the rice cooker pot, add all the ingredients including the shallots, then add water until it barely covers the pig feet chunks. Close the rice cooker and push the "cook" button.

5 When the "cook" button pops up, let it sit to cool for about 20 minutes. Stir the contents well. The water will have evaporated in the cooking. Scrape the dark brown sauce from the bottom and mix well with the pig feet.

6 Taste to see if the pig feet is soft enough for you. If it is still too tough, add more water to again barely cover the pig feet. Push down the "cook" button again. When it pops up, check to see if the pig feet chunks are done.

7 When the softness is right, let it cool a little and serve warm. If you want it to be softer, again add water to barely cover the pig feet chunks and push down the "cook" button a third time. When it pops up a third time, you will surely have perfect brown pig feet. This method is an easy way to make this dish.

Recipe Variation C

This is the conventional way of "red cooking" pork feet or pork butt. It uses exactly the same ingredients as Recipe Variation A, but is cooked with water instead of wine.

- 2 pig feet (2 lbs) or pork butt (*Ask the butcher to chop into approximately 2-inch cubes for you if it comes in one piece.*)

- 3 Tbsp. canola oil

- 1 Tbsp. sugar (or rock sugar) *Rock sugar brings a shine to the pig feet after it's cooked.*

- 4-6 cloves of shallot

- 1 medium size onion (optional), peeled, cut into 4 wedges, then sliced. *The onions add a natural sweetness to the dish.*

- 1-1½ cup Sauvignon Blanc or other favorite wine

- 5-6 Tbsp. soy sauce

- ½ tsp. black pepper

- 1 tsp. five spice powder (五香粉)

- 2-3 cloves (茴香)

- ¼ tsp salt

- 2 cups canola oil (optional), *for deep frying as in step below.*

1 Bring a large pot of water to a boil. Add pork feet and butt to the boiling water and cook for 3-5 minutes. Remove the pork feet and butt and rinse clean with cold water. Discard the water inside the pot. This step is to remove the raw smell from the pork.

2 (Optional step) Pat dry the pork butt with paper towels. Heat up 2 cups canola oil over high heat for about 3 minutes. Slowly add pork butt to the hot oil. Cover to avoid splattering. After 3-5 minutes, remove the cover and turn over the pork butt to deep fry on the other side for 3-5 minutes until the pork butt turns golden brown. With this extra deep frying step, the finished pork butt will have a skin that tastes chewy yet very soft. This is the very taste that modern Taiwanese desire and is called 彈牙 "tan ya" literally meaning "spring between teeth."

3 Place the pork feet and butt into the large pot, add water so it covers the pork feet and butt entirely. Add the browned shallot (see Recipe A Step **2**) and the rest of the ingredients. Bring the entire pot to a boil. Skim off the foam on top. Reduce heat to low and cook in total for 2-2½ hours. Every 20-30 minutes, gently stir the pot thoroughly from the bottom to the top so it won't burn at the bottom of the pot. Use a timer to measure the time interval. After cooking for 30 minutes, taste the liquid and adjust the salt.

To save time for modern day cooking, you can use a Slow Cook Crock Pot to finish Step in Recipe C. The only difference is when cooked in a crock pot, the liquid from pork butt ends up as a clear broth, and is not so saucy as when cooked on a stovetop.

Fettuccini with Ground Pork & Prosciutto 意式寬麵炒火腿肉片 (yi shi chao mian) **

This version is adapted from a Japanese Iron Chef recipe. Using the same technique, you can substitute other ingredients.

Yield: 4-6 servings

6 oz. ground pork

Pork Marinade:

1 Tbsp. cornstarch

1 tsp. soy sauce

1 pinch of black pepper

A few drops of canola oil

3 strips bacon

2 Tbsp. canola oil

1 shallot (optional)

¼ tsp salt (or more to taste)

5-6 leaves Chinese cabbage (also called Napa cabbage)

¼ cup water

¼ lb. imported Italian prosciutto from De Parma, Italy

1 tsp. soy sauce

½ lb. fresh fettuccini or ¼ lb. dried fettuccini *(Following the cooking instructions on package.)*

1 Mix the pork with the marinade above and set aside.

2 Slice the bacon into ½-inch pieces.

3 Peel the shallot and slice thinly.

4 Wash and cut the Chinese cabbage crosswise into thin strips.

5 Slice the prosciutto into one-inch pieces.

6 Bring about 2 quarts of water to a boil, and add the fettuccini. Using a fork or a pair of chopsticks, mix to separate the noodle so they won't stick together. Cook until al dente, following the directions on the package. Drain the water and rinse with cold water to keep the noodles from sticking and set aside.

7 In a wok or frying pan, heat up 2 Tbsp. canola oil, add bacon and shallot and stir fry until golden, about 3-4 minutes. Add the ground pork, stir and chunk it up until the meat changes color to a pale pink. Some meat may stick to the bottom of the wok as a caramelized residue will stick to the bottom of the wok, but it's OK.

8 Add the cabbage and salt, stir and scrape the caramelization on the bottom of the wok and mix with the cabbage. Add ¼ cup water. Cover for about 4 minutes then mix and taste. If the cabbage is still not soft enough, cook a few more minutes.

9 Remove the cover and stir thoroughly. Reduce heat to medium, add fettuccini and mix well. Turn off the heat, add the prosciutto, and mix well. Do not add any more salt, as the prosciutto is quite salty. It adds to the natural saltiness of the dish. Serve.

This dish can be prepared ahead of time. The leftovers are quite good.

Ma Po Tofu 麻婆豆腐 (ma po do fu) ***

The legend has it that CHEN Ma Po (陳麻婆), a lady from Sichuan Province (四川) in China, started to serve this dish to coolies (laborers) who passed by, and they in turn paid her. Later she opened an eatery serving this dish. Her face was "dotted" (Ma 麻) and Po (婆) means an older woman. So she was nicknamed Ma Po, this dish, Ma Po Do Fu, was named after her. Sichuan is located in the middle of China and is surrounded by mountains. As it is hot and humid in the summer, it's no accident that Sichuan food is spicy. Eating spicy food makes people sweat, providing relief from the unbearable heat and humidity. The Sichuan peppercorn (四川花椒) is famous for leaving a tingly numb feeling in the mouth. 麻, the same character as "dotted," refers to this numbness. Ma Po Do Fu is not authentic unless it is served piping hot in a real Sichuan restaurant using real Sichuan peppercorn. Chen Ma Po (陳麻婆) has become a registered trade name in China. I have found a small authentic Sichuan Restaurant in the suburb of Taipei (Ban Qiao 板橋) called "Chue Ye" (春野). The owner Mr. Guo (郭主義) regularly goes to Sichuan to learn Sichuan cooking techniques. He has won many cooking awards in Beijing and Shanghai. Their Ma Po Do Fu is the best that I've ever tasted.

For convenience, most Chinese restaurants in the States use spicy bean paste (四川豆瓣醬) although that ingredient is not used in the original dish.

Yield: 4-5 servings/One plate presentation

8 oz. ground pork *(Although pork is traditionally used, you can substitute with ground beef. Since beef has less fat, add 1 Tbsp. of vegetable oil to give the beef a more tender and smooth pork-like texture.)*

Meat Marinade:

1 Tbsp. soy sauce

1 Tbsp. cornstarch

1 tsp. Cognac or other favorite wine

1 tsp. sesame oil

¼ tsp. black pepper

1 Tbsp. vegetable oil (if marinating beef)

2 pieces soft tofu (豆腐), cut into one-inch cubes

3 Tbsp. cooking oil

3 stalks scallion

3 cloves garlic

¼ tsp. sugar

1 Tbsp. soy sauce

1 Tbsp. Sichuan bean paste (四川豆瓣醬) or Spicy Sichuan bean paste (四川辣豆瓣醬) (optional)

1 tsp. Cognac or other favorite wine

1 tsp. chili sauce 辣椒醬 adjust the amount to suit your taste (*I recommend Sriracha Hot Chili Sauce, 是拉差香甜辣椒醬. It comes in a see-through plastic bottle with a rooster on the bottle and a green dispenser cap. It's made in California by Huy Fong Foods 匯豐食品公司, and is available in any Chinatown grocery store.*)

1½ cup water

Black pepper to taste

1 tsp. sesame oil (optional)

1 Mix pork with marinade ingredients and set aside.

2 Prepare the scallion by peeling off any damaged layers and cutting off the top and any damaged ends. Chop finely and set aside.

3 Using the flat side of a cleaver, crush the garlic and the outer skin will come off easily. Discard skin, chop finely, and set aside.

4 Cut tofu into one-inch cubes and add to a pot of boiling water for about 1-2 minutes and drain the water. Pre-boiling the tofu will extract some water from the tofu so that it does not dilute the taste of the dish. This pre-boiling technique is also used for frying tofu to help it turn golden brown more quickly.

5 Heat up the wok about 3-4 minutes over high heat. Add 3 Tbsp. oil to the wok with the garlic and scallion. Let garlic and scallion become lightly golden.

6 Add the marinated ground pork and stir thoroughly until the pork changes color. Turn heat to medium. Add Sichuan bean paste (optional) or chili sauce, ¼ tsp. sugar, 1 Tbsp. soy sauce, 1 tsp. Cognac or other favorite wine, 1½ cup water, and tofu. After bringing the mixture to a boil, reduce heat to low and simmer for 5 minutes. Try not to break up the tofu. If using, add 1 tsp. sesame oil. Taste before serve. Sprinkle with freshly ground black pepper. Serve hot. (You may not need to add any salt if you use Sichuan bean paste as it is quite salty.)

This dish is especially good with rice. However, it is also good served over spaghetti.

Steamed Pork Liver 蒸豬肝
(zhen zhu gan) **

Traditionally, the Chinese believe in using food for its medicinal healing power (食療). Besides meat, liver, kidney, bone marrow, stomach and even coagulated blood are all good for people who are weak in that part of their body. My mother used to steam pork liver so that it was still rare inside, as to remedy for her anemia (貧血), which caused dizziness. This is a very simple and full-flavored recipe.

Yield: 3-4 servings/One plate presentation

- 1 lb. pork liver in one piece or cut into two pieces (or substitute with chicken liver)
- 2 Tbsp. soy sauce
- 1 tsp. Cognac or Chinese Shao Xing Wine, Maotai, or Gao Liang wine (紹興酒, 茅台酒, 高粱酒)
- ½ cup water
- 1 tsp. sugar
- A pinch of five spice powder 五香粉
- A pinch of black pepper
- A pinch of salt

Variation: You can replace the pork liver with chicken liver. In that case, decrease the steaming time to about 15 minutes.

1 Rinse the liver clean. In a pot, combine and mix well all the ingredients except for the liver. Place the liver in the pot with the mixture.

2 Bring the steamer pot of water to a boil. Place the pot with sauce mixture and liver in the steaming rack. Turn heat to medium high and steam 25-30 minutes. (Or, steam just 15 minutes if using chicken liver). Turn off the heat, and let it cool down for 10-15 minutes.

3 Remove the liver from the pot, slice thinly, and serve warm or at room temperature. This dish is a great item as a cold platter first course for a banquet. The sauce from the liver in the pot is great for serving with hot rice.

Pearl Balls 珍珠丸子
(zhen zhu wan zi) **

When the meatballs are cooked up, they look like pearl coated meatballs, hence their name. It is easy to make and can make a good impression on guests. It is usually served on special occasions, but of course it can be served as a daily dish. Kids love it. It's delicious and finger licking good.

Yield: 20 pearl balls

- 1 cup sweet rice, soaked overnight (*Substitute with regular short grain rice if sweet rice is not available. The original recipe calls for sweet, glutinous rice, which is more chewy and shiny than regular rice.*)
- 1 piece medium firm tofu (optional) *The original recipe does not call for tofu. I add tofu to make the meatballs lighter. The tofu is sold in plastic containers at the supermarket.*
- 10 oz. ground pork
- 1½ Tbsp. soy sauce
- 1 tsp. sesame oil
- 1 Tbsp. cornstarch
- A pinch of black pepper
- Salt to taste

Equipment:

Chinese steamer

Cheese cloth or a few Napa cabbage leaves

Variation: Add about 6 oz fresh shrimps either mashed or cut into small chunks to the meatball mix.

1 Soak the rice for at least 8 hours or overnight. Drain for at least 1 hour or until the rice looks dry.

2 Drop the tofu in boiling water for about 1-2 minutes and then drain. Let the tofu cool down to room temperature and then crush it into a paste. Pre-boiling the tofu extracts water making it easier to make meatballs after the tofu is added to the pork.

3 Mix the ground pork with the rest of the ingredients except the rice. Mix the meatball mixture in one direction by hand for 3-4 minutes until the texture becomes somewhat sticky.

4 Make meatballs about the size of a small Italian meatball using about 2 Tbsps. of the mixture. Roll each meatball in the rice to coat. Gently press the rice onto the meatball. Place each coated meatballs on a plate or directly on a steamer rack lined with cheesecloth or Napa cabbage leaves. While making meatballs, pre-boil the water for the steamer. Make sure that you have enough water for steaming 20 minutes.

5 Place the plate filled with meatballs on the steamer rack. Place the steamer rack over the steamer pot and steam over medium high heat for 20 minutes. Turn off heat and open the cover. Let the hot steam escape. Remove the rack from the steamer before removing the plate. Be careful, as the steam is very hot. Serve hot or at room temperature.

Lion's Head Crab Meatball Soup
蟹粉獅子頭白菜湯
(xie fen shi zi tou bai cai tang) ***

"Lion's head" literally means big. Every Chinese understands Lion's Head Crab Meatball Soup refers to the large size meatball. This dish is very simple, yet difficult to get exactly right. Just the pork could provoke a scholarly discussion. First, the pork has to be 70% lean meat and 30% fat, and any sinew has to be completely removed. The pork has to be cut uniformly into small pieces, then roughly chopped, using the so-called "cut finely and chop roughly" technique (細切粗斬). The point is not to chop the meat into a finely ground mass.

Nowadays, it is very hard to get the specific meat cut from the markets. Here I use ground pork. If you have time and want to make a really gourmet lion's head, get a piece of country-style pork (with some fat) and cut it into small pieces. Do not add breadcrumbs to it. It will make the meatballs hard. The best lion's head is tender like tofu, not hard and dry.

After tasting a wonderful lion's head dish in Guang Ling, Jiang Su Province (江蘇省廣陵), a Chinese poet once declared, "The playboy has no heart adorned with gold and jade/The poet enjoys the wine with flowery fragrance/Taste lion head in Guang Ling/One felt like riding on a crane[5] forgetting homesickness." (公子無腸金玉鑲，騷人有酒菊樺香，廣陵嘗品獅頭肉，騎鶴樓頭忘故鄉。)

The original dish calls for pork bones and pork skin. The pot is layered with pork bones, pork skins, cabbage, meatballs, and cabbage. The whole pot is then covered and brought to a boil, and simmered or steamed for over an hour over medium to medium high heat. This is truly a scrumptious soup. The cabbage, meatballs, and the soup are simply out of this world. Because of the large meatballs, it is usually presented with four "lion's heads" in one dish. It is also called "Four Happiness Meatballs" (四喜丸子).

Yield: 4-6 servings/One pot presentation

　　4 oz. crab meat (fresh or frozen) (optional)

　　4 oz. fresh water chestnuts (optional)

　　8-10 leaves Chinese (Napa) cabbage

5　*"Riding on a crane" refers to a carefree life.*

Meatball Mix:

1 lb. ground pork

1 tsp. Cognac, Sauvignon Blanc or your favorite wine

1 egg white

1 Tbsp. soy sauce

A pinch of black pepper

A pinch of salt

2 Tbsp. water

1 tsp. cornstarch

¼ cup canola oil

1 tsp. soy sauce

1 cup water

Salt to taste

Equipment:

One large heat-resistant CorningWare ceramic pot

Chinese steamer

1 If using fresh water chestnuts, cut off the top and bottom of the water chestnut, then peel the rest of the skin with a knife or peeler. Cut off any yellowish or rotten parts until the chestnut is all white. Once you have peeled and washed the fresh ones (or if using canned water chestnuts), use the flat side of a cleaver to crush the water chestnut into smaller pieces. To prevent splattering, you can do this inside a plastic bag.

2 Drop cabbage leaves into boiling water for 2 minutes and then cut crosswise into 2-inch wide pieces. Add more cabbage if the pot is big enough. The cabbage shrinks in volume after cooking for a while.

3 Mix ground pork with soy sauce, egg white, Cognac, black pepper, salt, 1 tsp. cornstarch, and about 2 Tbsp. water, and briskly stir the mixture in one direction until it becomes sticky in texture. Taste by touching a finger to the mix and tasting your finger. Salt to taste. Mix in the crushed water chestnut. Sprinkle some cornstarch on both your hands and make lime-sized meatballs. Press about ½ -1 tsp of crab meat into the meat ball.

4 Heat up the wok over high heat for about 3-4 minutes. Add ¼ cup canola oil, and reduce heat to medium high. Place the meatballs into the wok one by one, but do not crowd them. Pan fry for about 2 minutes. There is no need to cook the meat through. The goal is to just make sure the meatball stays together and doesn't fall apart. Gently turn to the other side and lightly fry the other side about 2 minutes. Fry each side about 2 minutes or until golden brown.

5 In a large ceramic pot (such as CorningWare), line the pot with all the Napa Chinese cabbage except for 6 pieces. On top of the cabbage, layer the meatballs. Cover the meatballs with the rest of the cabbage. Sprinkle with some salt, 1 tsp. soy sauce, and add about 1 cup of water. Do not fill the pot more than about 80% full so that the water will not boil over.

6 Place the uncovered pot (or just cover with a piece of parchment paper) in a steamer. Bring the steamer water to a boil. Turn heat to medium and steam for 60-80 minutes. Make sure there is enough water in the steamer pot for the steaming time, or check the water level and add more water later if needed. Alternatively, bring the whole ceramic pot to a boil over the stove top, and turn to low heat and simmer for one hour.

7 Bring the whole pot to the table when it's ready. Open and serve bubbling hot.

Taiwanese-Style Homemade Sticky Spare Ribs 台式排骨酥
(bai gu suo - Taiwanese pronunciation) ****

One of my fondest memories of the dishes my mother made for me is this one. This is her recipe. The best starch to use is the coarsely ground Taiwanese yam starch (labeled "Sweet Potato Starch" 蕃薯粉), which is only available in Chinatown. Cornstarch will also do the job, but yam starch makes a stickier coating so it tastes better.

Yield: 4-5 servings

> 2 lbs. baby back pork ribs *(Whole Foods has the best one. It's a complete strip of baby ribs)*
>
> 4-5 cloves shallot (optional)

Spare Rib Marinade:

> 1 Tbsp. soy sauce
>
> ½ tsp. sugar
>
> 1 tsp. sesame oil
>
> ¼ tsp. black pepper

> 4 Tbsp. coarsely ground type Taiwanese Sweet Potato Starch 蕃薯粉 (or cornstarch)
>
> 2 cups canola oil
>
> 1-2 Russet potatoes or 1 taro root (optional)

Equipment:

Wok and Chinese steamer

1 The spare ribs usually come in a sealed plastic package about 4-inches by 14-15-inches. Do not get the one with the extra top part which has to be cut off. The real baby ribs are about 3 inches long. Cut into individual ribs, about 13 ribs total. Whole Foods Market has the best baby spare ribs

2 Peel the shallot, thinly slice, and then coarsely chop.

3 Mix and coat the spare ribs with the soy sauce, sugar, shallots, sesame oil, and pepper. Let them sit for 20 minutes or longer (keep in the fridge if the weather is warm). While waiting, you can pre-boil the water for the steamer in p **8** below.

4 Sprinkle 4 Tbsp. Taiwanese Sweet Potato Starch or cornstarch over the spare ribs and mix to evenly coat.

5 Heat up 2 cups cooking oil for 3 minutes over medium high heat. Throw in a little piece of meat. If it just sizzles and does not turn brown right away, it is a good temperature. If it turns brown very quickly, then it is too hot. Turn off the heat for 5 minutes to cool off the oil, and then turn it back on again. Fry six ribs at a time. Let them fry for about 3-4 minutes before turning them over, otherwise the spare ribs will stick to the bottom of the wok.

6 When the spare ribs become golden brown, remove and let drain on a rack. Wait another 3-4 minutes until the oil is hot again before frying the next batch of spare ribs.

7 After the oil has mostly drained from the ribs, put them in a bowl. I recommend using a stainless steel mixing bowl. Optionally, line the bottom of the bowl with ½-inch cubes of Russet potato or taro root, and layer the deep fried spare ribs on top. The potatoes will come out soft and delicious, flavored by the juices of the spare ribs.

8 Fill the steamer pot with plenty of water as it will have to steam for 50 minutes. Bring the steamer to a boil, and then turn off the heat. This is so you don't burn your hands when you place the bowl of spare ribs into the steamer rack. Turn the heat to medium high and steam for about 50 minutes or until tender. The meat should slip easily off the bones. Serve hot.

9 If you did not add the potatoes to the bowl in S p **7**, the greasy sauce that collects at the bottom of the pot can be added to a vegetable stir fry. Let the sauce stay in the refrigerator for a couple of hours or overnight, so you can skim off the top layer of grease before you use it to cook vegetables.

10 This dish can be prepared ahead of time and then just heated up by steaming over medium heat for 10-15 minutes before serving.

This is one of the so-called Taiwanese "old days' taste" "古早味" (gou za bi in Taiwanese) banquet dish. In the original presentation, after the spare ribs and chunks of taro root are deep fried, a large bowl is lined with spare ribs in rows, and then filled with the fried taro root to the rim. The bowl is steamed for 50-60 minutes. When it's done, the chef places a bigger bowl over the spare rib and taro root bowl and flips the contents into the bigger bowl. Then stock is prepared and poured over the resulting dome of spare ribs and served to the banquet table. Nowadays, this dish is disappearing from banquets, perhaps due to its complicate preparation.

Bell Peppers with Shredded Pork
青椒肉絲 (qing jiao rou si) **

Colorful bell peppers are everywhere. Pick up a couple with different colors. Fresh peppers should be firm to the touch with a skin that's shiny, not wrinkly. Colorful bell peppers, like red, orange and yellow tend to be sweeter than the deep green ones. The long-shaped light green one is also very good. Try a few colors to see what kind you like better.

Most homemade stir fry dishes are cooked this way. You can substitute with other kinds of vegetables found in your refrigerator, such as celery, Chinese Napa cabbage, and broccoli. If using broccoli, blanch the cut vegetable in boiling water for 1 minute before stir frying.

Yield: 3-4 servings/One plate presentation

- 2 bell peppers in different colors, remove seeds and core, thinly slice
- 6 oz. pork loin, remove the sinew on the surface, and cut into thin strips

  Marinate With:

  ½-1Tbsp. soy sauce

  1 tsp. Sauvignon Blanc or your favorite wine

  1 Tbsp. cornstarch

  A few drops canola oil

- 6 Tbsp. canola oil (divided)
- A pinch of black pepper
- 2 shallots
- A pinch of salt
- ¼ cup water

1 Remove the seeds from the bell peppers, and cut into thin strips.

2 Remove the sinew from the surface of the pork loin and cut into thin strips. Then mix well with marinade ingredients and set aside.

3 Peel shallots and slice thinly.

4 Heat up the wok over high heat about 4 minutes. Add 3 Tbsp. canola oil, add marinated pork strips, stir and separate the strips until color changes to pale white. Remove the meat from the wok.

5 Without washing the wok, turn heat to medium high, add 3 Tbsp. canola oil, add shallot slices, and stir until golden. Add bell peppers, sprinkle with a pinch of salt, stir and add ¼ cup water or less. Turn down heat to medium and cover for 3-4 minutes. Remove the cover when the water has almost evaporated. cooked pork from step **4**. Mix well for about 1 minute. Salt to taste. Serve hot.

Tender Spare Ribs with Rice Powder 粉蒸排骨
(fen zhen pai gu) **

This dish uses special crushed rice powder to make the spare rib tender. It is available in Chinatown grocery stores. If you cannot get it, you can soak the regular long or short grain rice overnight. Drain the water and let the rice dry at room temperature for a few hours and blend it in a food processor (no water) with some five spice powder and a pinch of salt and black or white pepper (for aroma) and coat the spare ribs with it. This dish is usually presented in a small bamboo steamer with a few pieces in a dim sum (appetizer) fashion.

This dish can also be prepared using boneless pork chunks. The pork should be cut into bite-size pieces. In this case, the dish is called Pork with Rice Powder 粉蒸肉 (fen zhen rou).

Yield: 3-4 servings

One 1.75 oz. (50 g) package Five Spice Rice Powder, specifically for steaming meat 五香蒸肉粉

If the Five Spice Rice Powder is not Available, Substitute with:

½ cup regular rice (long or short grain)

¼ tsp. five spice powder

10-12 oz. baby spare ribs or regular spare ribs cut in half crosswise (*Ask the butcher to do it for you.*)

Spare Rib Marinade:

1 Tbsp. soy sauce

Pinch of sugar

Pinch of salt

Pinch of black pepper

1 tsp. Sauvignon Blanc

Equipment:

Chinese steamer

1 *Preparing homemade rice powder:* Soak the rice for at least 4 hours or overnight. Drain in a sieve for 30 minutes. Spread the rice out in a paper-towel-lined plate and let the rice dry at room temperature for a few hours. Place in a food processor with no water, and pulse a few times until rice is broken into very small bits. Add ¼ tsp. five spice powder, and mix well.

2 Cut the spare ribs into separate ribs. Marinate with the marinade ingredients and let sit at room temperature for 30-60 minutes, or overnight in the refrigerator.

3 Bring a large steamer pot of water to a boil. Make sure there is enough water to steam for 50-60 minutes over medium high heat or check the water level half way through the steaming.

4 Add the rice powder to the marinated spare ribs, and mix to coat well.

5 Turn steamer pot heat to low. Place coated spare ribs in one layer on a plate and place in the steaming rack, making sure there is space between the spare ribs to let the steam in. Turn the heat to medium high and steam for 50-60 minutes. After 30 minutes, turn the heat to low to make sure the steamer pot still has enough water. Add water if needed, then turn to medium high again. Be careful of the steam; it is very hot. Serve hot. If you have a mini bamboo steamer, you can transfer the spare ribs to it to serve at the dining table.

Dong Po Pork 東坡肉
(dong po ro) ****

This dish is named after a brilliant Song Dynasty (宋朝 960-1279 AD) writer, SU Dong-Po (蘇東坡). He was not only a poet but a sharp and witty essayist. His open criticism of public policy angered the Song Emperor and court officials. As a result, time after time he was demoted to remote areas to serve as local magistrate. Once, he was sent as far away as Hainan Island (海南島) in the South China Sea. With his wit and unyielding spirit, his experience fueled his poems and essays. He was immensely popular with the common folks.

This dish is credited to him, honoring his gourmet expertise. The story goes that he left meat in a pot to cook while he was playing Go (圍棋) (Chinese chess) with a friend. He totally forgot about the meat until he finished the game. He expected to find the meat burned and ruined, but to his surprise, the meat was tender and aromatic. He even wrote a poem about how to cook this dish: "Heat up low flame/Place less water/Wooden flame low and red with no smoke/Let meat cook by itself/Do not rush the cooking process/Beautiful meat done with just right flame time" (慢著火，少著水，柴頭爐煙焰不起，待他自熟莫催化，火燒足時他自美。).

The cut of pork used here—called Five Layer Pork (五花肉) in Chinese because of its alternating layers of fat and lean meat—is what is used to make bacon. It is surprising that this cut is difficult to find in supermarkets except in Chinatown. After being slow cooked for a long time, the fat changes texture, and it does not feel like one is eating fat. This meat is MAO Ze-Dong's favorite. If you cannot get this meat cut, you can substitute with some sort of pork with skin, such as pork butt. In Taiwan, commercially made Dong Po Pork is sold in the traditional markets in 3-inch cubes of meat.

Yield: 5-6 servings

1 lb. pork belly with skin (Five Layer Pork 五花肉) or substitute with pork butt with skin

2 stalks scallion

2 cloves garlic

4 Tbsp. soy sauce

1 tsp. sugar

¼ tsp. five spice powder (五香粉)

3 slices fresh ginger

1 tsp. Cognac or Sauvignon Blanc

A few drops balsamic vinegar or black Chinese vinegar

1½ -2 cups water

A pinch of black pepper

1 Crush garlic with the flat side of the knife to loosen and remove the skin.

2 Cut off the tip and ends of the scallions and cut into ½-inch lengths.

3 Five Layer Pork is usually packed as one large piece about 1¼ lbs. with one rib on top. The bone can be cooked with the meat. Cut pork with skin into two-inch cubes.

4 Bring a pot of water with a pinch of salt to boil and drop in the pork chunks. Let cook for about 2 minutes. Remove the pork from the pot and rinse with water. Discard the water.

5 Place the boiled pork chunks in a pot or a CorningWare pot. Add the rest of the ingredients with 1½-2 cups water. Bring the whole thing to a boil, reduce the heat to very low, cover, and simmer for 2 to 3 hours. Mix well occasionally, at least once every 30 minutes. If it looks like it's going to boil dry, add ¼ cup water. A half hour before it finishes cooking, raise the heat to medium low to thicken the sauce. The pork chunks will become a beautiful brown. When it's done, the meat and skin will be really soft. It will literally melt in your mouth.

If this dish is cooked right, the meat and skin will be so tender that it can be separated with chopsticks. To make it more tender, 3 hours simmering is necessary.

Sweet and Sour Pork 咕咾肉 (gu lao rou) ***

Polynesian-style Chinese restaurants are notorious for this dish. It is terrible most of the time. Whenever I see this dish on the menu, it takes away all my appetite and makes my stomach turn "sour." Here I use canned pineapple chunks instead of sugar to get a naturally sweet flavor. This dish will also please non-Chinese taste buds.

You can adjust the degree of sweet and sour by varying the amount of sugar and white vinegar. However, the juice from the pineapple can is pretty sweet. To me, no additional sugar is necessary.

Yield: 4-5 servings/One plate presentation

8-10 oz. pork loin

Pork Marinade:

1 egg white

4 Tbsp. cornstarch

A pinch of salt

1 Tbsp. Sauvignon Blanc

2 cloves garlic

1 yellow bell pepper

1 light green long bell pepper, green bell pepper, or red bell pepper

1 medium-sized tomato

One 8-oz. can pineapple rings *(Reserve the syrup)*

2 cups canola oil

Sauce Ingredients:

Juice from the pineapple can *(Using sugar makes it taste unnaturally sweet.)*

2 Tbsp. unsalted ketchup *(The taste is unusually good.)*

1 Tbsp. white vinegar

A pinch of salt

1 Tbsp. cornstarch

¼ cup water

1 Use the spine of a cleaver to pound both sides of the pork loin. Slice pork into one-inch length slices. Marinate pork slices with one egg white and 4 Tbsp. cornstarch.

2 Remove top stem and seeds from the bell peppers and cut into irregular cubes.

3 Score the tomato from the top to bottom in a few places, then drop into a small pot of boiling water for one minute. Remove tomato and place in a pot of cold water. Peel off the skin, cut in half from the side, and squeeze out the seeds. Cut into one-inch cubes.

4 Remove the pineapple from the can and reserve the syrup. Cut the pineapple into one-inch chunks.

5 Pound the garlic with the flat side of a cleaver to remove the skin, and cut off the root end of the garlic clove.

6 Combine the sauce ingredients in a separate bowl and set aside.

7 Heat up the wok over high heat for about 3-4 minutes. Add 2 cups canola oil, slide pork slices into the oil. Deep fry pork pieces until golden brown. Remove the pork and drain the oil. Leave about 3 Tbsp. oil in the wok.

8 Turn the heat to medium high, and add garlic. When the garlic turns golden brown, remove it. Add cut up bell peppers, and stir fry about 3-4 minutes. Add tomato, pineapple chunks, ¼ cup water, and mix well. Cover for 2-3 minutes. Add fried pork slices, sprinkle 1 Tbsp. Sauvignon Blanc, and salt then quickly mix, and reduce heat to medium. Add the sauce ingredients, and mix well. While stir frying, if you see the wok is too hot or dry, add ¼ cup water to kind of "steam" the vegetables. Be careful as it releases the hot steam. It also quickly brings down the temperature. This is a common practice for this kind of cooking method. Adjust the sweet and sour taste. Serve hot.

Ground Pork Steamed with Chinese Pickles 花瓜蒸肉 (hua gua zhen rou) *

Unlike American pickles which are usually sweet and sour, Chinese pickles are salty and a little sweet. They come in cans and jars with a range of textures: crunchy, soft, and very soft. Chinese pickles are usually served with rice porridge for breakfast. Regardless of which Chinese pickles you use for this dish, the results are fairly similar. This dish can be prepared with great ease.

This cooking method can be applied to quite a few dishes, like Ground Pork Steamed with Salty Egg, Ground Pork Steamed with Fermented Black Bean Sauce. You can also substitute with baby spare ribs. In that case, the steaming time needs to be longer, about 50-60 minutes for spare ribs.

Yield: 4-5 servings/One plate presentation

> 10 oz. ground pork (I prefer coarsely ground.)
>
> One 6 oz. can or jar of Chinese pickles (花瓜)
>
> 1 Tbsp. soy sauce
>
> 3 Tbsp. water
>
> A pinch of black pepper

Equipment:
Chinese steamer

1 Coarsely chop the Chinese pickles.

2 In a stainless steel bowl, mix ground pork with 1 Tbsp. soy sauce, 3 Tbsp. water, one pinch of freshly ground black pepper, and the chopped pickles with its liquid. (Add ¼ cup more water if you prefer a lighter taste.) In the same bowl you used to mix, press hole-like indentations into the meat with your fingers to make it cook through more easily.

3 Bring the steamer water to a boil. Turn off the heat and open the cover. Be careful as the steam is quite hot. Place the bowl with the meat mixture on the steamer rack and cover. Turn on the heat and steam over medium high heat for 25-30 minutes. Or, if you don't have a steamer, put the stainless steel pot directly in the water in the wok and cover, steaming for 20 minutes. This method cooks faster than on a steamer rack. Serve hot or at room temperature with rice. The sauce from the dish is appetizing and delicious.

Shredded Pork with Fish Aroma 魚香肉絲 (yu xiang rou si) ***

This dish has a distinctively Sichuan taste. Sichuan dishes are well known for their spicy and Sichuan peppercorn taste—the numb sensation "麻" created by the Sichuan peppercorn). Originally the sauce was used for a fish dish, but making any dish with the same cooking technique, the taste develops the "fish aroma" (yu xiang 魚香) taste.

The key to success with this dish is to have the scallion, ginger, and garlic all very finely chopped. The distinctive aroma that comes out of this finely chopped trio is like nothing else! I got this tip from Mrs. Duan (段小毅太太) a Sichuan native and owner of the Sichuan Garden (四川飯莊) in Brookline, MA.

Yield: 3-4 servings/One plate presentation

> 8 oz. pork loin

Pork Marinade:
> 1 Tbsp. soy sauce
>
> A pinch of Sichuan peppercorn or black pepper
>
> A few drops Cognac or your favorite wine
>
> 1 tsp. cornstarch

> ½ cup dried tree ears
>
> 2 cloves garlic
>
> 3 slices of fresh young ginger (Young ginger is only available during the summer. Do not substitute with ginger powder; it is bitter and does not have the distinctive fresh ginger aroma.)
>
> 4 stalks scallion
>
> 1-2 fresh or dried chili peppers
>
> 2-3 sticks celery
>
> 3 Tbsp. canola oil
>
> Salt to taste
>
> ½ cup water

Sauce Ingredients:
> 1 Tbsp. soy sauce
>
> 1 tsp. balsamic vinegar or rice vinegar
>
> 1 tsp. sugar

1 tsp. cornstarch

A pinch of Sichuan peppercorn or freshly ground black pepper

A quarter of the mixture of finely chopped scallion, garlic, and ginger

1 Reconstitute the dried tree ears by soaking them in hot water for one hour. Remove the stem-like tough part with a knife. Then, use both hands to rub the tree ears against each other inside a pot of water. Lift the tree ears from the water and discard the water. Repeat this step a couple of times, and then coarsely chop the tree ears.

2 Cut the pork loin into thin strips and combine with marinade ingredients.

3 Smash the garlic cloves with the flat side of a cleaver or knife, remove the skin, and finely chop.

4 You can easily rub off the skin of the ginger by scraping the spine of a small knife against the skin. Finely chop the deskinned ginger.

5 Cut off the scallion top and the dark green ends. Finely chop the white and half green portions.

6 From the chili peppers, remove the seeds, and finely chop.

7 Peel off the tough strings of the celery and slice thinly.

8 Combine the sauce ingredients and set aside.

9 Heat up the wok over high heat until very hot, about 3-4 minutes. Reduce heat to medium high. Add 3 Tbsp. canola oil, the rest of the finely chopped scallion, garlic and ginger, and stir a few times.

10 Add the marinated shredded pork. Stir and cook until the pork changes color to a pale pink, and then add the celery slices and tree ears. Mix well.

11 Add a little salt, and ½ cup water. Reduce heat to medium and simmer for 5 minutes. Drizzle the sauce mixture evenly over the pork mixture and stir well. Serve hot.

Ground Pork Steamed with Salted Eggs 鹹蛋蒸肉 (xian dan zhen ro) **

*Salted duck eggs are available in Chinatown grocery stores packed in a jar of salted water. However, you can make your own easily (see Salted Egg 鹹蛋 (xian dan) ** on page 204). The French use eggs to make all kinds of pastries. The Chinese change the egg's taste and texture to make it into delicacies, like brown eggs (滷蛋 lu dan), salted eggs (鹹蛋 xian dan), tea eggs (茶葉蛋 page 188) and thousand year eggs (皮蛋).*

Another variation of brown eggs is "iron eggs" (鐵蛋 tie dan), which is popular in the northern Taiwan town of Dan Shui (淡水). The brown eggs are cooked over one week, and in between the eggs are air dried. The egg becomes totally black because of the shrinkage, and looks quite small.

Yield: 4-5 servings/One plate presentation

1 salted egg (raw)

10 oz. ground pork sirloin (or chop it yourself),

Pork Marinade:

A few drops soy sauce (for flavor only)

1 tsp. Sauvignon Blanc

½ tsp. sugar

½ tsp. balsamic vinegar from Modena, Italy

A pinch of black pepper

4 Tbsp. water

1 Tbsp. cornstarch

Equipment:

Chinese steamer

1 Using a plate with some depth, like a soup plate, combine the ground pork with marinade ingredients and mix well. Crack a salted egg on top of the pork mixture. The egg yolk will be a brilliant orange/red color in one solid ball. Leaving the egg yolk whole in the center, carefully mix the egg white into the ground pork using your hand or a spoon. (Salted egg is quite salty, so no additional salt is necessary.)

2 Fill the steamer pot with enough water to steam

30 minutes over high heat. Bring water to a boil. Place the plate of pork mixture on the steamer rack. Be careful of the hot steam. Cover and turn heat to medium high.

3 Turn off the heat and let it cool down for about 10-15 minutes before removing from the steamer. Serve hot or at room temperature with rice.

Pork Strips with Dried, Marinated Mustard Greens
梅菜扣肉 (mei cai kou ro) *****

This Cantonese delicacy requires quite a few steps, and is quite hard to get right. After you have gone through the steps, you may feel like just going to a restaurant to order it, but most of the time, the restaurant version is too sweet. The homemade one is always better. This is an exotic dish even for the Chinese. The best part is the pork skin. I have had the best mei cai kou ro at a 30-year-old restaurant in Hsin Chu City, Taiwan, called Sing Tao Fang 新竹市新陶芳. The fatty pork tastes tender and greaseless. The skin glistens with a soft and chewy texture. It was a real treat.

This is such a complicated dish that it is not worth cooking just a small amount. You can double the portions in this recipe. Leftovers can be kept in the freezer and steamed again to great effect. The meat and the dried mustard green make a great combination. This is not a daily homemade dish. If you cook this dish for your guests, everybody will be so impressed that they will think you are a professional chef!

Yield: 4-5 servings/One plate presentation

Dried Mustard Greens Preparation:

One 2.29 oz./65 g package of dried mustard greens (台灣新東陽紹興梅乾菜) *Buy the one from Taiwan. Once I tried a package from China; it was tasteless. If you can't find dried mustard greens, substitute with kale. Kale is a very inexpensive vegetable and always sold in a big bunch.*

2 cloves garlic, peeled and crushed

Ingredients for Kale Prepared as Substitute for Dried Mustard Greens

1½ lbs. kale

1 tsp. salt

2 cloves garlic (*Crush with the flat side of a cleaver and discard the skin*)

4 Tbsp. soy sauce

½ tsp salt

1 Tbsp. sugar

A pinch of MSG

1 strip pork belly (五花肉) with skin on (approx. 1-1¼ lbs.) from Chinatown (*This is the pork cut used to make bacon.*)

½ cup soy sauce

1½ cup canola oil

1 Tbsp. sugar

A pinch of salt

A pinch of MSG

Equipment:

Chinese steamer

1 *Preparing dried mustard greens:* Soak dried mustard greens in water for 30 minutes, then stir vigorously to loosen any sand or foreign objects. Rinse a few times and soak again for 30 minutes. Drain for about 10 minutes.

2 *Preparation for kale as a substitute for dried mustard greens:* By accident, my son-in-law Katsuya was cooking kale with soy sauce and sautéing it until it was dry in a frying pan. The end result was incredibly similar to fresh dried mustard greens. At first he thought the dish was a total failure, but I tasted it and it was simply terrific, just like fresh dried mustard greens. Kale prepared this way is a good substitute if you can't find dried mustard greens.

   a. Cut the kale into one-inch lengths. Put the kale into a large pot (or two smaller pots) and fill it with enough water to cover the kale, and add 1 tsp. salt. Bring to a boil over high heat, then reduce heat to medium low and simmer for one hour until the kale is all cooked. As it cooks, the green kale will turn somewhat yellowish. Kale is a tough vegetable so don't worry. Just cover and let it simmer for 1 hour.

b. Kale preparation continued: Drain the water, brown 2-3 cloves garlic in a wok. Drain the kale and add 4 Tbsp. soy sauce, ½ tsp. salt, 1 Tbsp. sugar and a pinch of MSG. Stir over medium heat until all the liquid evaporates, about 20-30 minutes. It is better to cook it drier than leave it wet. The effect and taste is better and more intense. The kale will shrink in volume as it cooks.

3 Cut the pork belly into roughly three equal pieces (about two-inches each). Bring about 3 cups of water to a boil in a pot and add the pork belly. Bring it to another boil, and reduce heat to medium low. Cover and cook for 30 minutes. Remove the meat from the pot and drain dry. Save the cooked water for later use.

4 In a large shallow pot, add ½ cup soy sauce. Add the chunks of meat to the pot one by one and fully coat in the soy sauce on both sides so the meat become light brown in color. Use a hand-held sieve or colander to let the meat drain thoroughly for about 15 minutes over a large plate. Save the soy sauce drippings from the meat.

5 Use a paper towel to pat dry the meat chunks thoroughly, so when they are deep fried, the splattering will be kept to a minimum.

6 Heat 1½ cups canola oil in a wok, for about 3-4 minutes until hot. Gently add meat chunks, sliding them away from your body, and into the hot oil. Be careful; the oil will still pop and splatter. Cover the wok right away (to keep from splattering yourself) for 3 minutes. Remove the cover and gently turn the meat to the other side and cover for another 3 minutes. At this point, it may suddenly splatter because of the skin, so be careful not to hurt yourself.

7 Turn off the heat and remove the meat chunks, immersing them in a pot of cold water. Run cold tap water over the pot with the deep fried meat chunks for about 5 minutes. This is a rather interesting technique. Not only does it get rid of the grease from the meat chunks but also makes the skin texture very "chewy, bouncy" and yet soft, an effect caused by the sudden hot to cold temperature change which expands and shrinks the skin.

8 Traditionally, the meat is sliced thinly lengthwise into rectangles about 3-inches by 1½-inches, but I find it's rather difficult to slice lengthwise if the knife in your kitchen is not restaurant sharp. You can slice it crosswise, but then slice the meat a little thicker, maybe ¼-inch thick.

9 (Skip this step if you are using freshly made kale.) Pour off the oil in the wok, leaving about 3 Tbsps. Heat the oil until hot, add crushed garlic, and stir fry until brown, then remove and discard. Add the water soaked Dried Marinated Mustard Green (梅乾菜) with 1 Tbsp. soy sauce, 1 Tbsp. sugar, a pinch of MSG, a pinch of salt, and mix well with the Dried Marinated Mustard Green. At this point the dried mustard green does not have too much taste.

10 In a large bowl, line sliced meat from step **8** skin side down one after the other in a neat row. Line up all the meat this way. Place all the cooked Dried Marinated Mustard Green from step **9** or the freshly made kale from step **2** on top of the lined meat pieces.

11 In a small pot, add 1 cup soup from step **3** and the soy sauce from step **4**. Bring to a boil then reduce heat to medium and let cook for about 5-10 minutes until the liquid is reduced to about ½ cup. Sprinkle the sauce over the bowl of meat slices and dried mustard from step **10**.

12 Bring to boil a steamer pot filled about two-thirds full with water. Turn down the heat, place the bowl with meat and dried marinated mustard green on the steaming rack. Turn heat to medium and steam for 2 to 3 hours. Check the steamer pot water level every 30 minutes, and add more water to the steamer if it runs low. (To make the skin more tender, it may need to be steamed longer.) Turn off the heat and open the cover a little to let it cool down for about 10-15 minutes.

13 Some water will have accumulated in the bowl during the steaming. Gently tip the meat bowl to pour off the liquid into another bowl.

14 Have a large plate with some depth cover the meat bowl tightly. Hold the plate and bowl together and quickly flip the meat bowl contents onto the large plate. It is a beautiful design with neatly lined skin side up meat pieces. Drizzle the liquid from step **13** all over the flipped plate.

Tofu Cubes with Pork Filling
醸豆腐 (niang do fu) ****

This dish is very popular in the South of China especially among the Hakka minority people (客家人). Hakka literally means "guests." In the old days, this minority group migrated from central China all the way to southern China, to Canton and its vicinity over a rather long period of time. There is a group which settled in the central Miao Li (苗栗) and the northwest corridor Hsin Chu (新竹) of Taiwan as well as in the southern part of Taiwan Ping Dong (屏東). They speak their own dialect, which is different from the Taiwanese and Cantonese dialects.

There is a story about this dish. The first emperor of the Ming Dynasty, ZHU Hong-Wu (明太祖朱洪武) was very poor when he was little and had to beg for food. One restaurant in Feng Yang, Anhui (安徽省鳳陽縣) gave him this dish, and he liked it a lot. After he toppled the Yuan Dynasty (The Genghis Khan Dynasty) (元朝) in 1368 AD and became the Ming Emperor, he took the chef to his palace to cook for him. Feng Yang Tofu (鳳陽醸豆腐) is a variation of this recipe in which two pieces of tofu are hollowed out and filled with a meat mixture, then put back together and deep fried.

Yield: 3-4 servings

2 squares of firm tofu *(Use the traditional Chinese tofu, or the firm tofu in supermarkets.)*

Filling Ingredients:

3 oz. pork loin, finely chopped or ground

4 oz. shrimp with shells on

1 tsp. soy sauce

1 tsp. sesame oil

1 tsp. Sauvignon Blanc

A pinch of salt

A pinch of black pepper

1 Tbsp. cornstarch

Cornstarch

3 Tbsp. canola oil

Iceberg lettuce or Boston lettuce leaves

1 *Tofu preparation:* This step ensures a successful deep fried tofu. Drop the tofu into a pot of hot water with a pinch of salt for 2 minutes, and then drain the water. Cut the tofu to half its thickness so you have two thinner squares of tofu. Then cut each slice into four triangles or squares.

2 *Shrimp preparation:* Peel the shrimp and devein by running a knife along the "spine" of the shrimp and removing the sandy black vein inside. Rub shrimp with some salt and rinse clean. Drain and sprinkle with a little salt. Put the shrimp inside a plastic bag (to prevent splattering) and smash each shrimp with the flat side of a cleaver

3 Mix the ground pork and shrimp with 1 Tbsp. cornstarch, 1 tsp. soy sauce, 1 tsp. sesame oil, a pinch of salt, a pinch of black pepper, 1 tsp. Sauvignon Blanc. Mix in one direction briskly until well mixed. By mixing in one direction, the chopped pork/shrimp mixture will become sticky and have a chewy texture after it's cooked. The meat will kind of "bounce back" when you bite into it. In Chinese, this chewy texture is called *jiao jing* (嚼勁) or a presently popular Taiwanese term "spring between teeth" (彈牙 *tan ya*). In the Taiwanese dialect it's called "Q." (The word in Taiwanese sounds like the English letter "Q.")

4 Scoop out a little of the middle of each tofu triangle to fill in the pork/shrimp mixture but do not make a hole on the other side. (This is pretty tricky; if you do not handle it right, the tofu will break.) Sprinkle a pinch of cornstarch into the hollow (so the filling will stick to the tofu), and fill with about ½ to 1 Tbsp. pork/shrimp mixture.

Do the same with the rest of the triangles. Any leftover pork/shrimp mixture can be made into meatballs to fry or cook in soup.

5 Heat up a non-stick frying pan to medium high for 2-3 minutes. Add 3 Tbsp. canola oil to the frying pan. Gently place each tofu filling side down in the frying pan. Let fry for 2-3 minutes, then gently flip to the other side and fry for another 2-3 minutes until golden. Remove and place on a plate.

6 Mix the leftover pork/shrimp mixture with the tofu pieces that were dug out to make meat balls and deep fry them.

7 To serve, place one fried tofu on a lettuce leaf on a plate. Top with catsup or chili sauce. Or, simply serve alone without the lettuce.

8 As an alternative to deep frying, the filled tofu pieces can be placed on a plate and steamed on a steamer rack over medium high heat for 8-10 minutes. Serve hot, or cool to room temperature to serve as an appetizer.

Pork Slices with Garlic Paste
蒜泥白肉 (suan ni bai rou) ***

Pork Slices with Garlic Paste is a very well-known classic Sichuan dish. In the old days, having a plate of thinly sliced pork was a luxury. The best cuts to use are pork butt and pork belly which are tender and soft. If those cuts are not available, you can get country style pork. I asked the owner of Sichuan Garden, Mrs. DUAN, who grew up in Sichuan (四川) about Sichuan dishes. She told me that the mixture of scallion, ginger, garlic (蔥薑蒜) and Sichuan peppercorn is the essence of the distinctive Sichuan flavor. Most Chinese restaurants use Sichuan bean paste as a substitute. Those so-called Sichuan dishes are not authentic at all. Sichuan Garden (四川飯莊) in Brookline, MA near Boston has the best Pork Slices with Garlic Paste. The sauce is simply fantastic. The chef is directly from Sichuan, China.

Yield: 3-4 servings/One plate presentation

10-12 oz. country style pork or pork loin

2 stalks scallion, cut off tips, cut off half the green part, and finely chop

4 cloves garlic

2 Tbsp. unsalted, roasted peanuts

2 pickling cucumbers (optional)

***Sauce Mix:**

2 Tbsp. soy sauce

1 tsp. balsamic vinegar or black vinegar

½ tsp. sugar

2 Tbsp. boiled water

½ tsp. chili oil

¼ tsp. freshly ground black pepper. *(The original one uses Sichuan peppercorn 四川花椒 that is hard to get even in Chinatown grocery stores.)*

**The sauce tastes better if it is somewhat spicy.*

1 **Pork preparation:** Trim off any sinew and place in a pot of boiling water. Bring to another boil, cover, reduce heat to medium low and simmer for 10-15 minutes. Turn off the heat, let the pork sit in the covered pot for at least 30 minutes before slicing. (It is important to cook meat this way so that it will come out tender and moist.)

2 *Vegetable preparation:* Cut off the scallion tops and trim the damaged ends. Cut off and discard half the green part and finely chop the rest. Use the flat side of a cleaver to smash the garlic cloves and remove the skin. Put the garlic in a ceramic mortar and use the pestle to pound it until the garlic becomes like a paste. Use a glass bottle or rolling pin to grind the roasted peanuts. Another easy way is to put the peanuts inside a plastic bag, and then grind it into a powder.

3 Remove the pork loin from the pot, let it cool down for 5-10 minutes, and then thinly slice into pieces 1-inch by 2-inches. Neatly line a plate with the pork slices.

4 Mix together the finely chopped scallion and the garlic paste with the sauce mixture ingredients. Drizzle the sauce over the pork slices, then sprinkle with ground peanuts and serve at room temperature.

Pork Slice Rolls Variation: Slice two fresh pickling cucumbers then stack and cut into thin strips. It's all right to keep the skin on. Spread out a pork slice and roll it around a small bunch of cucumber strips. Neatly line up the pork rolls on a plate and drizzle with the sauce mixture, and then sprinkle with ground peanuts.

Egg Caps Over Vegetables/ Mu Shu Pork 合菜戴帽/木樨肉/木須肉 (he cai dai mao/mu xi ro/mu shu ro) ***

When this dish is completed, the mixture looks like a cinnamon blossom (桂花) called "mu xi" (木樨) in Chinese. The Chinese characters for mu xi are hard to write, so it becomes mu shu (木須) the easier word, which appears in restaurant menus. This recipe was originally presented with a round egg pancake covering the whole dish in a dramatic presentation. That is the original mu shu dish. (It is also a way to prevent the dish from getting cold in a beautiful way.) The ingredients can vary, but pork, egg, tree ears, and cellophane noodles are the main ingredients. The other ingredients can be substituted with other vegetables.

Yield: 10-15 rolls

8 oz. pork loin, cut into thin slices,

> **Pork Marinade:**
>
> 1 Tbsp. soy sauce
>
> 1 Tbsp. Cognac or your favorite wine
>
> A few drops of canola oil
>
> 1 Tbsp. cornstarch
>
> A pinch of black pepper

2 cloves of shallots

One 1.76oz/50g package of dried cellophane noodles

¼ cup dried tree ears

4 oz. fresh bean sprouts

2 stalks celery hearts

4 oz. Chinese yellow chive (韭黃) (optional) *(The pale yellowish chive has a very distinctive fragrance and is quite crunchy, although it can be a little expensive.)*

6-8 fresh water chestnuts (optional)

¼-½ cup canola oil

10-15 Mandarin pancakes (see Pancakes for Peking Duck 北京烤鴨 and Mu Shu Dishes 薄餅 (bo bing) /荷葉餅 (he ye bing) **** on page 115) *A substitute is Mexican flour tortillas or French crepes*

1 egg, beaten

Hoisin sauce or your favorite chili sauce, such as Tabasco (海鮮醬/辣椒醬)

1 *Pork preparation:* Combine thinly sliced pork loin with marinade ingredients and set aside.

2 *Vegetable preparation:* Soak dried tree ears in hot water for 30 minutes, then rub them against each other to get rid of the sand, and cut off the hard stem tip. Soak the cellophane noodles in hot water for 10 minutes, and then pull it into shorter strands. It can be cut, too, but the pulling makes the cellophane noodles come out in more interesting irregular lengths. Peel the strings from the celery hearts and cut into small slices. Cut the yellow chive into ½-inch lengths. Peel off the brown skin of the fresh water chestnuts and remove any yellow parts, and then thinly slice. Peel shallots and then thinly slice.

3 Heat up the wok over high heat for about 3-4 minutes. Add ¼-½ cup canola oil then the marinated pork loin. The more oil the better, as the idea is to "slide" the meat through the oil. This method makes the meat tender. Stir and separate the pork slices, about 2 minutes, and remove from the wok and drain the oil. Turn off the heat. There may be some meat crystallization sticking to the bottom of the wok. That is called faun and is quite tasty. Do not wash the wok.

4 Turn heat to medium high. Add 3 Tbsp. oil to the wok; add shallot slices; and stir until golden. Add celery heart, tree ears, water chestnut, and sprinkle with salt. Stir and add 1 cup water and reduce heat to medium. Let the mixture cook for 5 minutes.

5 Add cellophane noodles and cook for 3-4 minutes. If the water dries out, add ¼-½ cup water. Add chives, bean sprouts and the cooked pork. Stir for about 2-3 minutes until the ingredients have blended well. Salt to taste. Remove to a large plate.

6 Heat up a non-stick frying pan over medium high for 2 minutes; add 1 Tbsp. canola oil, then slowly pour in the beaten egg. After a few seconds when the egg has set, flip it to the other side for a few seconds to make an egg pancake. Cover the ure

from step **5** with the egg pancake.

7 Wrap Mandarin pancakes in a piece of aluminum foil on a steamer rack and set over a pot of boiling water. Steam for 10 minutes.

8 At serving time, cut the egg pancake on top of the mu shu pork like a pizza. To eat, put about 2-3 Tbsp. of mu shu pork on a Mandarin pancake in a rectangular pile in the lower third of the pancake. Roll the pancake around the filling and fold in both ends at the halfway point, then finish by brushing a little swish of hoisin sauce across the upper third. Roll up and eat.

Taiwanese-Style Stewed Fatty Pork Sauce with Rice
滷肉飯 (lu ba beng - Taiwanese pronunciation) ***

Every Taiwanese knows this dish. In the old days, not every family had the luxury of eating meat every day. My mother used pork belly—the pork cut used to make bacon—cut into large chunks. She would then add soy sauce and other spices and let the fatty pork simmer on the stove for a pretty long time until the pork chunks became soft and tender, blending in with all the sauces. Each person would have a bowl of hot rice topped with some of this meaty sauce. It was the most satisfying feeling. Nothing else is needed to finish the rice. It was good, economical and a little meat would go a long way.

Drop the meat strips and skin in the boiling water and cook for a few minutes before cutting into small chunks. This way it is easier to cut through the tough skin. I got this tip from my friend in Hsin Chu, Taiwan (新竹), Ms. LU Siu-Mei (盧秀美), an ardent organic food lover and a retired home economics teacher.

In this dish, traditionally the meat chunks are pretty fatty and cut into large chunks; however after cooking for a long time, the fatty meat becomes soft and not greasy. I read a book that said after fatty meat is cooked for a long time, it is good for our skin. I don't know if it has any scientific basis. This kind of dish has regional variations, and many Chinese love it, including MAO Ze-Dong (毛澤東). It is best served with fluffy, hot, white rice.

Yield: 6-7 servings

  2 strips raw, unsalted pork belly (五花肉) or about 1¾ lbs. *(Or, use pork butt pieces with some fatty parts.)*

  One piece pork skin, about ½ pound (optional)

  6 dried Chinese black mushrooms

  ¼ cup small dried shrimps (optional)

  6-10 cloves of shallots (the more the better)

  5-6 Tbsp. canola oil

  1½ Tbsp. soy sauce

  2 Tbsp. Sauvignon Blanc, Cognac or your favorite wine

  1 tsp. balsamic vinegar or black vinegar

  1 tsp. sugar

  1 tsp. Sichuan bean paste (豆瓣醬) (optional)

  1 tsp. black pepper

  A pinch of five spice powder (五香粉) *(Available in Chinatown grocery stores and online. Sometimes it can be found in the supermarket spice section.)*

  A pinch of salt

1 Soak the dried Chinese black mushrooms in 1½ cups hot water for 1 hour, and reserve the water. Remove the stem, slice into thin strips, and then cut into tiny pieces.

2 Soak the dried shrimp in 1 cup hot water for 30 minutes. Reserve the water, and coarsely chop the shrimp.

3 *Pork belly preparation:* Remove the skin and the spare rib bone on top. (If the skin is too hard to remove, just leave it there.) The meat left will be about 1 lb. 4 oz. Cut the meat into 3 to 4 large pieces. Cook the meat and the skin in a pot with 4 cups boiling water for about 3 minutes over medium high heat (Meat is easier to cut after having been boiled first.) Remove the meat from the pot (saving the water from the pork skin preparation). Let it cool down about 10 minutes. Cut meat into roughly one-inch cubes. (In the Chinatown grocery, this is a very popular item in the meat section.)

4 *Pork skin preparation:* Boil the skin for 5 minutes in the water that was used for boiling the pork belly in the previous step. Remove the skin from the water and reserve the water. Cut the skin into one-inch squares.

5 Peel the shallots and slice thinly.

6 Heat the wok over high heat about 3 minutes. Reduce heat to medium high. Add 5-6 Tbsp. canola oil and thinly sliced shallot to the wok. Stir until golden, but not brown. When the shallots are done, they will be light, golden, and aromatic. Add the mushrooms, the dried shrimps, and the meat chunks to the wok; stir well.

7 Transfer the contents of the wok to a pot and add the pork skin. Add the water used to boil the meat chunks plus the soaking water for the mushrooms and dried shrimp, and the rest of the ingredients. The water should cover all the entire contents. Bring the pot to a boil. Taste the liquid; it should be on the salty side. Turn heat to low and simmer for 30 minutes.

8 Check to see if it is too dry. If so, add ½ to 1 cup water, and simmer for another 30 minutes or longer until the mixture still has some sauce but is not too watery. Serve warm but not hot.

9 To reheat any leftovers, add ½ to 1 cup water and simmer the second day again for 10-15 minutes or longer. It becomes even better, softer, and juicier the next day.

Sichuan Pickled Mustard Greens with Pork 榨菜炒肉絲 (zha cai chao rou si) **

Sichuan pickled mustard green (四川榨菜) comes in a can or packed into plastic bags. The canned one comes either already shredded or in chunks. When you buy it, make sure you check the label to get the kind in chunks. The shredded kind tends to have some coarse parts mixed in it. Sichuan pickled mustard green is quite salty and spicy. You can dilute its flavor by washing off the spicy chili pepper powder that coats it. When it is cooked with meat, especially pork, it enhances the flavor tremendously with its distinctive taste. I have not been able to find fresh pickled mustard greens in the U.S. You can either get the one from China or Taiwan. I have tried both and found the one from Taiwan is fresher, lighter in color, and crunchier in texture. It is packed in a clear plastic bag, but the one from Taiwan is not available in all Chinatown groceries. You have to really look and ask the store people. There is no need to add any salt to a dish with Sichuan pickled mustard greens.

Sichuan pickled mustard green can keep quite a while, for one or two months. After opening the can or plastic bag, transfer it to a glass jar. Each time you cook, just use a small chunk. It is enough for a whole dish.

Yield: 3-4 servings/One plate presentation

10 oz. pork loin, cut into thin strips,

> **Pork Marinade:**
>
> 1 tsp. soy sauce
>
> A few drops canola oil
>
> 1 Tbsp. cornstarch

½ cup Sichuan pickled mustard greens (四川榨菜), cut into thin strips

3-4 sticks celery hearts (optional)

2 cloves garlic

3 Tbsp. canola oil

1 Cut the pork into strips and mix with the marinade ingredients and set aside. Cut off both ends of the celery and peel off the stringy part. Remove the leaves. Slice thinly. Using the flat side of a cleaver, smash the garlic and the skin will come off easily

2 Heat up the wok over high heat until very hot, about 3-4 minutes. Reduce heat to medium high and add 3 Tbsp. canola oil, and garlic. Stir fry until the garlic turns golden brown and discard the garlic. However, if you like the garlic, you can leave it in, but do not cook it until it turns brown and burns. When the garlic is golden, add the marinated pork shreds. Stir and separate until the pork has changed color, but not quite fully cooked. Add Sichuan pickled mustard green; stir and turn heat to medium. Add celery slices, stir and sprinkle with about ½ cup water. Cover for about 3-5 minutes. Stir well and remove. Serve hot. No need to add salt. The Sichuan mustard green can take care of the whole dish's flavor.

Chinese Red Barbecue Pork-*Cha Shao* Pork 叉燒肉 (cha shao ro) ***

In the word cha shao, "cha" is the iron hook holding the meat strips, and "shao" means "roast." The restaurant version "cha shao" is roasted with the meat strips hanging on iron hooks over a large commercial oven. This is one of the most well-known Chinese food items in the States. Here I try to come up with a version as close as possible to the Chinese restaurant one. The result is delightfully better. The red is food coloring so you can skip it.

There is one ingredient—fermented glutinous rice—which you can only get from the refrigerated section of a Chinatown grocery store. It is packed in a glass jar with fermented sweet rice floating in a clear liquid. Because of the fermentation, the sweet rice has a sponge-like soft texture with the aroma of wine. You can skip it and still get similar result, but of course that "mysterious" taste will be missing. It is also used to tenderize meat.

The Hakka people are very fond of fermented sweet rice. They come in white and red, but only the white one is available in Chinatown grocery stores. It is supposed to be very good to build up one's energy and body strength. One butcher in Hsin Chu, Taiwan told me that cooking an egg with fermented sweet rice is the easiest way to boost one's energy, especially in the winter time. The cha shao can be sliced thin and presented in a plate. It can also be sliced and cook with other ingredients, like cha shao fried rice. Sometimes steamed bun fillings also contain cha shao. It is also one of the main ingredients in Japanese ramen noodle soup.

Yield: 4-8 servings

- 1-2 lbs country-style pork strip, cut into 2-4 long chunky strips
- 2 Tbsp. fermented sweet rice, 甜酒釀 (optional) *sold in the Chinatown grocery's refrigerated section*
- 2 Tbsp. hoisin sauce 海鮮醬 *(sold in supermarkets and Chinese groceries)*
- 5 Tbsp. soy sauce
- 1-2 Tbsp. Sauvignon Blanc or your favorite wine *(Wine is also a tenderizer.)*
- ¼ tsp. five spice powder 五香粉

2 star anise 八角

4-5 whole cloves 丁香

A pinch of cinnamon powder 肉桂

2-3 pieces fresh ginger

2 stalks scallion, cut off top tip, cut off half green part, cut into 1" lengths, pound flat with the flat side of a knife

Orange peel from half an orange (use the leftover orange peel from an orange, 橘子皮 ju zi pi)

A pinch of black pepper

1-2 tsp. sugar

A pinch of salt

1 cup water

A couple drops of red food coloring (optional)

1 In a pot, add all the ingredients except the red food coloring and the pork strips. Bring the mixture to a boil, reduce heat to medium low and simmer for 15-20 minutes. Let the mixture cool down to room temperature. (Mix in the food coloring at this point if you are using it.) Add the pork strips to the mixture, thoroughly coat the pork strips in the sauce. Cover with plastic wrap and place in the refrigerator for 3-4 hours or longer, even overnight.

2 Preheat oven to 375° F. Remove pork strips from the marinade, removing any solids that may cling to the pork strips.

3 Place pork strips on a wire rack over a baking pan lined with aluminum foil, so that it will not make a mess while roasting. Bake about 60-70 minutes. If the edge of the pork strip burns a little, that is okay.

4 Slice pork thinly and arrange neatly on a plate. Serve at room temperature.

Pork Liver Cold Platter Appetizer 紅燒豬肝 (hong shao zhu gan) **

This dish frequently appears on the platter of cold appetizers (冷盤). The cold platter is usually the first dish in a banquet. Other popular cold platter items are red cook beef (滷牛肉 lu niu rou), thousand year eggs, drunken chicken, smoked fish, vegetarian duck, and red barbecue pork cha shao. Everyone is sure to like this liver dish.

My mother always cooked the pork liver so that there were still some traces of blood in the middle. It is supposed to be good for people who have anemia.

Yield: 4-5 servings

¾-1 lb. pork liver, cut into 3 large pieces

1 tsp. sugar

1 tsp. Cognac

2 Tbsp. soy sauce

2 tsp. Balsamic vinegar

1 tsp. canola oil or sesame oil

2 stalks scallion

A pinch of black pepper

¼ tsp. five spice powder

2-3 cups water

2 stalks scallion (for garnish)

1 With the flat side of a knife, pound the scallion flat and cut into ½-inch lengths.

2 In a pot, add all the ingredients except the pork liver with 2-3 cup water. Bring the mixture to a boil, add pork liver and bring to another boil. Skim off the foam on top. Cover and reduce heat to low and simmer for 15 minutes. Turn off the heat and let the pork liver stay inside the pot covered for one hour until ready to serve. Let it cool down to room temperature. Remove and cut into thin slices. If it is not served right away, it can be refrigerated in the pot with the liquid overnight, which enhances the flavor even more.

3 It is all right if the middle of the pork liver is still a little reddish. Pork liver is very tender this way. Thinly slice the pork liver chunks and arrange neatly on a plate. Cut off the green part of two scallions and thinly slice the white part at an angle to make the slices look longer and more aesthetically pleasing. Arrange sliced scallion around the side of the liver. Serve one piece of pork liver with one piece of scallion per person.

Taiwanese-Style Deep Fried Red Pork 台灣紅燒肉 (tai wan hong shao rou) ***

This dish brings back fond memories. Whenever there was a celebration of some sort, usually for the Buddha "bai bai," my mother would cook this dish with one piece of "five layer pork" (pork belly 五花肉 wu hua rou). A little red food coloring mixed in with the very grainy Taiwanese yam starch coated this meat. After the pork is deep fried, it looks really pretty displayed on the offering table for "bai bai" to the Buddha god or goddess.

Yield: 3-4 servings

> 1-2 pieces country style pork; or one piece pork loin (usually sold as two per package); or one 1-1¼ lb. piece of pork belly if available.
>
> 1-2 drops red food coloring (to create a festive mood for this dish)
>
> 6 Tbsp. Taiwanese yam starch (粒狀蕃薯粉), the grainy type, not the finely ground one. Cornstarch can be substituted, but it does not have the same crispy effect as yam starch (4 Tbsp. = ¼ cup)
>
> ¼ cup water
>
> 1 tsp. sugar
>
> ⅛ tsp. salt
>
> 1 Tbsp. Sauvignon Blanc or your favorite wine

1 Cut the meat into ½-inch thick strips with the original meat chunk length about ½" x 6" so they cook through when fried.

2 Mix all the ingredients together except the pork. The mixture should be quite watery. Add pork to it and mix well.

3 Heat up 1-2 cup canola oil in a wok over high heat for 3-4 minutes. One by one, pick up each pork strip and let the watery starchy coating drip off. Then put three strips in the oil at a time. Turn the heat to medium and deep fry one side about 3-4 minutes. Do not turn the pork strips for at least 3 minutes. If the pork strip is turned too early, the meat will stick to the wok. Gently turn the pork to the other side and fry another 3-4 minutes. If it burns a little, it's okay as it will be crispy outside and juicy inside.

4 Let the pork strips cool for about 5 minutes, then cut into thin strips and serve. It can be dipped with soy sauce or other favorite sauce.

Pipa Tofu 琵琶豆腐
(pi pa dou fu) ****

This dish is a Cantonese delicacy. The ingredients are quite simple, just tofu and egg. However, it is not easy to handle. The tofu has to be the medium firm type. If the tofu is too soft, it is hard to put it together; and if the tofu is too firm, the dish will not come out as tender. This is a very popular dish in Cantonese restaurants. Try it yourself; you will love it.

Yield: 16 pipa tofu

2 eggs

2 pieces of tofu, medium firm

1 Tbsp. cornstarch

2 Tbsp. Chinese BBQ pork (*cha shao* 叉燒肉) or 3 strips of bacon

1½ to 2 cups canola oil

A pinch of black pepper

A pinch of salt

Soy sauce and Tabasco sauce for dipping

1 If you are using *cha shao,* dice it into small cubes. If you are using bacon, cut it into small pieces and pan fry until crispy and then chop into smaller pieces.

2 Cut each piece of tofu into four squares and drop into a pot of boiling water for 1-2 minutes. Drain the water and let it cool down. Without this step, the mixture will be watery and hard to mix into neat lumps later.

3 Crush the tofu and mix with eggs and cornstarch. Add Chinese *cha shao* pork pieces or fried bacon bits. Sprinkle with a pinch of salt and black pepper.

4 Heat up over high heat 1½-2 cups canola oil in the wok for about 3-4 minutes. Drop a tiny piece of tofu/egg mixture into the oil. If it sizzles, the oil is hot enough for frying. Turn the heat to medium high and shape about 2 tablespoons of egg mixture into a small olive-like shape, a little bigger than a meat ball. Gently slide each ball into the oil one by one. Do not fry too many at a time,

otherwise the oil temperature will drop.

5 Let each ball fry about 2 minutes before turning to the other side. When both sides have turned a light golden brown, remove and drain in a sieve. The finished tofu/egg mixture is shaped like a Chinese string instrument called a *pipa* (琵琶). So it is called pipa tofu. Dip with soy sauce mixed with a little Tabasco sauce.

.

CHAPTER 8

雞肉鴨肉主菜

Chicken & Duck Entrees

Chicken & Duck Entrees

Chicken Lettuce Package
生菜雞鬆 (sheng cai ji song) **

This is a variation of the original Squab Lettuce Song (鴿鬆) ("Squab Lettuce Package"). Song means "fluffy and dry." The original recipe is cooked with squab and its bones are finely chopped and sautéed with lots of oil so the meat and bone are dry and crunchy in texture. Then everything is all wrapped with a piece of bowl-shaped lettuce and served. Here the chicken is substituted for squab since it is more readily available.

Yield: 20 lettuce packages

> 12 oz. coarsely chopped chicken or ground chicken
>
> **Chicken Marinade:**
>
> 1 Tbsp. cornstarch
>
> A pinch of black or white pepper
>
> A pinch of salt
>
> 1 head iceberg lettuce
>
> 4 Tbsp. canola oil
>
> 1-2 cloves shallot, peeled and sliced
>
> ½ bunch celery heart (about 7 oz.)
>
> Salt to taste
>
> 2 Tbsp. cornstarch mixed with ½ cup cold water
>
> 3-4 oz. pine nuts (toasted, deep fried, or raw)
>
> Chili sauce or hoisin sauce
> *(optional, as condiments)*

1 Mix chicken with marinade ingredients and set aside.

2 *Lettuce preparation:* Grasp the lettuce with both hands and bring the stem end down hard on the chopping block. The center stem will then be easily removed. Peel off the lettuce leaves one at a time and rinse clean. Pat dry each lettuce leaf with a paper towel. Use a knife or a kitchen scissors to shape each leaf into a bowl-like shape.

3 For each celery stalk, peel off the tough strings. Cut into long thin strips lengthwise, then cut into small pieces crosswise and soak in cold water about 30 minutes or longer to bring out the crispiness. I got this great tip from Iron Chef CHEN Kenichi's cookbook.

4 Heat up the wok over high heat for about 3 minutes. Add 4 Tbsp. canola oil. Turn heat to medium high. Add shallot slices and stir fry until golden but not brown.

5 Add marinated chicken to the wok, and let it sit about one minute before stirring. Stir chicken until it turns a pale white. If the wok is hot enough, the wok bottom will not be sticky. If it sticks, do not panic. The residue, or the *faun*, is very tasty. Add the celery heart to the chicken. Scrape the wok bottom with a metal spatula and incorporate any burned part into the chicken and celery heart mixture. Turn heat to medium high. Cook the chicken and celery mixture for another 3 minutes. Some water will appear as the celery heart cooks. Salt to taste.

6 Mix ½ cup water with 2 Tbsp. cornstarch. Sprinkle all over the mixture and stir to mix well. Serve on a large plate sprinkled with pine nuts. It is not necessary to cook the pine nuts, but if you like, you can toast or deep fry them a little first, which will add extra aroma.

7 When eating, place some chicken in a lettuce leaf with chili sauce or hoisin sauce (海鮮醬) whichever you prefer. There should be enough chicken to wrap up in 20 lettuce leaves. Do not wrap too much filling, otherwise the lettuce will be hard to hold and the chicken will spill out.

Ants Over the Tree 螞蟻上樹
(ma yi shang shu) ****

This is a classic dish. It is full of interesting textures: crunchy fried rice sticks (or fried cellophane noodles), saucy ground pork, and crunchy tree ears. The fried rice sticks and tree ears combined with ground pork imitate trees and ants.

Chinese menus usually give beautiful names to dishes, such as "Whole Family Luck" 全家福,"Buddha Jumps Over the Fence" 佛跳牆 and "Ants Over the Tree" 螞蟻上樹 etc. Consequently, it's sometimes hard to tell what kind of ingredients are inside the dish.

I remember during my senior year of high school, we had an all school cooking competition. Tents were set up in the track field with hibachi stoves to do all the cooking. Our class chose the "Ants Over the Tree" dish for its dramatic title as well as for the simplicity of the dish. Teachers sat there and tasted all the dishes presented by the students. Our class did not win any prize, but it was a good competition. For one day, everyone was busy cooking, forgetting about the daily pressures of studying and taking exams. Students in Taiwan (except college students) are loaded with tons of homework and exams on a daily basis.

Yields: 4-6 servings/one plate presentation

- 1 cup loose, dried tree ears (東北木耳) or 2 small cubes packed tree ears (They come packed in small cubes 1 x 2 x ¼ inches from Northeast China; those are the best) — Get the one with soft tree ears, not the hard ones.
- 10 oz. ground pork

   ### Pork Marinade:

   - 1 Tbsp. soy sauce
   - 1 Tbsp. cornstarch
   - A pinch of salt
- 2 cups canola oil
- ½ piece of rice sticks (米粉) if packed in a plastic package with three pieces about 10 x 12-inches each, or one 7 oz./50 g package cellophane noodle (粉絲)
- 2 cloves garlic
- ½ cup water
- 2 Tbsp. soy sauce

1 Soak the tree ears in hot water for 30 minutes or more, then rub the tree ears against each other and remove the tough stem from the tree ears. Rinse clean with water three times to get rid of any sand and coarsely chop. Reconstituted tree ears expand a lot, maybe 4 times depending on which kind.

2 Mix the pork with the marinade ingredients and set aside.

3 Crush the garlic cloves with the flat side of a cleaver and remove the skin.

4 Heat up 2 cups canola oil in a wok. The oil is hot enough if when you drop in a tiny piece of rice stick it puffs up. Pull apart the rice sticks and drop them into the hot oil. When it puffs up, in about 2 seconds, quickly flip to the other side and deep fry. When rice sticks are all puffed up—this happens very quickly—remove the fried rice sticks with a hand-held strainer. Remove the fried rice sticks quickly otherwise they will be too deeply browned or burn. Place fried rice sticks in a large pot, push down gently with a spatula to break it into smaller pieces, and place in a large plate.

5 Drain oil from the wok leaving only 2-3 Tbsps. Turn heat to high, add crushed garlic until golden brown. Discard garlic. Add mixed ground pork, stir and separate. When pork turns a pale pink, add tree ears, stir, add ½ cup water, 2 Tbsp. soy sauce and reduce heat to medium. Cover and let simmer for 5-6 minutes. Cook a few minutes more if tree ears have not simmered enough. Add more water if it seems a bit dry. Remove the mixture and serve on top of the fried rice sticks.

Chicken with Spinach 雞片菠菜
(ji pian bo cai) **

This is a homemade dish that can be done with or without chicken. Most leafy vegetables, like cabbage, romaine lettuce, collard greens or bok choy *(the Cantonese pronunciation, literally means "white cabbage") can be stir-fried as follows. More than half of Chinese homemade dishes are done in this fashion.*

When you buy the spinach, get the kind with smooth small leaves which comes in small bunches with pink stems at the root, and not the crinkled leaf kind, which is not as tender. Spinach needs a lot of oil to make it taste good and not chalky.

This dish can be found on some Chinese restaurant menus. However, the restaurant version is usually quite greasy, because spinach tastes better with more oil.

Yield: 3-4 servings/one plate presentation

6 oz. boneless chicken breast

> **Chicken Marinade:**
>
> 1 Tbsp. cornstarch,
>
> 1 egg white (optional)
>
> 1 tsp. Sauvignon Blanc
>
> A pinch of salt
>
> A pinch of black pepper

5-7 Tbsp. canola oil, divided

1-2 cloves garlic

Salt

1 Here is a good way to wash the spinach. Fill the kitchen sink with a lot of water, and put all the spinach in the sink. Cut off the red root ends one by one with a small knife. Use both hands to stir and swish the spinach in a brisk motion — as if imitating the movement of a washing machine — to remove the dirt. Repeat the washing procedure two more times to make sure all the dirt is removed. Remove the spinach from the water and drain in a colander. This is the best method to remove dirt. Cleaning the leaves by running water over them one by one does not work. I found this method of cleaning by accident. There is no need to cut the spinach. If needed, you can simply tear any large leaves in two.

2 Crush the garlic cloves with the flat side of a cleaver and remove the skin.

3 Slice the chicken at an angle to get thin slices about ½ by 1 inch. When the meat is partially frozen, it is easier to cut into thin slices. Mix with the marinade ingredients and set aside.

4 Heat wok over high heat about 3-4 minutes. Add 3-4 Tbsp. canola oil and chicken slices and stir fry for about 2 minutes. When the chicken turns pale white, remove the chicken to a plate and turn off the heat.

5 Without washing the wok, heat up over high heat, and then add 2-3 Tbsp. canola oil to the wok. Add the crushed garlic and discard when it turns brown. Add spinach to the wok, sprinkle with a pinch of salt. Stir and cover for about 3-4 minutes. The spinach will turn limp and dramatically shrink in volume. Return the cooked chicken slices to the wok, mix with the spinach a little and remove. Serve hot.

Drunken Chicken
醉雞 (zui ji) ****

There are different versions of Drunken Chicken. You can use your favorite white wine to produce an aromatic dish. Some use beer. I like Sauvignon Blanc. It's not too strong, and it has a mild taste. The basic technique is not too complicated. This dish can be prepared ahead of time to serve as an impressive appetizer. At a few restaurants in Taiwan, Drunken Chicken is beautifully presented with the meat in, the middle and the skin wrapped around the chicken which is thinly sliced into round shapes and arranged on a plate.

Yield: 5-6 servings/One plate presentation

- 2 lbs. chicken breast with bones. *Boneless chicken breast can be used too, but chicken breast with bones tastes juicier. Other chicken parts are good too, like drumsticks, thighs or even one whole chicken. It all depends on what kind of meat you like. The meat with bones is always much more tender and juicy.*

- 3 Tbsp. salt

- 1-2 cups plus 1 Tbsp. Sauvignon Blanc, rice wine, or Chinese liquor Mao Tai 茅台酒 or Gao Liang 高梁酒 (which is strong and aromatic). *You can use the liquor you like, preferably a white wine so the white chicken meat will not be tinted.*

- 1-3 stalks scallion

- ½ tsp. salt

1 Cut off both ends of the scallion and chop finely.

2 Rub chicken breast with 1-2 Tbsp. salt, rinse clean, and then sprinkle with ½ tsp. salt all over the chicken breast along with 1 Tbsp. Sauvignon Blanc and the chopped scallion in a large bowl, and let sit in a refrigerator for 2-3 hours.

3 Bring a steamer pot of water to boil. Boil enough water for steaming 45 minutes. Place the bowl with the marinated chicken breast into the steamer and steam over high heat for 45 minutes.

4 Turn off the heat, open the steamer cover, and let the chicken breast cool down to room temperature. To make the chicken meat taste firmer and better, you can dunk the chicken breast into a pot of icy water for 10 minutes to bring down the temperature quickly.

5 When the juice from steaming the chicken breast cools down to room temperature, mix the juice with 1-2 cups Sauvignon Blanc. Immerse the chicken in the mixture. Cover with plastic wrap and leave in the refrigerator overnight or even over two nights to develop a stronger taste, but do not make it too "drunk" by using a stronger liquor or soaking even longer. It can give the meat a biting taste. Turn over the chicken breast if it is not totally immersed in the liquid. When it is ready to serve, remove the bones from the chicken. Slice the chicken into thin slices and serve cold or at room temperature. The Drunken Chicken served in the restaurants in Taiwan is sliced into neat slices with meat and skin together. That makes a really beautiful presentation.

6 The juice and Sauvignon Blanc mixture can be used again for another round of Drunken Chicken.

Chicken Chunks with Orange Peel
陳皮雞塊
(chen pi ji kuai) ***

I learned this dish at a potluck party from a lady from Wuhan City, China (武漢). The key to this dish is very finely chopping the fresh ginger, garlic, and scallion. In her words they should be chopped to "the size of a grain of rice" (米粒大). The mixture of ginger, garlic, and scallion produce an immense aroma with the chicken chunks.

She chopped a whole chicken into chunks. You can use boneless chicken for convenience, but the taste will not be as good as chicken chunks with bones. The chicken thighs sold in supermarkets are ideal for this purpose as they are already cut into chunks.

The aroma of fresh orange peel is very good. The recipe originally calls for "dried orange peel" (陳皮). The words for "dried orange peel" in Chinese literally mean "old skin," which is a Chinese medicinal herb made from orange peel. I find that the fresh orange peel produces better results than dried orange peel. Sometimes dried orange peel has a little mildew-like smell.

Yield: 3-4 servings/One plate presentation

1 lb. boneless chicken, cut into bite size pieces or chicken thighs

Chicken Marinade:

1 tsp. Sauvignon Blanc

A pinch of freshly ground black peppercorn

Fresh orange peel from half an orange, cut into one-inch square pieces

3 stalks scallions

3 slices of fresh ginger

3 cloves garlic

6 Tbsp. canola oil, divided

½ tsp. sugar

1-2 Tbsp. soy sauce

1 Tbsp. Sauvignon Blanc

¼ cup water

¼ tsp. Balsamic vinegar or rice vinegar

1 Mix the chicken with the marinade ingredients, cover, and refrigerate for 30-60 minutes.

2 Cut off the tops of the scallions and half of the green part, and then finely chop.

3 Crush garlic cloves with the flat side of a cleaver, remove the skin and then finely chop.

4 Remove the skin from the ginger slices by rubbing off the skin with the back of a small knife, and then finely chop.

5 Heat up the wok over high heat for about 3-4 minutes. Add 3 Tbsp. canola oil, turn heat to medium high, add chicken chunks and stir until the meat becomes a pale white, about 2 minutes. Remove to a plate. In this step the chicken chunks do not have to be cooked through.

6 Without washing the wok, heat the wok up again over high heat. Add 3 Tbsp. canola oil, the orange peel, and stir until golden but not brown. Add the partially cooked chicken chunks, the finely chopped scallion, ginger, and garlic, and stir. Sprinkle some freshly ground black pepper and ½ tsp. sugar, and stir. Add 1-2 Tbsp. soy sauce, 1 Tbsp. Sauvignon Blanc, ¼ cup water, and adjust to your taste.

7 Reduce heat to medium low and simmer for 5 minutes or until the liquid has evaporated. Add a few drops or about ¼ tsp. balsamic vinegar or rice vinegar and mix well. Serve hot.

Silvery Bean Sprouts with Shredded Chicken 銀芽雞絲
(yin ya ji si) **

This dish is called "Silvery Sprout with Chicken Shreds" in Chinese. The original dish calls for plucking off the root end of the bean sprouts. The legend has it that the Empress Dowager of the Qing Dynasty (清朝慈禧太后) demanded her royal kitchen to pluck off both ends of the bean sprout to satisfy her palate.

If you have time and want to experiment, you will find that without the stringy end, the bean sprouts come out with almost a shimmery look. Otherwise, you can just cook the bean sprouts as is. There are soy bean sprouts, too, which are usually cooked with soup.

You can grow bean sprouts by soaking green beans (mung beans) in cold water for a few hours, then draining the water and leaving them in the sieve in a dark, hot, and humid place. Sprinkle the beans with water every day, and let the water drain off all day and night. In a few days there will be bean sprouts you can collect and cook. It is fun, but not easy to get the beans to sprout just right.

This dish should only take 10 minutes. Don't overcook the bean sprouts. Remove them from the heat when they look half cooked.

Yield: 3-4 servings/One plate presentation

> 12 oz. fresh bean sprouts *(available in most supermarkets and quite inexpensive. Do not use canned bean sprouts.)*
>
> 8 oz. boneless chicken breast, cut into very thin strips,
>
> > **Chicken Marinade:**
> >
> > A pinch of salt
> >
> > One egg white
> >
> > 1 Tbsp. cornstarch
>
> 1 clove garlic
>
> 5 Tbsp. canola oil, divided
>
> Salt to taste
>
> One egg yolk *(leftover from the egg white for the marinade)*

1 Soak the bean sprouts in cold water for 30 minutes or more before cooking. Soaking will make the bean sprouts come out much crunchier. If the bean sprouts are very fresh, no pre-soaking is required.

2 Cut the chicken in very thin strips and combine with marinade ingredients.

3 Crush the garlic with the flat side of a cleaver and remove the skin.

4 Heat up the wok over high heat until hot, about 3-4 minutes. Add 3 Tbsp. canola oil and garlic and stir fry until golden brown, and then discard the garlic. Add marinated chicken and cook until it turns a pale white. Remove the chicken and set aside. Some brown residue from the chicken may be stuck to the wok. It is called *faun*, and is good, tasty stuff. Scrape it off the bottom with a spatula and leave it in the wok.

5 Without washing the wok, turn to high heat and add 2 Tbsp. canola oil. Drain the water from the bean sprouts and add to the wok. Sprinkle with some salt. Mix with the scraped off brown *faun* and mix in with the bean sprouts and add the egg yolk. Cook for about two minutes, add the cooked chicken, mix well, and serve hot immediately.

Foo Young Chicken
芙蓉雞片 (fu rong ji pian,
"foo young" is the Cantonese
pronunciation) *******

In Chinese restaurants here in the States, "foo young" (芙蓉) is a dish where the ingredients are cooked together and then mixed with a lot of cornstarch and water to make the dish saucy. The original "foo young" dish is named for the shape of the flower "hibiscous mutabilis" (芙蓉花), also called the "foo young flower" (芙蓉花) to describe the beauty of this dish, which is pure white and shaped like a flower. It is not the sauce that alludes to "foo young" but the shape of the chicken.

Yield: 4-5 servings/One plate presentation

- 10 oz. ground chicken
- 1 egg white
- 6 Tbsp. water
- A pinch of salt
- 10-12 snow peas
- 1 slice low salt ham, about ¼ inch thick, cut into small cubes
- 2 stalks scallion
- 1-2 Tbsp. cornstarch mixed with ½ cup water

1 Mix the ground chicken with the egg white, 6 Tbsp. water, and a pinch of salt, stirring in one direction. The mixture will be watery but thick.

2 *How to String Snow Peas:* From the leafless end of each snow pea, break off the tip and pull the string along the straighter side, then break off the other end to string both sides of the pod. Drop the snow peas into a pot of boiling water for 1 minute, remove and drop into a pot of icy cold water. Cut each snow pea in half with a diagonal cut.

3 Cut the ham into small cubes.

4 Cut off the tip of the scallions and half the green part, and then slice the remainder thinly.

5 Heat up the wok over high heat, about 3 minutes, and then add 1 cup canola oil and heat about 2-3 minutes. If it feels hot when you put the palm of your hand above the wok, but the oil is not smoking, drop a little of the chicken mixture in. If it sizzles, the temperature is right. Reduce heat to medium high and slowly slide in a flattened 1 Tbsp. or less of the ground chicken into the wok and deep fry. Let each spoonful fry without stirring for 2-3 minutes. When the shape has set, remove the chicken pieces. Let the fried chicken pieces soak in a pot of warm water to get rid of the greasiness. The chicken pieces will be very irregularly shaped, almost like a flower. You can also shape the chicken mixture into small patty-like shapes and pan fry in a wok, cast iron frying pan, or non-stick frying pan. The wok has to be hot so the chicken pieces will not stick to the wok.

6 Drain the oil through a sieve. Leave about 3 Tbsp. oil in the wok. Turn heat to high, add scallion pieces and stir fry until golden. Add ham and snow peas, stir a couple of minutes. Reduce heat to medium, remove chicken pieces from the warm water and add to the wok. Add the cornstarch and water mixture. Gently stir and remove right away. Serve hot.

Chicken Liver with Eggs
軟煎鳳肝 (ruan jian feng gan) **

This is a rather easy dish that can be prepared in less than five minutes. Do not add any soy sauce, as it will make the dish look "muddy." Liver is especially good for people with anemia.

Yield: 4 servings/One plate presentation

8-10 oz. chicken liver (*Chicken liver is usually sold in 20 oz. packages. You can double the recipe and cook it all, saving the leftovers for the next day*)

Chicken Liver Marinade:

1 tsp. Cognac or your favorite wine

A pinch of salt

A pinch of black pepper

2 cloves shallots

2 stalks scallions

2-3 Tbsp. canola oil

A pinch of salt

3 large eggs, beaten.,/

Freshly ground pepper

1 Remove the fat and sinew from the liver and slice thinly. You can save the fat and sinew to cook in soup or discard it. Mix with marinade ingredients.

2 Peel the shallots and slice thinly.

3 Cut off the tops of the scallions and half of the green end and then finely chop.

4 Heat up the wok over high heat until it is hot, about 3 minutes. Add 2-3 Tbsp. canola oil, add shallot slices, and cook until golden but not brown. Add sliced chicken liver, stir and turn until the liver has changed color but is not yet fully cooked. Sprinkle with a pinch of salt.

5 Turn heat to medium and gently pour the beaten egg over the liver, and let the egg sit and set for about 2 minutes without stirring. When the egg is set, gently turn over the liver and egg and cook the other side for 2-3 minutes without stirring until cooked. Gently remove and place on a plate. Sprinkle with the chopped scallion and freshly ground black pepper. Serve hot.

Fresh Spring Rolls
潤餅 (run bing)/

"Fried" Egg Rolls
春捲 (chun juan) ***

This dish originates from the Province of Fujian (福建) in southeastern China next to Canton and Hong Kong. People there emigrated to Taiwan, the Philippines, and Southeast Asia, including Singapore. You can find people speaking the dialect of southern Fujian in those locales, including Taiwan. Fujian is a rather large province with people speaking many different dialects because of the mountains separating each region.

The skins used in this dish are very skillfully made. The person constantly mixes a rather soft lump of flour dough with one hand, and in a single motion quickly smears the dough on a flat hot plate and lifts it off, leaving a film, which becomes the egg roll skin. After a couple of seconds, he lifts the skin off the iron plate with the other hand.

My mother used to tell me to bring home some freshly made egg roll skins to make fresh egg rolls. I once saw one guy working a sidewalk eatery in Taiwan. He had three hot plates and quickly smeared a skin on each plate, and then peeled each skin off one by one. He made three skins as quickly as I could count "one, two, three." Nowadays, egg roll skins are machine-made. (In Chinese restaurants in the U.S. they are called Shanghai egg rolls or spring rolls, but they are not from Shanghai.). In the Philippines, it's called lumpia. The skin is thinner than the pancakes used for Peking duck.

When you buy fresh egg roll skins, make sure you are getting the already cooked Shanghai egg roll skins, not the uncooked flour dough skins. There are many brands, but the best one is from Singapore called "Spring Home" TYJ Spring Roll Pastry. It comes in 12 oz. packages with 25 pieces and can be found in the Chinatown grocery store's freezer section.

Yield: About 25 vegetarian egg rolls

Fresh Egg Roll with Meat:

One package fresh egg roll skins (*Try to get "Spring Home" TYJ Spring Roll Pastry, which is made in Singapore and sold in 25-sheet packages in the Chinatown grocery's freezer section.*)

6-8 oz. pork loin

Pork Marinade:

½-1 Tbsp. soy sauce

1 egg white

1 Tbsp. cornstarch

A pinch of black pepper

3-5 dried Chinese black mushrooms

4-6 oz. snow peas (optional)

One package cellophane noodle (about 7 oz.)

2 pickling cucumbers, peeled and cut into 3" length strips and set aside on a plate

½ lb. ham (optional)

3 oz. of any combination of oyster mushrooms, crimini mushrooms, or white mushrooms (The oyster mushroom, if available, is a great ingredient with a modern touch.)

4 oz. roasted, unsalted peanuts or raw peanuts, which you will deep fry (Do not skip this ingredient. It adds a special flavor to the fresh egg rolls and it prevents the egg roll from becoming soggy. It is also a traditional ingredient in egg rolls.)

2-3 cloves shallot

One head of Taiwanese cabbage (about 1-1¼ lbs.) (If Taiwanese cabbage is not available, substitute with Napa Chinese cabbage; do not use regular cabbage. Taiwanese cabbage is finer and more tender than regular cabbage, and after cooking a while, it becomes soft and rather sweet in taste. Regular cabbage is too coarse and cannot be cooked down to a soft texture.)

1-2 carrots (4-6 oz.)

2-3 large eggs, plus the egg yolk leftover from the pork loin marinade

½ lb. fresh bean sprouts (If fresh sprouts are not available, skip it. Do not use canned sprouts.)

5 Tbsp. canola oil, divided

Salt to taste

Hoisin sauce 海鮮醬/chili sauce/catsup or your favorite BBQ sauce

1 Defrost the egg roll skin by simply leaving the frozen package at room temperature for 1 hour before serving time. If you forget to defrost ahead of time, remove skins from the bag then wrap with aluminum foil and leave it in a 100°F degree oven for about 10 minutes. The results are very good with this method, too.

2 Cut the pork loin into thin strips and mix with marinade ingredients and set aside.

3 Soak the dried Chinese black mushrooms in hot water for at least 1 hour. After soaking, cut off the tough stem, and slice into strips. Filter any sediment out of the soaking liquid and set aside to add to the cabbage later in step **16** .

4 If using snow peas, string them and then soak in cold water for 30-60 minutes before cooking to make them crunchy.

5 Soak the cellophane noodles in warm/hot water for 15 minutes, drain the water and cut into 3-inch lengths.

6 Peel the cucumbers and slice into 2-inch thin strips and set aside.

7 If you are using ham, cut into thin strips and set aside.

8 Cut off the bottom tough stem of the fresh mushrooms, but leave the mushroom whole for aesthetic looks. If it is large, cut it into two.

9 If you are using commercially roasted peanuts put them inside a plastic bag and grind them with a rolling pin until crushed to a coarse or fine texture depending on your preference. If using raw peanuts, deep fry them as follows, being very careful. In a wok, place 1 cup canola oil, add the raw peanut in the COLD oil. Do not add peanuts to hot oil, always add to them to cold oil. Turn the heat to medium low, and constantly stir the peanuts with a spatula. Do not leave the stove unattended. Stir the peanuts constantly or they may become brown on one side while the other side remains white. It takes about 10 minutes to deep fry. The aroma is definitely better with the freshly fried peanuts.

10 Peel the shallots and slice thinly.

11 To prepare the cabbage, slice the four sides and the bottom part as if you were coring an apple, and discard the hard core in the center. Remove and discard the outer two to three layers of coarser leaves. Shred the leaves.

12 Cut off both ends of the carrots, peel off the skin, and shred using a box shredder.

13 Heat up the wok over high heat for about 3-4 minutes. Add 2 Tbsp. canola oil to the wok, turn heat to medium high and add half of the sliced shallots, half of the Chinese black mushrooms, and cook until the shallots turned golden.

14 Then add the marinated pork loin. Stir with a spatula and separate the pork. Stir fry until the pork is thoroughly cooked, about 3 minutes. Remove to a plate. There are going to be many plates of filling ingredients for the fresh egg rolls. This is the first one.

15 Without washing the wok, heat the wok again over high heat and add 3 Tbsp. canola oil, the rest of the shallot and Chinese black mushrooms. Stir until the shallot becomes golden, then add the shredded cabbage, shredded carrots, and sprinkle with salt.

16 Add the reserved mushroom soaking liquid with ½ cup water; stir and cover. Reduce heat to low. Stir occasionally, so the cabbage will be cooked evenly. Cook about 20-30 minutes over low to medium low heat, the longer the better. But watch it carefully to keep from burning. If it looks like it will burn, turn the heat lower and add about ¼-½ cup water but not too much. The goal is to evaporate the liquid as the cabbage becomes very limp, soft, and translucent-like.

17 Add the cellophane noodles, ½ cup water and cook 3-4 more minutes. (The cellophane noodle will absorb the liquid.) Taste, and sprinkle on

some more salt if needed.

18 In a large bowl, place a smaller bowl with a smooth bottom (like a cereal bowl) face down in the middle. When the cooked cabbage is placed over the smaller bowl, any liquid will drain to the center of the large bowl, leaving the cooked cabbage dry for wrapping without soaking the egg roll skin. Place the cabbage in the bowl.

19 Bring a pot of water to boil, and sprinkle with a pinch of salt. Drop in the bean sprouts, stir about 1 minute, then scoop out the bean sprouts and set aside on a plate. Do not overcook the bean sprouts. You should literally drop the bean sprouts into the water, stir with chopsticks and remove right away. After the bean sprouts are removed, the lingering heat continues to cook the bean sprouts.

20 Bring the same pot of water to another boil, drop in the snow peas, stir one minute and remove the snow peas.

21 In the same pot of hot water—no need to bring to another boil—drop in sliced oyster/regular/crimini mushrooms, stir for 2 minutes and remove to a plate. The mushrooms are just dropped into the water to remove the raw taste, so it's okay if they are not fully cooked.

22 With 2-3 large eggs, plus the egg yolk leftover from the pork loin marinade, beat well and just like making breakfast pancakes, in a non-stick frying pan, make egg pancakes. Stack up the egg pancakes, and roll them into a cylinder and cut into thin strips crosswise. Set the egg strips aside on a plate.

23 When you serve, place all the prepared dishes of fillings on the table for people to pick from to fill their egg roll. Peel off one skin at a time. Position the egg roll skin with one corner pointed towards yourself. Sprinkle some ground peanuts in the center to keep the ingredients from making the skin soggy, then put on a little of each cooked ingredient, and again sprinkle with some ground peanut. Fold one corner over the ingredients then fold in the left and right sides. Then just before closing the roll, brush on Hoisin sauce or your favorite sauce, wrap it up, and eat. Try to use up all the skins in one sitting. The leftover skins tend to become hard and brittle. One person can usually eat 3-4 egg rolls with ease. One package of fresh egg roll skins can serve 5-6 people

The first-timer tends to put in too many fillings, making the roll hard to handle. A little of everything goes a long way. This dish is especially good with a big party. Everyone handles his or her own food with great satisfaction. You can add any kind of ingredients you like, e.g., chicken, shrimp, fried tofu, celery, cucumber, bacon bits, etc.

Fried Egg Rolls Variation

To make "fried egg rolls" or the so-called "egg rolls," follow the directions below.

Additional Ingredients

¼ cup water mixed with 3 Tbsp. flour or 1 beaten egg (to seal the egg roll)

2 cups canola oil

1 Mix all the fillings that were on separate plates together in a large pot except the skin and simply make rolls like the fresh egg roll.

2 Seal each roll with either the mixture of flour and water or beaten egg. Heat up 2 cups of canola oil over medium heat for about 3 minutes and deep fry the egg rolls. Gently slide the egg rolls down the side of the wok and use tongs or a pair of chopsticks to "roll" the egg rolls to fry evenly on all sides. Since the filling is already cooked, you only need to fry until the skin looks golden, about 6-8 minutes.

Vegetarian Egg Rolls

Taiwanese cabbage and Vidalia onions are "must have" ingredients to make this kind of egg roll totally delicious. This recipe is the easiest and most delicious way to make vegetarian egg rolls. The only requirement is to cook the cabbage and onion a really long time to get the full flavor out of them.

One package fresh egg roll skins (*Try to get "Spring Home" TYJ Spring Roll Pastry, which is made in Singapore and sold in 25-sheet packages in the Chinatown grocery's freezer section.*)

One head of Taiwanese cabbage (about 2 lbs.) (*If Taiwanese cabbage is not available, substitute with Napa Chinese cabbage; do not use regular cabbage. Taiwanese cabbage is finer and more tender than regular cabbage, and after cooking a while, it becomes soft and rather sweet in taste. Regular cabbage is too coarse and cannot be cooked down to a soft texture.*)

3 Vidalia onions (available in the summer), or regular yellow onion (not the white onions) shredded

1 package cellophane noodle (7oz.), pre-soaked in warm water for 20 minutes

3 eggs, beaten

¼ tsp. salt

¼ cup canola oil

2 cups canola oil (for frying)

1 beaten egg or 3 Tbsp. flour with ¼ cup water

1 Defrost the egg roll skin by simply leaving the frozen package at room temperature for 1 hour before serving time. If you forget to defrost ahead of time, remove from the bag and wrap with aluminum foil then leave it in a 100° F degree oven for about 10 minutes. The results are very good with this method, too.

2 Heat up the wok over high heat. Add ¼ cup canola oil (or vegetable oil) into the wok. Add shredded onion into the wok and cook for about 5 minutes. Turn heat to medium, keep stirring for about 25 minutes or longer until the onion is soft and limp with a touch of brown color. If it looks like it's going to burn, do not add any water but reduce the heat. Add shredded cabbage to the cooked onions, and mix over medium heat. Cover for 10 minutes. Open the cover and stir frequently until the flavors of all the ingredients are well blended, about another 20 minutes. If it looks like it's going to burn, add ¼-½ cup water each time.

3 Add salt and mix well. The vegetables will shrink to about half the original volume when cooked. Add the soaked cellophane noodles and ½ cup water to the mixture and cook for another 5 minutes. Mix well.

4 Dish the mixture to a large bowl in which you have place a smaller bowl with a smooth bottom (like a cereal bowl) face down. When the cabbage is placed on top, any liquid will collect underneath the smaller bowl, leaving the cabbage dry for wrapping in the egg roll skin without making it soggy.

5 Scramble the 3 beaten eggs in a frying pan. Mix the egg pieces with the cabbage mixture.

6 Peel off a spring roll skin and spoon 2 Tbsp. of filling in one corner of the skin, and brush the opposite corner with a mixture of water and flour, and roll the mixture up with the skin. When halfway rolled up, fold the left and right corners over the center, then continue to roll all the way up and seal with beaten egg or 3 Tbsp. flour mixed with ¼ cup water.

7 Heat up 2 cups of canola oil over medium heat for about 3 minutes and deep fry the egg rolls. Gently slide the egg rolls down the side of the wok and use a tong or a pair of chopsticks to "roll" the egg rolls to fry evenly on all sides. Since the filling is already cooked, you only need to fry until the skin looks golden—not brown—about 6-8 minutes.

Kung Pao Chicken 宮保雞丁 (gong bao ji ding) **

Kung Pao Chicken is a favorite Chinese restaurant dish here in the States. The legend has it that it was created by the family of Mr. DING Bao-Zhen (丁寶楨), a governor of Sichuan Province in the Qing Dynasty (清朝1644-1910 AD). He was bestowed the official title "Gong Bao" (宮保) by the Qing Emperor for his outstanding work. He liked spicy food, chicken, and peanuts. His family cook put together this dish, which he liked so very much it was presented every time there were guests in his house. So it's called Kung Bao Chicken (or Gong Bao Chicken, which is the correct pinyin spelling.)

Most Chinese restaurants cook this dish with Sichuan bean paste (or chili Sichuan bean paste 四川豆瓣醬/四川辣豆瓣醬). You can do that, too, but it's not authentic. It tastes better without the bean paste as it lets the natural flavor of the chicken come through.

Yield: 3-4 servings/One plate presentation

    1 lb. boneless chicken breast, remove sinew, cut into ¼-inch cubes

    Chicken Marinade:

    1 Tbsp. light or regular soy sauce

    1 Tbsp. rice wine or Sauvignon Blanc

    1 Tbsp. cornstarch

    A pinch of black pepper

    2-3 slices fresh ginger

    2-3 cloves garlic

    1-2 stalks scallion

    3-5 fresh or dried red chili pepper

    3 Tbsp. canola oil

    ½ tsp. freshly ground black pepper or Sichuan peppercorn (if available)

    ¼ cup roasted, unsalted peanuts

    ½ tsp. Sichuan bean paste or soy sauce (optional)

1 Remove the sinew from the chicken breast and cut into ¼-inch cubes. Mix chicken cubes with marinade ingredients and set aside.

2 Rub off the skin from the ginger slices using the spine of a small knife against the skin, and then finely chop the ginger to the size of rice grains.

3 Smash the garlic with the flat side of the cleaver to remove the skin and then finely chop.

4 Cut off the tops of the scallions and half of the green portion and finely chop the rest.

5 If you are using fresh chili peppers, cut a slit and remove the seeds. That way, when it's placed in the hot wok, it will not "pop up and jump," causing an accident. After cutting the chili pepper, do not rub your eyes before washing your hands thoroughly!

6 Chop together the finely chopped fresh ginger, garlic, and scallion after each is finely chopped individually. Mix well and place in a bowl.

7 Heat up the wok over high heat, about 3-4 minutes. Reduce heat to medium high, and add 3 Tbsp. oil and red chili pepper. Stir fry until almost brown in color, and add half the ginger/garlic/scallion mixture. Stir quickly and add the marinated chicken chunks. Sprinkle the rest of ginger/garlic/ scallion mixture over and some freshly ground black pepper or Sichuan peppercorn.

8 Stir until the chicken turns pale white. Taste, and adjust the saltiness with more soy sauce or Sichuan bean paste. Stir a couple more minutes until the chicken is cooked, but not overly cooked. Remove to a plate and sprinkle with roasted, unsalted peanuts. Serve hot.

Bang Bang Chicken 棒棒雞 **

In the old days, people had to kill a chicken to get meat. The original recipe calls for a whole chicken. Nowadays we have the luxury of getting just the parts we want. I like chicken breast with bones. You can use the chicken part that you like. For this dish, originally a small stick "bang zi" (棒子) was used to lightly pound the chicken to tenderize it, so it was called Bang Bang Chicken. The way they use a stick to pound the chicken is really very ingenious. After the meat is pounded, it is very easy to separate into thin strips. Here I use a long, thin rolling pin which produces very good results.

Yield: 3-4 servings/One plate presentation

> 10-12 oz. chicken breast with bones
> (Chicken tastes much more tender with
> bone. Follow the cooking instructions in step
> **3** exactly for tender meat.)

> A pinch of salt

> 2 small fresh pickling cucumbers, peel off
> skin, cut into 1" length thin strips

> 5 stalks scallion

> ### Sauce Ingredients:
>
> 6 level Tbsp. creamy peanut butter (Peter
> Pan brand is the best) or sesame paste
> (sesame paste is pretty bland, so mix in
> 1 tsp. sugar. It is available in Chinese and
> Japanese grocery stores.)
>
> A pinch of black pepper
>
> 2 Tbsp. sesame oil
>
> 1 Tbsp. soy sauce
>
> 1-2 tsp. chili sauce
>
> A few drops balsamic vinegar or Chinese
> black vinegar

1 Cut off the tops of the scallions and the green parts, and cut lengthwise into very thin strips and then into 1 to 1½ inch lengths. Soak in cold water for 10 minutes. If the scallions were sliced thinly enough, after soaking in the cold water, the scallions will curl up.

2 To make the sauce, put the peanut butter in a small pot over low heat, then add the rest of the ingredients one by one and mix well with chopsticks or a spoon.

3 Remove the skin from the chicken. Place the chicken breast with bone or the boneless chicken breast in a pot with four cups of water. The water should be barely covering the chicken. Add a pinch of salt to the pot. Bring the water to a boil, and skim off the foam. Reduce the heat to medium low, cover, and simmer for 10-15 minutes. Turn off the heat and let the chicken stay covered inside the pot for 30 minutes to 1 hour.

4 Drain the soaked scallions and pat dry with a paper towel. Line the outer edge of a plate with the scallions.

5 Place the cucumber strips in the middle of the plate.

6 Remove the chicken from the pot. Let it cool down for about 15 minutes. Remove the meat from the bones. Use a small rolling pin to lightly pound the meat. The meat will separate easily. Use your hands to break the chicken into thin strips. Place chicken strips on top of the cucumber strips. Drizzle the sauce over the shredded chicken and serve warm or at room temperature.

The recipe above uses the basic ingredients of Bang Bang Chicken. You can adjust the taste or spiciness to your liking. With the broth created from boiling the chicken, you can make an easy egg flower soup or Sichuan pickled mustard green soup (see page 63).

BBQ Sauce for Chicken Wings, Baby Spare Ribs, or Beef
烤肉滷汁 (kao ro lu zhi) *

There are many types of BBQ sauce. This one is a typical homemade Chinese-style BBQ sauce which can be used with any kind of meat, be it chicken, beef, pork, or fish.

Yield: 4-5 servings

> 1½ lbs. chicken wings (about one package from the supermarket) or other kind of meat
>
> ½ cup regular or low sodium Kikkoman soy sauce
>
> 5 Tbsp. rice wine or Sauvignon Blanc
>
> 3 Tbsp. sugar
>
> ¼ tsp. five spice powder
>
> ½ tsp. rice vinegar or Balsamic vinegar
>
> 4 cloves star anise
>
> 2 stalks scallion
>
> 4 fresh ginger slices (Do not substitute with powdered ginger. If you cannot get it, skip it.)
>
> ¼ tsp. black pepper
>
> ¼ cup water

1 Cut off the scallion tops and half of the green part, then lightly pound with the flat side of a knife, and cut into one-inch lengths.

2 Place all the ingredients into a pot except for the chicken wings. Adjust the taste. Reduce to the lowest heat and simmer for 15 minutes. (There is no need to bring it to a boil.) Let the mixture cool down to room temperature.

3 Rinse clean the chicken wings and drain the water completely. Add the chicken wings to the cooled down mixture and refrigerate for 4 hours or longer. Marinating overnight is even better.

4 Depending on your available equipment or personal preference, finish the chicken by barbeque, broiling, or baking.

5 *Barbeque Option:* Once the briquettes have turned red, barbeque the chicken wings for 5-6 minutes on the first side and then just 3-4 minutes on the other side.

6 *Broiling Option:* The chicken wings can be broiled for a charred look. Since the broiler is quite hot, you don't need to flip it. Just broil for 5-7 minutes or until golden brown.

7 *Baking Option:* Bake the chicken wings in a preheated 400°F oven for 15-20 minutes. For a charred look, after 15 minutes at 400°, change the oven setting to broil and broil for 5 minutes.

Deep Fried Game Hen 炸子雞 (zha zi ji) ***

Game hens are usually sold two in a package. Each one weighs about 1½ lbs. This is a comparatively easy deep fry dish. Not much preparation is needed. My daughter Clara loves to eat the hen with her fingers. One time, probably for her birthday, I specially fried one just for her so she could eat the whole chicken with her fingers. She tore into it, and ate it all by herself.

Deep frying a regular-size chicken is not easy. Frying a game hen is easier, and it's lighter and tastier. And, if you just want to use your hands to pull it apart to eat like "Robin Hood" did. It is not hard, too. Enjoy!

Yield: 3-4 servings

> One game hen
>
> 1 tsp. salt
>
> ½ cup flour or cornstarch *(either will produce pretty much the same effect)*
>
> 2-3 cups canola oil. (Or enough oil to immerse half of the hen)

1 Remove the paper package with neck, liver, and gizzard inside the game hen cavity. Use those for making soup. Rinse clean the game hen, and use paper towels to pat it dry inside and outside. Place about 1 tsp. salt in the palm of your hands and rub both hands together, then rub your hands all over the game hen, inside and out. Over a sink, sprinkle the flour or cornstarch all over the game hen, lightly press a little, and shake off the excess flour in the sink.

2 Heat up 2-3 cups canola oil over medium high heat for 3 minutes in a wok or a deep fryer. It is easier to use a wok to turn the hen to other side. Add enough oil so that at least half of the hen is immersed in oil when you put it in. Gently place the floured game hen into the oil. Reduce heat to medium and let it deep fry for 5-6 minutes on each side.

3 Use a spatula to see if the bottom part is golden or not, but not burned brown. If there are some burned spots, gently hold a spatula in one hand, and a pair of long chopsticks or a large ladle in your other hand to hold one side of the game hen, and gently turn over the game hen. Be very careful, to turn the game hen away from your body. Fry another 5-6 minutes. When it's all golden brown, it's done. It's better to be a little overcooked than undercooked. Remove the game hen and drain in a sieve for a few minutes. Transfer to a plate and let it cool down for 10-15 minutes. Cut off the wings and legs. Then cut from the center into two by pressing a knife into the center. Cut each half into 4 pieces.

Peking Duck Homemade Style
北京烤鸭 (beijing kao ya) ****

Everybody loves Peking duck. It is very hard here to find a duck. Whenever our family feels like having Peking duck, I go to Chinatown to get a roasted duck hanging in the window of a barbecue place. You simply prepare some hot canola oil in a wok, heated up over medium high heat—make sure the inside cavity of the duck is totally drained of all liquid and patted dry with paper towel—and deep fry both sides for 4-5 minutes on each side. Let it cool down for 5-10 minutes. Then slice it so each slice has a little piece of skin and meat. (If it's too hard to slice, peel off the skin and cut into small pieces, then cut the meat.

In each Mandarin pancake, fill with one piece of skin, one to two pieces of meat, a few julienned pickling cucumbers and couple stalks of scallion. The pancakes are available commercially, or you can make your own; see Pancakes for Peking Duck 北京烤鸭 and Mu Shu Dishes 薄餅 (bo bing)/荷葉餅 (he ye bing) **** on page 115.

At most Chinese restaurants Peking Ducks are done in this fashion, only a few roast their own ducks. It is easier to deep fry a duck in a wide, open wok. You can turn the duck around with ease. Of course if you have a deep fryer that can immerse a whole duck in the hot oil, that is even better, but you'll need to use a lot of oil. The oil can be reused. It is very aromatic after deep frying the duck. One skilled chef at the famous Peking duck restaurant in Beijing, Quan Ju De Restaurant (北京全聚德), can slice 105 pieces of meat from one Peking duck. I was once at Quan Ju De Restaurant several years ago trying out their Peking duck, but it wasn't that impressive at all.

The leftover duck bones can be cooked into soup. The leftover meat can be stir fried with vegetables or used to make fried rice. In Chinese this is called "Peking Duck Three Ways" (烤鸭三吃).

Yield: 6-8 servings

- One roasted duck (烤鸭) from a Chinatown barbecue place *(It will be a reddish brown color.)*
- 12-15 pancakes 薄餅/荷葉餅 *(See page 115 for recipe)*
- One jar or bottle of hoisin sauce (海鮮醬) or your favorite sauce *(It usual comes in a 15 oz. jar. Keep it refrigerated after opening.)*
- 1-2 pickling cucumbers

3-4 stalks scallions

4 cups canola oil

1 Peel the pickling cucumbers and slice thinly, then stack the slices to cut into a julienne. Set aside

2 Cut off the tops of the scallions and the green part, and then cut into one-inch lengths. With the tip of your knife, cut the top third of the scallion lengthwise in thin slices for a julienne-like cut. Soak the julienned end scallion in cold water for 10-15 minutes, and it will curl open like a flower.

3 In a wok, heat 4 cups canola oil over high heat for about 3-4 minutes. Drop a little piece of scallion into the wok. If it sizzles, the oil temperature is good.

4 Use a paper towel to wipe the skin of the roast duck to get rid of any collected moisture or liquid from inside the cavity. Gently place the duck in the oil, the breast side down. (The breast is the side with more meat.) Be careful, as it will splatter. Reduce heat to medium/medium-high. Let the duck fry about 4 minutes, but do not over fry. It is already cooked. You are just frying it until the skin becomes crispy. Gently use tongs and a spatula to turn the duck over to the other side. Turn the duck away from your body. Be careful not to turn it too fast, otherwise the oil might splatter out. Fry about 4 minutes more. Remove the duck to a large sieve and let the excess oil drip off. The oil can be reused for cooking vegetables and meat; it is very aromatic.

5 Let the duck cool down a little, about 10-15 minutes. Slice the duck meat at an angle, like slicing a turkey. You can separate the skin from the meat or make slices of meat and skin together. A lot of people love the skin. It is the best part.

6 *To Reheat the Pancakes:* wrap pancakes with a piece of aluminum foil and place them in a steamer, readied with boiling water, and steam for 10 minutes. Or wrap pancakes inside a couple of layers of cheesecloth to steam.

7 *To serve:* each person places a pancake on a plate, then adds to the center, two pieces of duck meat, a little cucumber julienne, and one piece of scallion.

Roll up the pancake from the lower edge to cover the ingredients and fold in the left and right edge when you reach the center, then brush hoisin sauce or other favorite sauce (Personally, I prefer spicy chili sauce) on the far edge of the pancake. Finish rolling up the pancake and eat.

Pancakes for Peking Duck
北京烤鴨 and **Mu Shu Dishes** 薄餅 (bo bing)/荷葉餅 (he ye bing) ****

The pancake that is beloved by everybody takes a little skill to make. Unlike the Mexican tortilla, each pancake becomes two pancakes when it is peeled apart. This ingenious method is why the pancakes come out so thin. The Chinese name of the pancake is "thin cake" (薄餅) or "lotus leaf pancake" (荷葉餅) because its shape is similar to a lotus leaf. Also, the Chinese like to give beautiful names to any dish. It can be used for wrapping Peking duck or mu shu dishes. Although available commercially, if you make it at home, it is thin, fresh, soft, moist, supple, and delicious.

Yield: 24-30 pancakes depending on the size

- 3 cups all purpose flour
- 3 Tbsp. canola oil (for dough)
- A pinch of salt
- 1 cup lukewarm water (the ratio of flour to water is the same as for Pot Sticker Dumplings 鍋貼與餃子 (guo tie yu jiao zi) *** page 196)
- ¼ cup canola oil (for brushing)
- 2 Tbsp. sesame oil (optional; for brushing)

1 Mix flour, salt and 3 Tbsp. canola oil together in a bowl. Mix lukewarm water with the flour. Transfer the flour mixture to a mixing board. Mix until the dough is very smooth, like bread dough. Place the dough in a mixing bowl and cover with a few layers of moist cheesecloth or plastic wrap. Let it sit at room temperature for 60 minutes. It is all right if the dough is on the softer side.

2 Cut dough into three portions. Roll one portion into a cylinder. Place the other two pieces back in the bowl and cover with a cheesecloth or plastic wrap again. Cut the cylinder into about 8-10 equal pieces. With the cut side down, press each piece into a round flat disk with the palm of your hand.

3 Use a rolling pin to roll out each disc into a 3-inch diameter disc. Brush the canola/sesame oil mixture generously on one piece and sandwich another on top. If the two pieces do not match very well, just pull the smaller piece to fit the larger one. Use one hand to press the two pieces together. Use a rolling pin to roll the two pieces into a 6-inch diameter pancake. Repeat the same steps until all the dough is used up.

4 You can work in batches, making a few, cooking them and then making some more. This way the finished pancakes will have a chance to stick together. As long as you brush a good amount of oil in between the two pancakes, you can make the pancake thinner and they will still be easy to peel apart later.

5 Heat up a non-stick frying pan over medium to medium high heat about 3 minutes. There is no need to add any oil to the frying pan. When the frying pan is hot, place one pancake into the frying pan, cooking about 2 minutes on each side. The pancakes will have a few light brown spots on each side. Do not overcook; otherwise the pancake will become hard and brittle. The pancakes will puff up between the two layers. Flip the pancake and when it gets very puffy, use a spatula to hit the pancake, deflating the bubble and loosening the two layers from each other. The edge of the pancakes will automatically open up. Remove the pancake from the frying pan and let it cool down a little. (The flour from the pancakes tends to burn after you cook a few, so wipe off the flour from the pan with a paper towel once a while.)

6 Open the pancake from an open edge. Do not let the pancake cool down too much before peeling them apart or they will be hard to peel. Be careful, as the steam in the middle of the pancake is quite hot. Serve immediately, or stack them on a plate and cover with a piece of moist cheesecloth.

Any leftover cooked pancakes can be frozen. To heat up frozen pancakes, wrap the pancakes in a piece of aluminum foil and steam for 10 minutes over medium high heat.

Curry Chicken with Potato

馬鈴薯咖哩雞 (jia li ji) **

Have you ever wondered why you rarely find dishes with potatoes in a Chinese restaurant? Before I came to the U.S., I never really like potatoes. They are traditionally considered peasant food, and not fitting for a banquet table. However, every time I dine in American restaurants, potatoes are everywhere. My kids love potatoes, too. Here is a delicious and easy dish with potatoes you can try. No deep frying is required. I use the curry made in Japan. It is very interesting to me that the Japanese love curry so much. You can find vending machines selling curry dishes on the streets of Tokyo. Drop in a coin, and out comes a piping hot curry dish! Amazing!

Yield: 4-5 servings/One plate presentation

2 medium-size Russet potatoes *(Use only Russet for this dish; it has a fluffy, soft texture perfect for this dish.)*

10-12 oz. boneless chicken breast
(about 1 whole boneless chicken breast)

Chicken Marinade:

A pinch of salt

1 Tbsp. cornstarch

A few drops canola oil

1 egg white (optional) *(adds to the tenderness of the chicken)*

A pinch of salt

3 Tbsp. canola oil

1-4 cloves shallot (optional, to add aroma)

2 cubes medium hot curry, Japanese brand S&B Golden Curry or House, or use 1 Tbsp. Indian curry powder mixed with ¼-½ cup hot water (to make the curry easier to dissolve). *I think the Japanese curry has the best taste. You can find it in Japanese or Chinatown grocery stores. The Japanese curry comes in hot, medium hot and mild. You can start with the mild one and go on to medium hot. I like the hot one.*

½ cup hot water

Salt to taste

1 Peel the potatoes and soak in water with a little salt so they will not oxidize and change color. Cut the potatoes into ½-inch cubes

2 Cut the chicken into ½-inch cubes and coat with marinade. Set aside.

3 Peel the shallot by making a slit on the surface. It will be easier to remove the skin this way. Slice thinly crosswise.

4 Add potato cubes to a pot with enough water to barely cover the potatoes. Sprinkle with a pinch of salt, stir and cover. Bring the pot to a boil, and then reduce heat to medium low and let it cook for about 8 minutes. Occasionally check the doneness with a chopstick or a fork. Do not overcook, otherwise potato will fall apart and become like mashed potatoes. (Save the water used to boil the potatoes.)

5 Heat up the wok until it is quite hot, about 3-4 minutes. Add 3 Tbsp. canola oil, turn heat to medium high. Add shallot and stir. Quickly add marinated chicken cubes, and stir until it changes color to a pale white. Turn heat to medium, and add all potato cubes plus the liquid the potato was boiled in and mix well.

6 Break off two cubes of Japanese curry—it is packed like a chocolate bar—and cut into tiny pieces and put into ½ cup hot water (or use the dissolved curry powder). Use a spoon to break up and dissolve the curry in the water.

7 Turn heat to low. Slowly pour the dissolved curry into the wok. The Japanese curry has a little starch. After it is added to the mixture, the mixture will thicken a little. Let the mixture simmer over low heat for about 2-3 minutes. Mix well and salt to taste. Serve hot.

Easy Chicken Gizzard 簡易雞肫
(jian yi ji zhun) **

I got this recipe from my college classmate Stella Weng.

Total cooking time about 1 hour;
Yield: 4-6 servings

> About 1 lb. chicken gizzards (get more than
>   1 lb. if the gizzards are packaged with
>   chicken hearts and livers)
>
> 3 cloves garlic
>
> 2 Tbsp. canola oil
>
> 2 Tbsp. soy sauce
>
> 1 Tbsp. Cognac or your favorite wine
>
> 1 tsp. sugar
>
> ¼ tsp. black pepper
>
> ¼ tsp. five spice powder (五香粉 wu xiang fen)

1 Wash and drain the gizzards (and heart and liver if
using). If gizzards come with hearts and livers, hold
them aside in a separate bowl to add at the end of
the cooking time. Chicken hearts and livers cook
in about 5 minutes. Cut the chicken hearts open on
one side like a butterfly, or make a shallow cut to
make it cook through more evenly and quickly.

2 Crush the garlic with the side of a cleaver to
remove the skin and then coarsely chop.

3 Heat 2 Tbsp. canola oil over high heat in a pot
that has a lid. Add the garlic and stir until it turns
golden brown. Discard the garlic or reserve if you
prefer. Reduce heat to medium high.

4 Add the gizzards only, stir until the color changes
to a pale white. Reduce heat to medium. Do not
add any water. Water will come out from the
gizzard during the cooking.

5 Add 2 Tbsp. soy sauce, 1 Tbsp. Cognac, 1 tsp.
sugar, black pepper, and five spice powder; mix
well. Cover and let cook about 5 minutes. Taste
the sauce and adjust seasoning to your taste.

6 Reduce heat to very low. Simmer for 30 minutes,
stirring occasionally. Do not walk away, otherwise
it might burn.

7 After another 20-30 minutes, the mixture will
become kind of sticky. Add the chicken heart and
liver at this point if you are using them, and cook
another 10 minutes.

8 Try one piece of gizzard. If it is tender, it is done.
Let it cool down a little. Slice and serve hot or at
room temperature. The dish will keep up to one
week in the refrigerator. It is great as an appetizer
or as a main dish served with hot rice.

Chop Suey

雜碎 (za sui) **

Chop Suey literally means "mix little pieces" in Cantonese. The story of its invention is credited to Mr. LEE Hong Zhang (李鴻章), who was a prominent Qing Dynasty (清朝) court officer (the equivalent of a present day prime minister) in the late 19th century. He represented the Qing Dynasty when it signed many defeated agreements (不平等條約) with the aggressive foreigners, like Great Britain, Russia, France, Germany, and Japan, and had to pay huge sums of money and give away cities and land of China, including Hong Kong and Taiwan.

Legend has it that once Mr. LEE had some unexpected guests arrive well after dinner time, but he ordered the family cook to come up with some decent dishes. The cook assembled whatever was left in the kitchen and chopped and mixed everything together to present a colorful dish. The delighted guests asked the cook for the name of the dish. After a moment's pause, the cook hesitantly replied "Chop Suey."

The idea behind "chop suey" is to turn the leftovers in your fridge into a brand new dish so that no one suspects that it's made from leftovers. Ingredients can vary based on what's available in your fridge, both cooked or fresh ingredients. Chop Suey is such a household name here in the States that the famed American artist Edward Hopper has a masterpiece called "Chop Suey." In the painting, two women are sitting in the 2nd floor of a "Chop Suey" Chinese restaurant with the restaurant sign visible.

Yield 3-4 servings.

¼ lb. chicken or ground chicken

¼ lb. pork or ground pork

Meat Marinade:

1 tsp. Sauvignon Blanc or your favorite wine

1 Tbsp. soy sauce

1 Tbsp. cornstarch

1 carrot, diced

2-3 stalks celery heart

1 piece of fried tofu or five spice tofu, which is dry and brownish in color, cubed

5-6 snow peas, cut into half at an angle to create a triangular shape

4-5 mushrooms, quartered

One egg, beaten

4 Tbsp. canola oil, divided

A pinch of salt

A pinch of black pepper

1 Lightly pounded the chicken and pork with the spine of a knife and cut it into pieces about ¼" x ¼" pieces. Or, you can use ground meat.

2 Mix chicken and pork together with 1 Tbsp. soy sauce, 1 tsp. Sauvignon Blanc, 1 Tbsp. cornstarch and set aside.

3 Dice the carrot into small cubes.

4 Peel off the stringy layer of the celery, and then cut crosswise into small pieces.

5 Cut the tofu into small cubes

6 Cut the mushrooms into quarters.

7 Heat up the wok over medium heat for 1 minute. Add 1 Tbsp. canola oil and the beaten egg. Use a spatula to briskly stir the egg in the wok, breaking it up into small pieces. Remove to a plate.

8 Heat up the wok over medium high heat for 3-4 minutes, and add 2-3 Tbsp. canola oil and the meat mixture, and stir for 2 minutes or until the meat changes color to a pale white. Add carrots and mix. Sprinkle ¼ cup water, mix and add tofu, celery pieces, and mushrooms. Turn heat to medium and cover for 3-4 minutes. Remove the cover; add egg and snow peas, a pinch of salt and black pepper. Stir for one minute. Taste, remove and serve hot.

CHAPTER 9

海鮮主菜

Seafood Entrees

Seafood Entrees

Fish (魚) is a main dish in Chinese New Year celebration feasts as turkey is for Thanksgiving. Since "fish," pronounced *yu* (魚) in Mandarin Chinese sounds exactly the same as "extra" or "more" *yu* (餘), having fish for the New Year, means the family will have "more" of everything in the coming year, than the previous year, so fish symbolizes prosperity in the coming year.

A traditional Taiwanese-style banquet usually serves an even number of courses, whether it's 8, 10, 12 or more; but when the fish is served, usually a whole fish, it signals the end of the banquet. The next dish will be a "dessert soup," such as pineapple or almond jelly soup. The Taiwanese are very hospitable—with a tropical weather-like kind of passion—so they are always urging guests to eat as much as they can. Even you say you are full to the gills, they still keep cooking to please the guests. One time I remember my mother cooked up 16 dishes for her high school classmates when they came to our house.

Shrimp with Broccoli
蝦仁炒青花菜
(xia ren chao qing hua cai) **

This dish is a very typical homemade stir fry. Broccoli can be replaced with cauliflower, snow peas, celery hearts, or asparagus with similar results. Reduce the cooking time for snow peas.

Yield: 4-6 servings

> 2-4 stalks scallion, in ½-inch lengths
>
> 1-1¼ pounds broccoli
>
> 1 lb. raw shrimp with or without shells (*This dish will not work with pre-cooked shrimp.*)

A pinch of salt

1 Tbsp. cornstarch

3 Tbsp. canola oil

2-4 slices of fresh ginger

¼ cup water

Salt to taste

Black pepper to taste

1 Tbsp. cornstarch in ½ cup cold water (optional)

Pasta Variation:

Mix in cooked spaghetti at the end for a shrimp and pasta dish.

1. Peel off any damaged layers on the scallions then cut off the tops and any damaged or wilted green ends. Cut into half-inch lengths. Set aside.

2. Cut off broccoli flowerets and cut into bite-size pieces. Peel the tough outer skin from the main stems and slice thinly at a slight diagonal.

3. Put the broccoli into a pot or metal bowl and pour boiling water over the broccoli. Let soak about 5-10 minutes, drain the hot water and cover the broccoli with icy cold water for another 2-5 minutes and drain the water. Soaking in cold water keeps the broccoli crunchy when it is cooked later. Set aside. Next, shell and devein the shrimp.

4. *How to Shell and Devein Shrimp.* There is a very neat plastic tool on market for shelling shrimp. It costs only a couple dollars. You just stick the tool into the tail of the shrimps and lift the shell off whole. KitchenEtc. carries this item. Slice open the back of the shrimp (along its spine) to devein. Soak the shrimp in a pot of cold water.

5 Rub the shrimp between your hands to quickly devein them without having to pick out the veins one by one. Lift the shrimp from the water so that the sand remains at the bottom of the pot. Repeat this step.

6 Finally let the shrimp drain in a colander for about 10 minutes. In a bowl, mix a pinch of salt and 1 Tbsp. cornstarch with the shrimp.

7 Heat up the wok over high heat for about 3-4 minutes. Add 3 Tbsp. canola oil. Reduce heat to medium high. Add ginger slices and sautée until golden brown and discard the ginger.

8 Add the shrimp and stir fry until they turn a pale pink. If they stick together, separate them. Reduce the heat to low.

9 Holding a colander or strainer over the wok, scoop the shrimp into the colander and let the oil drip back into the wok. Put the shrimp in a plate.

10 Without washing the wok, turn the heat to high, add scallions and cook until golden brown.

11 Add broccoli and ¼ cup water, turn heat to medium and stir thoroughly and cover for about 5 minutes. Remove cover, taste to see if the broccoli is soft enough, otherwise add a little bit of water (if needed) and cover for a few more minutes.

12 When the broccoli is cooked but still firm, turn the heat to low, add shrimp, stir thoroughly and salt to taste. Sprinkle with black pepper. Continue to next step if you prefer a dish with sauce. Otherwise, serve hot.

13 *(Optional)* If you prefer a little bit of a sauce with the dish, just before you remove the shrimp from the heat, mix 1 Tbsp. cornstarch with ½ cup cold water. Turn heat to medium low, pour cornstarch mixture over broccoli and shrimp, mix well and serve. Do not overcook the shrimp or it will become hard. Serve hot.

Shrimp with Ginger & Scallion
薑蔥蝦 (cong jiang xia) ***

This Cantonese dish is served widely in Boston Chinatown restaurants. Asian Garden (香滿園), a restaurant located on Harrison Ave. in the heart of Boston Chinatown cooks this dish to perfection. I used to order it as takeout once every week. Later I talked with my second sister WU Shu-Ying (吳淑英) in Taipei to figure out how to cook this dish. She gave me a few tips to follow. I practiced a few times and this recipe is my successful result. It is quick, easy, and good. The best part is you don't have to peel the shrimp shells or even take off the heads. If you can get shrimp with heads it is even better.

Yield: 3-4 servings

¾ lb. shrimp with shells and head (*If you can't find it at the supermarket, it's available at Sun Sun Company (新新公司) on Oxford Street in the heart of Boston Chinatown.*)

4 Tbsp. canola oil

2-3 slices of fresh ginger

Sauce to Toss with Shrimp:

3-4 cloves garlic, peeled, crushed, finely chopped

4 slices of fresh ginger, skinned and julienned

3 stalks scallion, finely chopped

1 Tbsp. sesame oil

A pinch of freshly ground black pepper

1 tsp. salt

A few drops chili oil (optional)

2-3 lettuce leaves, shredded, for garnish

1 Use the side of the knife to crush the garlic and remove the skin, then finely chop.

2 For the sauce, peel off the skin of the ginger slices using the spine of a small knife to scrape/rub it off. Slice four of the slices into thin strips.

3 Cut off the tops of the scallions and half of the green part, and then finely chop.

4 Mix 1 Tbsp. salt with the unshelled shrimp. Mix and rinse clean with water. Drain the water, mix in a pinch of salt, and pat dry with a paper towel.

5 In a large stainless steel mixing bowl, add chopped garlic, julienned fresh ginger, finely chopped scallion, a pinch of black pepper, 1 Tbsp. sesame oil, 1 tsp. salt, and chili oil, and mix well.

6 Add about 4 Tbsp. canola oil to the wok, heat over high heat and when the wok is hot about 3-4 minutes, add 2-3 slices fresh ginger and stir until golden brown. Add shrimp and immediately cover for about 2-3 minutes to avoid splattering. Remove cover and stir shrimp well and cover again for about 2-3 minutes or until the shrimp have all turned a bright orange color.

7 Remove shrimp from the wok, and add to the mixing bowl mixture. Toss shrimp a few times in the mixture until coated evenly. Sprinkle with fresh ground black pepper. Serve hot. Place tossed shrimp on a bed of shredded lettuce on a large plate.

Shrimp Wrapped in Bacon

培根包蝦仁 (pei gen bao xia ren) ***

This dish is considered an East meets West creation. In traditional Chinese cooking, bacon did not exist except as the Chinese equivalent of Virginia Ham called Jin Hua Huo Tui (金華火腿Jin Hua Ham). This recipe uses bacon instead and raw shrimp. In Taiwan, bacon is translated as pei gen *which sounds like "bacon."*

This dish is very simple yet fancy, except that the shrimp shells have to be removed. I once bought some shrimp from a supermarket only to discover that the shells had already been cut open. They also tasted like they had been mixed with baking soda. Do not use that kind of shrimp; buy shrimp whose shells are intact, or get shrimp from a local fish merchant that you trust. Freshness is everything. This dish is excellent as a party appetizer. It is an exquisite and fine dish that partygoers will appreciate a lot.

Yield: 25 shrimp wraps

- 8 oz. package of bacon strips
- ½ lb. of shrimp with shells (sized at 25-30 shrimp per pound)
- A pack of toothpicks
- Salt
- 1-1½ cup canola oil (if frying instead of broiling)

1 Shell the shrimp and devein (see steps **4** and **5** in Shrimp with Broccoli on page 121). Add some salt, rub and rinse with water. Drain well and add a pinch of salt. Mix well and place shrimp in a sieve to drain.

2 Cut each strip of bacon in half. Then, placing one bacon strip on a plate, put one shrimp at one end, wrap the bacon around the shrimp, and stick in a toothpick to hold the shrimp and bacon together. Place the wrapped shrimp on an aluminum tray. Repeat with all the shrimp until they are used up.

3 ***Broiling Method:*** Set the oven to the High Broil setting. Place the aluminum tray in the oven and broil for about 8 minutes.

4 ***Deep Frying Method:*** They can be deep fried, too. Place 1-1½ cup canola oil in the wok, heat up the oil over high heat about 3 minutes or until hot. Drop a bacon shrimp roll into the oil; if it sizzles, it is hot enough. Fry about half the shrimp rolls at a time. When they turn golden, remove and drain. Deep fry the rest of the batch until all done. Serve hot.

Shrimp Toast

蝦仁土司 (xia ren tu si) ***

This is a dish perfect for appetizer. It may be a little greasy if you use regular soft sandwich bread like Wonder. Use hard crusty bread, like French or Italian bread, it is not as greasy because of French and Italian bread's dense texture and crusty outer shell.

Yield: 12 pieces shrimp toast

> 8 oz shrimp (shelled); or 10 oz. raw shrimp with shells, but no heads
>
> 1 tsp. salt
>
> 1 baguette of French bread
>
> A pinch of salt
>
> 1 Tbsp. cornstarch
>
> A pinch of black pepper
>
> ¾ cups canola oil

1 Shell the shrimp and devein (see steps **4** and **5** in Shrimp with Broccoli on page 121). Add 1 tsp. salt, mix and rinse clean with water. Drain the water. Sprinkle with a pinch of salt. Put shrimp into a plastic bag (to avoid splattering) and crush shrimps with the flat side of a cleaver into a paste-like texture.

2 Slice the bread into 12 slices, ½-inch thick. Slices will be about 1½" x 3".

3 Mix the cornstarch and pepper with the shrimp paste.

4 Spread about 1 Tbsp. of shrimp paste on one side of each bread slice until you've used up all the paste. It makes about 12 pieces depending how much shrimp paste you put on each slice.

5 Heat up ¾ cup canola oil over medium heat for about 2-3 minutes. Put the shrimp-paste-coated bread into the oil one by one, shrimp side down. You can fry about 6 pieces at once. Deep fry for 1 minute. Use a spatula to turn the toast over when the shrimp paste side is golden after about 1 minute. Turn over the piece and remove. It's not necessary to fry the side without paste, otherwise it will be too greasy. Serve warm or at room temperature.

Shrimp with Tofu

蝦仁豆腐 (xia ren dou fu) **

This dish is easy except the shrimp have to be shelled. The tastiest shrimps are from the Gulf of Mexico. However, it is not always easy to find out where the shrimp at the market are from. Go to your local fish market and ask; they will be happy to tell you. If the shrimp is not good, the dish won't come out right.

Yield: 4 servings/One plate presentation

> 1 lb. raw shrimp with or without shells (Do not use pre-cooked shrimp.)
>
> **Shrimp Marinade:**
>
> A pinch of salt
>
> 1 Tbsp. cornstarch
>
> 2 pieces soft tofu
>
> 4 Tbsp. canola oil, divided
>
> 2-3 fresh ginger slices (*Ginger is used like lemon to get rid of the fishy smell; do not use ginger powder*)
>
> A pinch of salt
>
> 1 shallot
>
> 1 Tbsp. light soy sauce or a pinch of salt
>
> 2 stalks scallion, cut into ¼-inch lengths
>
> A pinch of black pepper

1 Shell the shrimps and devein (see steps **4** and **5** in Shrimp with Broccoli on page 121). Mix with a pinch of salt and 1 Tbsp. cornstarch and leave shrimp in a colander to drain.

2 Cut tofu into ½-inch cubes and drop into boiling water for about 2 minutes and drain. Pre-boiling the tofu means water will not come out when you cook it in the dish, diluting the taste.

3 Peel the shallot by making one cut on the skin, remove the outer film, and then slice thinly.

4 Cut off the tops of the scallions and half the green part, and then cut into ¼-inch lengths.

5 Heat up the wok over high heat, about 3-4 minutes.

Add 2 Tbsp. canola oil in a wok, add 3-4 fresh ginger pieces and let it turn golden brown. Discard the ginger. Add shrimp and stir until they turn pale pink, then stir another 2 minutes. Remove to a plate.

6 Heat up 2 Tbsp. canola oil, add shallot slices and cook until golden brown, add tofu cubes, 1 Tbsp. light soy sauce. If you cannot get light soy sauce, just add a pinch of salt. Stir and add cooked shrimp back to the wok, mix and salt to taste. Sprinkle with scallion pieces and black pepper. Serve hot.

Shrimp with Snow Peas
雪豆蝦仁 (xue dou xia ren) **

If cooked correctly, the snow peas turn out beautifully green and crunchy. It is best to blanch them first, and then add them to the cooked shrimp at the last minute. The shrimp is better with shells. Do not use pre-cooked shrimp; this dish will never work.

Yield: 3-4 servings/One plate presentation

> 12 oz. medium size shrimp with or without shells (about 25 shrimp per pound size)

> **Shrimp Marinade:**

> One egg white (optional)

> 1 Tbsp. cornstarch

> A pinch of salt

> 8-10 oz. snow peas (or substitute with sugar peas)

> 4 Tbsp. canola oil, divided

> 2-3 slices of fresh ginger

> Salt to taste

1 Shell the shrimp and devein (see steps **4** and **5** in Shrimp with Broccoli on page 121).

2 String the snow peas by breaking off one tip and peeling off the string on one side then doing the same at the other end for the string on the other side of the pod. Soak stringed snow peas in cold water for 1-2 hours before cooking

3 Heat up the wok over high heat, about 3-4 minutes. Reduce heat to medium high; add 3 Tbsp. canola oil and ginger slices; and stir fry until golden brown. Discard the ginger slices. Add marinated shrimp; stir until the shrimp changes color, about 2 minutes, and remove the shrimp to a plate. There's no need to wash the wok. Add 1 Tbsp oil to the wok over medium high heat, and add snow peas. Stir a couple times and sprinkle a little water so the snow peas will not burn. Stir for another minute and add the cooked shrimps, sprinkle with a little salt, stir and quickly remove. Do not let snow peas stay in the wok too long or they will become limp and yellow.

Asparagus with Shrimp

蘆筍炒蝦仁 (lu sun chao xia ren) **

Asparagus comes in different sizes. Buy ones that are plump and bigger. The skinny ones sometimes are tender, but sometimes are not. When asparagus is in season in the spring, it is the best time to cook them.

Yield: *3-4 servings/One plate presentation*

> 12 oz. shrimp with shells (sized at about 25 per pound)

> **Shrimp Marinade:**

> A pinch of salt,

> 1 Tbsp. cornstarch,

> 1 egg white (optional)

1-1½ lbs. asparagus

4 oz. oyster mushrooms or your favorite mushrooms

2 cloves garlic

6 Tbsp. canola oil, divided

2-3 slices fresh ginger (optional)

1 egg yolk

Salt to taste

1 Tbsp. cornstarch with ¼ cup water (optional)

1 Shell the shrimp and devein (see steps **4** and **5** in Shrimp with Broccoli on page 121). Add 1 tsp. salt, mix and rinse clean with water. Drain the water.

2 Snap off the top tough end of the asparagus. Start at the bottom and gently bend the asparagus. It will break at the point where it is no longer tough. Peel off the lower part of the asparagus skin with a peeler. If the asparagus is very tender, you can skip peeling the skin. Peeling the skin makes the asparagus taste sweeter. If you do peel the asparagus, you may need to get 1½ lbs. of asparagus. Slice the asparagus at an angle or use a bias cut, where you make a diagonal cut, turn the asparagus a quarter turn and make another diagonal cut at the same angle as the first. Continue turning and slicing.

3 Cut off the tough bottom part of the mushroom stem. For mushrooms bigger than bite-size, cut them in half.

4 Use the flat side of a cleaver to pound the garlic and remove the skin.

5 Heat up the wok over high heat, about 3-4 minutes, add 3 Tbsp. canola oil and fresh ginger slices (if using) and brown. Add shrimp and stir about 1-2 minutes until it turns pink. Remove from the wok and set aside.

6 Reheat the wok without washing, and add 3 Tbsp. oil with garlic and stir until golden brown. Discard the garlic. Add asparagus to the wok; stir; sprinkle with some salt and ¼ cup water. Cover for about 3 minutes or until asparagus is tender but not too soft. Add oyster mushrooms, reserved shrimp, and egg yolk (leftover from using the egg white in the marinade). Stir well with a pinch of salt. If it is too dry, sprinkle a few drops water to prevent the wok from burning at the bottom. Serve hot.

7 *(Optional Sauce):* Mix 1 Tbsp. cornstarch with ¼ cup water and pour over the mixture, stir and serve hot.

Fish with Miso Sauce

魚塊加日本醬

(yu kuai jia ri ben jiang) **

A well-seasoned heavy cast iron frying pan or non-stick pan works well for this homemade dish to prevent the fish steak from sticking to the pan. My children love it. For best results, use a firm fish steak like halibut, salmon, or swordfish. Miso can be purchased from Asian markets. It is a fermented soybean paste and comes in many colors, yellow, beige, a coffee-like, dark-colored one, and low salt ones. It is widely used in Japanese and Taiwanese cuisines.

Yield: 3-4 servings

> ¾ lbs. salmon, halibut steak, or swordfish
>
> Salt
>
> 3 Tbsp. canola oil
>
> 3-4 slices fresh ginger
>
> 4-5 stalks scallion, in one-inch lengths
>
> 1-2 tsp. miso (I prefer the lighter colored one or a low salt miso.)
>
> ¾ cup hot water

1 Trim off the tops of the scallions and cut off any damaged ends, then cut into one-inch lengths.

2 Rub the fish steak with plenty of salt, and rinse clean with cold water. Pat dry with paper towels then sprinkle and rub with a little salt on both sides.

3 Heat a non-stick pan or wok over high heat for 4 minutes. Add 3 Tbsp. canola oil and ginger slices, turn heat to medium, and cook until golden brown. Discard ginger slices. Add scallions and cook until wilted. Make sure the wok is hot to lessen the possibility of the fish sticking to the pan. Add the fish steak, cover and let it sit on one side for at least 3 minutes. Do not flip it too soon; otherwise the fish will stick to the wok.

4 Remove the cover; use a spatula to loosen the bottom of the fish from the pan before flipping. Gently flip the fish steak away from you so the oil will not splatter on you. Cover and let it cook for 3-4 minutes more until the fish steak is golden brown on both sides. Turn heat to low.

5 Mix 1-2 tsp. miso in ¾ cup hot water until dissolved. Pour the miso and water over the fish, and let it simmer on low heat for 2-3 minutes on one side. Turn over the fish, and let it simmer for another 2 minutes. Use the spatula to ladle sauce over the fish a few times. Remove and serve hot. The sauce is very good when served with hot rice.

Fried Whole Fish
炸全鱼 (za quan yu) *****

Most fried fish in Chinese cooking is whole, rather than as fillets or steaks. It is a fact that a fish cooked whole with the bones in is much more tasty and delicious. (Italians cook fish whole, too.) I grew up eating whole fish. When someone takes the fish head away before I dig my chopsticks into the fish, I feel "not complete." My husband Leo loves to do that all the time.

There are two kinds of people eating whole fish. One kind, like me, only eats the fish meat. The other kind, like Leo, loves to eat the fish meat from the head and the bones. Beautifully frying fish is notoriously difficult— except if you deep fry. With a shallow fry or pan fry, every cook has the tendency to flip the fish too soon, making a mess. This dish needs a very patient cook to accomplish the job.

A successfully fried whole fish is not only delicious; it is also glorious. Sea bass is the best fish for this task. The sea bass is readily available in Chinatown groceries. One pound is about $5.00. Sea bass sold in supermarkets usually is Chilean sea bass. The taste is somewhat different from the one sold in Chinatown. You can use that for convenience. Otherwise get it from Chinatown. When eating a whole fish, be careful as there are bound to be tiny fish bones in the meat. Examine each piece of fish meat before you put it into your mouth—although sea bass usually has few tiny fish bones in the meat.

Yield: 3-4 servings

- 1-1¼ lbs. sea bass with head (If the fish is too big to fit in the wok, cut it in half crosswise, otherwise it is very hard to handle in a small, home-use wok.)
- 2-3 Tbsp. salt
- 4-5 slices fresh ginger
- 3-4 Tbsp. canola oil for shallow/pan fry
- 2-3 cup canola oil for deep frying, varies depending on the size of the fish
- ½-1 cup cornstarch, for deep frying only (to prevent the fish from splattering while being deep fried.)

Sauce for the Fish:

1 Tbsp. soy sauce

¼ cup water

1 tsp. balsamic vinegar

½ tsp. sugar

3 stalks scallions, finely chopped

3 slices of fresh ginger, finely chopped

1 tsp. cornstarch mixed with ½ cup of water (optional)

1 *Fish Preparation:* A 1-1¼ lbs. sea bass is easier to handle. The fish is usually cleaned by the vendor. However, there are usually some scales left. Get a small serrated knife and scrap the entire fish to get rid of any remaining scales on the fish skin. Under running water, clean both sides thoroughly. Use a lot of salt to rub the fish inside and out. Rinse clean with water. Sprinkle with a little salt on both sides and inside the fish body. Let the fish drip dry. Cut three diagonal or horizontal slits on both sides of the fish so that the fish will cook through the middle. Pat dry the fish inside and out with paper towels before placing it into the pan to fry.

For Pan Frying: (煎鱼)

To make the pan frying fish easier, use a non-stick frying pan to avoid a sticking mess. Otherwise use the following technique:

1 *Pan Fry Only Method:* Let the wok heat up to the point where you can see faint smoke coming up from the wok. Pat dry the whole fish with paper towels inside and outside. Add oil, and then the fish to the wok and cover immediately to prevent splattering. This technique is called "hot pan, cold oil" (熱鍋冷油). Turn heat to medium high. Let the fish cook on one side for 3-3-½ minutes without moving the fish. Remove the cover and gently turn the fish to the other side, turning the fish away from your body. Cover and fry for another 2-3 minutes. Do not stir; do not move the fish around. Remove the cover, and use a spatula to remove the fish to a plate. The fish is not easy to handle. To make it easier, I would rather you use a non-stick frying pan.

2 *Pan Fry Only Method:* Or pan fry the fish on one side for 4 minutes, and then remove the fish to a jelly roll pan. Preheat the oven to 450°F degrees. Bake the fish on the tray in the oven for 15 minutes. Traditionally the fish is fried on both sides, since the home-use wok is not big enough to retain the heat, the second side usually cannot be pan fried satisfactorily to a crispy skin. This alternative is a good way to completely pan fry fish with very successful results.

3 Enjoy your gloriously cooked whole fish. One side is crispy and the other side is tender with white flesh. It is truly a piece of culinary art. Serve with the sauce described below.

For Deep Frying: (炸魚)

1 Pat dry the fish with paper towels. Sprinkle with cornstarch or flour all over the fish, inside and out. Use both hands to press the cornstarch against the fish. Shake the excess cornstarch off over the sink.

2 Heat up the wok over high heat for about 4 minutes. Add 2 cups canola oil and reduce heat to medium high. Gently slide the fish into the hot oil and fry for 3-4 minutes. Do not turn or move the fish. Occasionally use a Chinese spatula to "baste" hot oil over the fish if the oil does not cover the entire fish. Gently turn the fish away from you to the other side and fry for 3-4 minutes, or until golden brown. Remove and serve hot.

Sauce for the Fish

1 Mix soy sauce, water, balsamic vinegar, sugar, finely chopped scallions, finely chopped fresh ginger, and simmer over medium heat for 2 minutes. Turn off the heat, and add 1 tsp. cornstarch mixed with ½ cup water to the mixture to thicken the sauce. Remove the sauce and drizzle over the fish and serve. Or simply mix the sauce together without the cornstarch and serve as a dipping sauce.

This is the most satisfying dish you will ever taste. It is perfect to serve with fluffy hot rice. The Golden Dragon Chinese Restaurant in Foxwood Casino, Connecticut has the best Deep Fried Flounder (酥炸龍俐) on their menu.

Steamed Fish
蒸魚 (zhen yu) ***

The best fish to steam whole is flounder or sea bass. However, you can use the same technique to steam boneless fish chunks, like tilapia, salmon, halibut, haddock, swordfish, or clams. Steam the fish for 10 minutes over high heat. (The fish is placed on a plate inside the steamer when the steamer pot water is boiling).

When steaming a whole fish or part of a fish, be sure to put the fish in a plate inside the steaming rack. I saw a TV cooking show where the chef placed the fish fillet directly on the steaming rack. By doing so, the best part of the fish juice is lost. The fish juice can be saved and simmered with a little soy sauce, vinegar, sugar, ginger slices, and scallion pieces over low heat for 3-4 minutes or less and then drizzled over the steamed fish. It makes a perfect dish.

The fancy, tall stainless steel steaming pot used on cooking shows or in cooking school demonstrations is not practical for steaming. The fancy steaming tray (fitted to the steaming pot) is shallow and tiny. For steaming, it is more practical to buy a reasonably priced aluminum steamer with two steaming racks fitted on top of a steamer pot from any Chinese grocery store.

East Ocean City Restaurant (醉瓊樓) on Beach Street in Boston Chinatown has really good Steamed Flounder (清蒸龍俐).

Yield: 2-3 servings

> 1 lb. whole sea bass, flounder or fish steak with bone in (like halibut or swordfish, fish with bones is much juicier than just the fish meat itself)
>
> 3-4 slices fresh ginger, cut into thin strips (julienne)
>
> 3-4 stalks scallions, in one-inch lengths
>
> A few drops Sauvignon Blanc or your favorite white wine
>
> 2-3 Tbsp. canola oil

1 Cut the tops off the scallions and half of the green part. Then cut into one-inch lengths and slice thinly lengthwise.

2 *Fish Preparation:* Use a serrated knife to scrape off any remaining scales on the fish skin. Rub a generous amount of salt all over the fish, rinse clean, and then sprinkle with a little salt all over the fish. If steaming a whole fish, make 2-3 diagonal slits on both sides of the fish so it will cook through more easily.

3 Place the fish inside a plate with a little depth so it will catch the juice that comes out during steaming. Sprinkle a few drops of Sauvignon Blanc over the fish. Scatter julienned fresh ginger over the fish. Place the fish plate inside the steaming rack.

4 Pre-boil the water in the steamer pot with the cover on. Turn the heat to low, then place the steaming rack with the fish plate over the steamer pot. Turn the heat to high again. Steam for 8-10 minutes. If you are using a fish fillet that is thicker than a whole fish, steam 12 minutes, or make diagonal slits in the fillet to make it cook faster. If you don't have a steamer, use the wok. You can add some water to the wok, and put the fish plate on a rack inside the wok and steam.

5 Turn off the heat; open the cover. Be careful to not burn yourself with the hot steam that comes out. Let the fish cool down for about 5 minutes before removing the fish plate from the steamer. Carefully remove the fish plate without burning yourself. If you have a dish holder with 4 prongs, use that. Sprinkle the thinly sliced scallion all over the fish.

6 *(Optional)* Heat a wok over high heat to high, add 3 Tbsp. canola oil and heat until it is very hot and almost smoking, about 3 minutes. Using a Chinese metal spatula, drizzle the hot oil over the steamed fish and scallion. The scallion will make a "zi, zi, zi" noise.

You can place the steamed fish on the table before you drizzle the hot oil over the fish. It makes the presentation of the fish at the table more dramatic, seeing the fish gleaming with piping hot oil.

Smoked Fish
熏魚 (xun yu) ★★★★

This smoked fish is not smoked but deep fried. In the original recipe, the fish was actually smoked with either sugar or a special kind of wood chip, which has a certain aroma when they smoulder at the bottom of the wok. The fish was then placed over the chips, but nowadays that method is rarely used. In Taiwan it is widely believed that smoked food can cause cancer. I don't know if there is any scientific evidence to prove that, but probably more for convenience sake, deep frying is a popular way of cooking this dish today.

I have tried a few kinds of fish. Tilapia (鯛魚/吳郭魚) and snapper have produced satisfactory results. I have tried salmon not too successfully. Salmon's texture is too fine. It is better to use fish with a coarser texture. If you can get fish steak with a piece of bone in the center, it is better and it is also the more traditional cut for smoked fish.

Smoked fish is one of the items usually presented as a cold platter as the first course of a banquet.

Yield: 5-6 servings/One plate presentation

> 1½ lbs. tilapia or snapper, steak or fillet about ½-inch thick or more

Salt

> **Fish Marinade:**
>
> 2 Tbsp. soy sauce
>
> 2 Tbsp. Sauvignon Blanc
>
> 2 slices fresh ginger
>
> 2 stalks scallion, in ½-inch lengths
>
> 2 Tbsp. sugar
>
> 1 tsp. balsamic vinegar from Modena, Italy
>
> A pinch of five spice powder
>
> A pinch of cinnamon powder
>
> A pinch of freshly ground black pepper

1-2 Tbsp. cornstarch

2 cups canola oil

1 Tbsp. soy sauce (if needed) for sauce

1 Cut off the scallion tops and half the green part, and then cut into ½-inch lengths.

2 Cut each fish fillet into two large pieces, rub with some salt, rinse clean, and sprinkle with a pinch of salt. Cut into large pieces about 3-inches square.

3 Mix the fish pieces with the marinade ingredients. You can adjust the taste of the marinade to your liking; some like it sweeter. Leave marinated fish in the refrigerator for 2-3 hours. Once in a while, turn the fish pieces to marinate evenly.

4 Drain off the marinade and save it in a bowl. Remove the scallion pieces and ginger slices from the fish pieces. Use a paper towel to pat dry both sides of the fish pieces. Sprinkle some cornstarch over the fish steaks and shake off any excess.

5 Heat up a wok over high heat, about 3-4 minutes, and then add 2 cups canola oil. Reduce heat to medium high. Gently place half of the fish pieces one by one into the wok. Do not add too many pieces at once or it will bring down the oil temperature and the fish will not fry satisfactorily. Cover and let deep fry for 3-4 minutes or until golden brown. It is not necessary to turn the fish if it is completely submerged in the oil. Remove fish pieces to a sieve and let drain. Repeat, deep frying the rest of the batch. Make sure each time to deep fry 3-4 minutes without turning the fish pieces. Otherwise the fish will flake very easily into smaller pieces. Simply use enough oil to fry fish pieces. Remove the drained, fried fish pieces to a plate.

6 Taste the marinade sauce. If it is not salty enough, add more soy sauce (1 Tbsp. or so) and 1 Tbsp. water.

7 Pour off the oil from the wok, put the deep fried fish pieces back into the wok, and pour the reserved marinade over the fish pieces. Turn heat to high to bring the sauce to a boil, then reduce the heat to medium low and simmer for 5-7 minutes until the sauce is almost all evaporated. Remove fish to a plate and serve at room temperature. Or, leave in the refrigerator overnight and serve at room temperature the next day.

This dish tastes best when it is served the next day at room temperature. You can prepare it beforehand to achieve the best results.

Pan Fried Salmon
煎鮭魚 (jian gui yu) ***

When pan frying a whole fish or fish fillet, the wok has to be really clean and hot. This way the fish will not stick to the wok and you will cook up a beautiful piece of fish. Salmon is readily available at a reasonable price. Of course wild salmon tastes much better, but it's more expensive than farm-raised salmon. I have tried the American chef way of pan frying the fish on one side, and then finishing the cooking in an oven, but my husband says that the fish turns out dry, and not juicy like fish which is pan fried on both sides. Here is a method you can use with fish steaks such as halibut and swordfish, but not cod. The cod is usually sold skinless, and is too flaky and hard to handle.

Yield: 2-3 servings

　　1 lb. boneless fish steak or fillet (use salmon, halibut, or swordfish)

　　Salt

　　3-4 slices fresh ginger

　　3 Tbsp. canola oil (for pan fry method)

　　1 Tbsp. white wine (for baking method)

　　Black pepper (for baking method)

　　Sauce (optional):

　　2-3 stalks scallion, finely chopped

　　1 Tbsp. soy sauce

　　1½ tsp. sugar

　　1 tsp. Italian balsamic vinegar

　　4 Tbsp. water

　　1 tsp. canola oil

　　1 tsp. cornstarch with ¼ cup water

1 Scrape the skin of the fish with a serrated knife to remove any remaining scales. Rub the fish with a lot of salt to get rid of the fishy smell, then rinse clean and sprinkle with a pinch of salt on both sides. If the piece is thick, cut a couple horizontal slits in the thickest portion.

2 **Pan Fry Method:** Make sure the wok is very clean. Heat it over high heat for about 3-4 minutes.

Reduce heat to medium high, add 3 Tbsp. canola oil, and swirl it around the wok to coat the surface where the fish will touch the wok. Pat dry the salmon with paper towels. Add ginger slices to the wok and let them turn golden brown. Discard the ginger.

3 Put the salmon skin-side down in the wok and cover to prevent splattering for 3-3½ minutes. Open the cover, and use a spatula to turn the fish to the other side. Turn the fish away from you, so the oil will not splatter onto you. Again, cover for 2½-3 minutes. Remove to a plate. Serve with dipping sauce below.

4 *Baking Method:* Baking is another easy way to cook salmon steak. Line an oven pan with a piece of parchment paper, place the salmon steak in the pan, sprinkle with 1 Tbsp white wine and line with fresh ginger slices along the edge of the salmon steak. Sprinkle black pepper all over the top of the salmon steak and bake at 450°F for 20 minutes or until done. (A "Black Pepper Crab" dish which I ate while I was traveling in Singapore gave me this inspiration.)

5 *(Optional Sauce)* Cut off the tops of the 2-3 scallions and half the green part, and then finely chop. Sprinkle scallion all over the pan fried salmon. Mix the sauce ingredients (except cornstarch and water) in a small pot and simmer the mixture over low heat for 3 minutes, add 1 tsp. cornstarch dissolved in ¼ cup water. Stir well, remove from heat, and drizzle the sauce over the salmon that has been sprinkled with chopped scallions. Serve hot.

Fried Oysters
炸生蠔 (zhao sheng hao)

Oysters must be handled delicately, but it is so delicious after it's cooked. It is worth all the trouble. You can easily find this dish in any seafood restaurant. Most fried oysters presented in restaurants are heavily coated with flour. This homemade one is really light and good.

Yield: 3-4 servings

> 8 oz. shucked oysters
>
> 1½ cup canola oil
>
> 3 Tbsp. cornstarch or more
>
> A pinch of salt

1 Rinse the oysters in water, mix with a pinch of salt, and then let sit in a sieve for 30 minutes to drain.

2 Heat up 1½ cup canola oil over medium high heat, about 3 minutes.

3 Reduce heat to medium low.

4 Pat dry oysters with a piece of paper towel first before mixing with the cornstarch. Mix oysters with the cornstarch one by one. Add more cornstarch if needed. Make sure the cornstarch on the oyster is dry and does not get mixed with the oyster into a whole lump. Another way is to coat the oyster in a bowl with a lot of cornstarch, so the oyster stays fluffily coated with dry cornstarch. Place one oyster into the oil; if it sizzles, the oil is at the right temperature.

5 Carefully place about half the oysters into the oil *one by one* as they will splatter. Do not stir for 10 seconds—count from 1 to 10. Use a spatula to move the oysters around. They are done when they float. The oysters cook up pretty fast. Pick up the oysters and put in a sieve to drain. Continue to deep fry the rest of the oysters, also added to the oil one by one.

6 This is a very quick dish. Don't start the heat too high. As long as it sizzles, the temperature is good.

Egg Pancake Rolls with Fish and Pork

蝦肉蛋捲 (xia rou dan juan) ****

It's quite common to use egg pancake to wrap up some fillings and steam. This version is fancy. You can skip some ingredients to make a simpler version.

Yield: 8 rolls

Filling ingredients:

5-6 oz. fish fillet (haddock, sole, tilapia are all good choices) or shrimp

Salt

5-6 oz. ground pork

6 pieces fresh shiitake mushrooms, sliced

8 fresh water chestnuts, peeled and smashed (skip if unavailable)

3 stalks celery heart, finely chopped

Seasonings for filling

A pinch of salt

A pinch of black pepper

1-2 Tbsp. soy sauce

2 Tbsp. Sauvignon Blanc

1 Tbsp. sesame oil

1 tsp. rice vinegar or balsamic vinegar

2 Tbsp. cornstarch

6-7 eggs

6-7 tsp. cornstarch

4 Tbsp. flour mixed with ¼ cup water as sealer for rolls

Variation: The amount of meat can be reduced in favor of more celery in the filling. However, more meat with a sprinkle of vegetables is easier to wrap.

1 Rub the fish with some salt and rinse clean. Slice thinly. Then combine and chop with the ground pork into a paste. If using shrimp, shell and devein before salting, rinsing clean, and then chopping with the pork. (See steps **4** and **5** in Shrimp with Broccoli on page 121).

2 Clean, cut off the stem, and slice the shiitake mushrooms.

3 Peel water chestnuts with a peeler (remove all the yellow parts) then place inside a plastic bag, and using the flat side of the cleaver, smash the water chestnut.

4 Peel the strings off the celery and finely chop.

5 Roughly chop together the filling ingredients (meat, fish, shrimp, mushrooms, water chestnuts, and celery) and mix with the filling seasoning ingredients.

6 *Making Egg Pancakes:* Mix one beaten egg with 1 tsp. cornstarch and 1 Tbsp. water. Using a non-stick frying pan, pour the beaten egg mixture into the pan. About 1 egg will make one egg pancake if the egg is small. If the eggs are large, you can make three pancakes out of two eggs. Make enough pancakes for eight rolls.

7 Place 2 Tbsp. of filling shaped like a cylinder on each egg pancake. Roll up the egg pancake all the way, leaving both ends open. Seal the long edge with the flour/water mixture. Alternatively, spread the mixture in a thin layer all over the egg pan cake and roll it up. (This method creates a distinctive design when the rolls are sliced.) Line up the rolls on a plate without overlapping the rolls. Do not stack them as the bottom ones will be squashed flat.

8 Bring the steamer pot of water to boiling. Reduce heat to low and place the plate with rolls in the steaming rack. Be careful not to be burned by the steam. Turn heat to medium high and let steam for 20 minutes.

9 Turn off the heat. Let rolls cool down for about 10 minutes before removing from the steamer. Cut into slices ⅓-inch thick and arrange nicely on a serving plate in rows or concentric circles.

West Lake Sweet & Sour Fish Fillet

西湖醋魚 (xi hu cu yu) ***

West Lake, located in Han Zhou, China (杭州西湖), is famous for its beautiful natural scenery and West Lake fish cuisine. West Lake Sweet & Sour Fish is one of the most well-known fish dishes. The area's cuisine emphasizes the natural taste of the fish, mostly steamed and boiled. This cooking method is especially good with fresh whole fish. It retains the natural fish flavor. In the area on the east coast of China near Shanghai in Jiangsu (江蘇) and Zhejiang (浙江) Province, the cuisine emphasizes the original flavor of the ingredients, not relying heavily on spices like Sichuan cuisine (四川).

Besides its fish, the West Lake is also known for Long Jing Tea (龍井茶) and pure spring water for tea making. The lake is also the site of a beautiful, legendary and tragic love story White Snake (白蛇傳).

In the story, the thousand year old White Snake BAI Su-Zhen (白素貞) wants to experience the human world. From the West Lake, she rises and becomes a beautiful young lady. As she is walking along the lake with her maid Green Snake Xiao Qing (小青) through the Broken Bridge (斷橋), a downpour soaks her through. Suddenly she is aware of an umbrella over her. There is a handsome young man, XU Xian (許仙), holding an umbrella for her. They immediately fall in love with each other. They get married and open a Chinese herbal medicine shop.

White Snake is good at curing people's ailments. A monk Fa Hai (法海) in the nearby Golden Mountain Temple (金山寺) finds out that White Snake was originally a snake. Fa Hai lures XU Xian to the temple. The pregnant White Snake reaches the Golden Mountain Temple and tries to rescue XU Xian being detained by Fa Hai. She uses her "kung fu" power to flood the temple, but without success. Finally she is "sucked" into Fa Hai's golden pot and buried alive at the bottom of the Thunder Mountain Pagoda (雷峰塔) by the monk. A movie "Green Snake" starring famous Hong Kong movie actress Maggie Cheung (張曼玉) tells this story.

Yield: 3-4 servings

- 1 whole fish (sea bass or red snapper), or for a less challenging dish, use 8-10 oz. salmon steak (with bone in the center) about ½" thick
- A few drops Sauvignon Blanc or your favorite white wine
- 3 slices of fresh ginger
- 3 slices of fresh ginger, cut into thin strips (julienne)
- 4 stalks scallion
- 1 Tbsp. soy sauce
- 1 tsp. balsamic vinegar or rice vinegar
- 1 Tbsp. sugar
- 1 Tbsp. canola oil
- ¼ cup water mixed with 1-2 tsp. cornstarch
- Salt to taste

1 Cut off the tops of all four scallion stalks. With two stalks, cut half the green part off and then cut into one-inch lengths. With the other two stalks, cut off all the green part, and then slice lengthwise into thin strips (julienne).

2 If using a fish fillet, rub the fish with some salt, rinse clean, and sprinkle with a little salt all over. (The dish usually is cooked with a whole fish.) If cooking with a whole fish, refer to the fish preparation instructions in Fried Whole Fish on page 128.

3 In a wok, combine 1½ cup water, 3 slices fresh ginger and the scallion cut into one-inch lengths, a few drops of Sauvignon Blanc and bring the mixture to a boil. Add the entire salmon steak (or the entire fish) and bring to another boil. Reduce the heat to medium high and cook for 8-10 minutes. If the fish steak is thick, cook a couple minutes longer. Turn off the heat. Remove the salmon. Remove the ginger and scallion pieces, and leave the water in the wok.

4 Turn the heat to medium to heat up the liquid in the wok. Add the julienned ginger and scallion, 1 Tbsp. soy sauce, 1 tsp. balsamic vinegar, ½-1 Tbsp. sugar (add more or less depending on how sweet you like it) and 1 Tbsp. canola oil to the wok. Let the mixture simmer over low heat for 2 minutes. Adjust the salt to taste. Add ¼ cup water mixed with 1-2 tsp. cornstarch to the mixture and cook about 1 minute until the sauce thickens. Remove and drizzle the sauce over the salmon steak and serve hot.

Fish Maw, Black Mushrooms, Dried Scallop Soup

花膠 (魚肚) /香菇/干貝湯 (hua jiao, yu du)/xiang gu/gan bei tang) ***

Fish maw is called fish stomach in Chinese 花膠/魚肚. The English label is sometimes "dry fish" or "baked fish maw." Fish maw is a pale yellowish white color with a hard puffy texture, similar to the texture of fried pork rind. It's a lightweight ingredient and costs about $13 for a large plastic bag with 3 oz. One piece is about 10" x 12" or smaller and crinkly in shape. It is very tasty.

Dried scallops are a symbol of the rich life. They are the very essence of exotic Chinese food at the same level as shark fin, swallow's nest or even higher. It is not in the everyday menu. Serving dried scallops is the highest honor a host can give to a guest. When dried scallops are used in a dish, no other taste enhancer is necessary. One pound costs $90-$140 depending on the size of the scallops. Each one is about ¾ inches in diameter and a ½ inch thick. There is a small-size dried scallop, which costs much less, about $9 for a half pound. The small dried scallops I have used have some kind of saltiness that does not have the pure taste of the large dried scallops.

I haven't found any Chinese restaurant in Boston area serving dishes with dried scallops. This soup is the ultimate in Cantonese cooking.

The Cantonese love soup. They are known for making Chinese herbal soups to strengthen one's health called "food cure" (食療). "Food cure" (食療) is another important category in Chinese cooking, that could easily fill a thick volume of Chinese cooking recipes. This recipe is a Cantonese soup, but not a "food cure" soup.

Yield: 4-6 servings

> 1 piece fish maw, about 5" x 5"
>
> 3-6 dried Chinese black mushrooms
>
> ¼ cup small/large sized dried scallops
>
> A pinch of salt

1 Soak the fish maw in boiling water for 60 minutes, and then cut into pieces about ½" x 1". Save the soaking water.

2 Rinse the black mushrooms clean with cold water and soak in boiling water for 60 minutes. Remove the center tough stem and cut into thin slices. Save the soaking water.

3 Rinse clean the dried scallops with cold water, and soak in boiling water for 60 minutes or even overnight. Save the soaking water. Then use a rolling pin to pound flat the reconstituted scallops. Use your hands to tease apart each scallop into thin strings. Another easy way to reconstitute dried scallops is to steam them inside a rice cooker. After pour the boiling water over the dried scallops, place the dish inside the rice cooker with a rack at the bottom. Add 1 rice cooker cup of water, cover, and push down the "cook" button. When the "cook" button pops up, let them sit inside the rice cooker for 10-15 minutes. Remove the scallops and save the water. Then use a rolling pin to pound flat the dried scallops and tease apart each scallop into thin strings.

4 Fill the steamer pot with about enough water to steam for one hour over medium heat, and bring to a boil. Combine the fish maw pieces, black mushroom slices, dried scallops and the soaking waters together in a pot. Add a pinch of salt. Place the pot in the steamer rack, and steam for one hour over medium heat.

Enjoy the clear soup without any other condiments. It will clear your mind with its pure taste.

Fish Head Casserole
砂鍋魚頭 (sha guo yu tou) ****

Every Chinese loves this ultimate soup, but is scared to cook it at home. Fish head is not easy to come by. Whenever a fish is cooked, it is traditionally a whole fish. For this dish, the cook has to get a fish head by itself. There is one fish head very popular among Cantonese called Buffalo Carp. It is the one you see in the fish section of a Chinese grocery usually displayed with the fish body open, and red with fish blood all over.

People who are not familiar with this kind of fish will feel it's a little fishier than other kinds of fish. Sometimes at the supermarket you can buy salmon fish head for a very reasonable price or even free. I used to get fish heads free from Captain Marden in West Newton, MA, which is now closed, although their store in Wellesley, MA is still open. Or you can use a red snapper fish head. The soup is simply great and very tasty. The fish head is usually served with the soup. Here I separate the fish head for people who are not used to seeing fish heads.

Yield: 4-5 servings/One pot presentation

One fish head (salmon, buffalo carp, or
   red snapper)

Salt

1-2 Tbsp. Sauvignon Blanc or your favorite
   wine, for broiling the fish

1-2 pieces soft tofu, cut into one-inch cubes

1-1½ lbs. Napa Chinese cabbage

4-6 slices of fresh ginger

1 tsp. Sauvignon Blanc, for the soup

A pinch of salt

1 Tbsp. rice vinegar

4-6 oz. pork loin, cut into thin strips,

   Pork Marinade:

   ½ Tbsp. soy sauce

   1 tsp. Sauvignon Blanc

   1 Tbsp. cornstarch

5 Tbsp. canola oil, divided

2 stalks scallion, cut off two tips, cut into
   1" lengths

1-2 Tbsp. balsamic vinegar or rice vinegar

1 Cut the tofu into one-inch cubes

2 Slice the Napa Chinese cabbage crosswise into one-inch pieces.

3 Slice the pork loin into thin strips and mix with marinade ingredients, and then set aside.

4 Cut off the scallion tops and any damaged ends, and then cut into one-inch lengths.

5 Rub the fish head with some salt and rinse clean. Sprinkle the fish head with a little salt and then place in a jelly roll pan and sprinkle with 1-2 Tbsp. Sauvignon Blanc. Turn on the oven to broil on high for 15 minutes.

6 In a stainless steel pot, place the broiled fish head with its juices, and enough water to just barely cover the fish head. Add ginger slices, 1 tsp. Sauvignon Blanc, a pinch of salt, and 1 Tbsp. rice vinegar. Bring the whole pot to a boil, and then reduce heat to medium low and simmer for 20-30 minutes. Place a sieve on top of a large pot. Pour the whole contents of the pot into the sieve. (If you like to eat the fish head, you can skip this step and keep the fish head cooked with the following ingredients.) Save the broth and place in a heat-resistant ceramic pot such as CorningWare. Discard the fish head unless you like to eat the meat left on it. Some people like to pick the meat from the fish head. They say it's the best part of the fish. My husband Leo enjoys it tremendously.

7 Heat up the wok over high heat, about 3-4 minutes. Add 3 Tbsp. canola oil, add scallion pieces and stir until lightly golden. Add the marinated pork strips and stir until the color changes to pale white. Remove to a plate. The pork does not have to be cooked through at this stage.

8 Without washing the wok, reheat it over high heat, add 2 Tbsp. canola oil to the wok, then the cabbage pieces, a little salt, and stir and cover. Reduce heat to medium, add 1 cup of water, and let it cook about 5-10 minutes or until the cabbage becomes

limp. Stir occasionally. Remove and place inside the ceramic pot with the fish head broth (or the fish head and its broth).

9 Place the tofu cubes on top of the cabbage. Place the cooked shredded pork on top of the tofu and the cabbage. Sprinkle with 1-2 Tbsp. balsamic vinegar or rice vinegar. Add water to barely cover the very top of the whole mixture. Bring the mixture to a boil, cover, reduce heat to medium low, and simmer for 20-30 minutes. Serve hot.

As an alternative to fish head, you can use a fish with bone like halibut or salmon steak. First broil the fish on high heat for about 10-15 minutes in the oven to give the fish a slightly charred aroma). Then place the fish at the bottom of the ceramic pot and proceed to layer cabbage, tofu and pork on top. Bring to a boil and cover and simmer for 20-30 minutes or longer. The result of this method is also good. Fish head and the pork give the flavor to the soup. The best part is the tofu and cabbage. Bring the ceramic pot directly to the dining table with the soup bubbling hot. It is especially good on a cold wintry night.

Taiwanese-Style Pan Fried Oysters with Egg (or Oyster Omelette)
蚵仔煎 (er ah jian - Taiwanese pronunciation) ****

There are many stories about how this well-known Taiwanese local dish came about. In one story, a retired seaman looking to make a living created this dish, which he served in a sidewalk eatery in a southern seaport, Lu Gang (鹿港), outside the Tian Hou Temple (天后宫; "Heavenly Queen Temple").

Traditionally the square outside a temple is a local marketplace especially for food vendors, which people flock to especially at night. During a festival, a temporary, open air stage would be set up on bamboo poles to showcase Taiwanese opera (歌仔戲). As a child, I would go with my friends to watch the actors and actresses putting on makeup before the show. The back stage was only covered with a curtain flapping in the wind. As the show started, we would sit on the ground and watch the show. Inside the temple, a hanging stage for a hand puppet show 布袋戲 would be going on. My eldest brother WU Jian-Si 吳建熹 loved the puppet shows, which portrayed dramatic, historic stories.

Because oysters are quite fishy, a seaman created this recipe, which became quite popular. There are many eateries in Taiwan offering this dish.

The most famous one was located in Taipei at the site of the historic Circle Food Court (圓環) which used to be in the middle of a huge rotary with six avenues converged on the Circle Food Court. This place was near the site of the 2/28 Massacre in 1947. The incident happened at the present day intersection of Nanjing West Road and Yan Ping North Road.

When the Nationalist Chinese, led by CHIANG Kai-Shek 蔣介石 took over Taiwan from defeated Japan in 1945 after 50 years of Japanese occupation, conflict was inevitable. A Taiwanese woman was selling cigarettes at a sidewalk stand near the old Circle Food Court. A group of armed Nationalists claiming to be the Cigarette & Liquor officers ordered her to pay the cigarette tax. They confiscated her merchandise and a few dollars cash from her pocket. With the language barrier—the Nationalist Chinese spoke Mandarin Chinese, the Taiwanese woman spoke the Taiwanese dialect—

difficulty in communication created further tension.

Nearby Taiwanese gathered to protest to the arrogant Nationalists. The Nationalists opened fire on the crowd, which resulted in several deaths. The next day, February 28, 1947, the Nationalist authority declared a curfew, ignoring a group of 2,000 people protesting outside the Nationalist governing building. The Nationalist started to arrest Taiwanese intelligentsia on a wide scale.

My two eldest brothers WU Jian-Si 吳建熹 and WU Jian-Yu 吳建燠 were in their early 20s and had to go into hiding with a group of young Taiwanese. My second brother told me that he carried a Japanese sword to protect himself when they went into hiding. Unofficially, ten thousand Taiwanese intelligentsia were massacred by Nationalist Chinese. The father of one of my junior high school classmate, a physician, was one of the massacred.

In 1996 under the then-Mayor of Taipei, later the President of Taiwan Mr. CHEN Shui-Bian commemorated the incident by erecting a memorial in a park situated in the middle of Taipei that used to be called New Park (新公園), which was then renamed "Two Twenty-Eight Peace Park" (二二八和平公園).

The old Circle Food Court was demolished, and the modernized Circle Food Court officially closed on June 2006 for lack of business. At the site now stands an ugly, three-story circular glass building in the middle of a busy thoroughfare with only a couple of eateries offering Pan Fried Oyster. A piece of Taiwanese culture is gone forever because of the poor planning of the former Taipei Mayor MA Ying-Jeou, who later became the President of Taiwan.

Yield: 2-3 servings/One plate presentation

> 8 oz. shucked oysters
>
> Salt
>
> 2-3 Tbsp. canola oil
>
> 4 Tbsp. cornstarch or yam starch 蕃薯粉 mixed with ½ cup water (or less). *Yam starch, which is available in Chinatown, produces better results.*
>
> 1 large egg
>
> A half bunch of coriander
>
> Condiments: catsup or 2 Tbsp. catsup mixed with ¼ tsp. chili sauce, chili oil or Tabasco

1 Mix the oysters with a lot of salt and then rinse clean. Sprinkle with a pinch of salt. If the oysters are too large, cut them into ½-inch pieces. Let the oysters drain in a sieve for 30 minutes or longer.

2 Wash the coriander in a large pot filled with water. Shake the coriander briskly in the water to get rid of the dirt. Drain the water and repeat one more time. Soak in cold water one hour or more, and then coarsely chop. Instead of coriander, the vegetable used in Taiwan is called Tong Ou (茼蒿). Because it shrinks greatly in volume after it's cooked, it is nicknamed "wife beating vegetable."

3 Heat up a non-stick frying pan over medium high heat, and add 2-3 Tbsp. canola oil. Gently place drained oysters in the frying pan, and let them sit for 2 minutes without moving them. Quickly stir up the cornstarch or yam starch and water mixture before pouring the mixture over the oysters. Do not stir for a good 1-2 minutes until the starch has cooked a little, and the color changes. Scatter the coriander all over, and then crack an egg over the mixture. Gently break the egg yolk a little using a spatula and roughly spread the egg all over the oysters. Let it sit for another 1-2 minutes. Reduce heat to medium and flip the mixture over to the other side with a spatula and let it sit for 1-2 minutes. Remove to a plate.

4 Serve with catsup or 2 Tbsp. catsup mixed with ¼ tsp. chili sauce, chili oil or Tabasco. Adjust the spiciness to your taste. The original sauce served with this dish is called "ocean & mountain sauce" (海山醬) that is made from rice. This sauce is still available commercially in Taiwan.

This dish is a delicious seafood delight without any fishy smell, but also not greasy like fried oysters.

Clams with Fermented Black Bean Sauce
豆豉炒蜆 (dou chi chao xian) **

This is a good combination for people who do not like the fishiness of clams. A touch of black bean sauce makes this dish wonderfully tasty without the fishiness. Any kind of clams should be soaked in water with about 1 tsp. salt for 3-4 hours to let clams spit out the sand inside. Otherwise, when you remove the clam meat to eat, sometimes it still has sand inside.

Yield: 2 servings/One plate presentation

- 1-1¼ lbs. littleneck clams or your favorite clams *(The results are better if you use small-size clams.)*

- 3 cloves garlic, crushed

- 3 slices fresh ginger

- 2 stalks scallions, chopped

- 3 Tbsp. canola oil

- 1 Tbsp. fermented black bean sauce 陰豆豉 *(Get the one with semi-crushed black beans with sauce packed in a glass jar; do not get the dry one packed in a plastic bag without any sauce.)*

- 1 Tbsp. Sauvignon Blanc or your favorite wine

*Fermented black bean sauce is very salty, so it is not necessary to add any soy sauce or salt.

1 Rinse and soak clams in cold water with 1 tsp. salt (or more) for 3-4 hours.

2 Crush the garlic with the flat side of a cleaver and discard the skin.

3 Cut off both ends of the scallion and coarsely chop.

4 Heat up the wok over high heat, about 3-4 minutes. Add 3 Tbsp. canola oil, garlic and fresh ginger and stir fry until they turn golden brown. Add clams, stir 1 minute, add 1 Tbsp. fermented black bean sauce, stir and try to spread the black bean sauce evenly throughout. Turn heat to medium high and cover for 3 minutes. There is no need to add water, as water will come out from the clams. If water is added, it will dilute the taste and flavor.

5 Remove cover and sprinkle 1 Tbsp. Sauvignon Blanc. Quickly stir the clams, which should have all opened up by now. Turn off the heat. Sprinkle with coarsely chopped scallion, stir a few times and remove right away. Serve hot. Discard any unopened clams.

Mussels Steamed with Black Bean Sauce
貼貝蒸豆豉
(yi bei zheng dou chi) **

The mussels I use, PEI mussels are on the small side. You can also use the regular, larger size mussels.

Yield: 2-3 servings

1 lb. PEI mussel, rinsed and soaked in cold water with 1 tsp. salt for 3-4 hours to get rid of the sand.

1 Tbsp. fermented black bean sauce with sauce 黑豆豉醬 *(Get the one with semi-crushed black beans with sauce packed in a glass jar; do not get the dry one packed in a plastic bag without any sauce.)*

1 Tbsp. Sauvignon Blanc

1 tsp. Balsamic vinegar

2 slices fresh ginger, finely chopped

2 stalks scallion, finely chopped

2 cloves garlic, crushed and finely chopped

Equipment:
Chinese steamer

1 Rinse and soak mussels in cold water with 1 tsp. salt for 3-4 hours to let the mussel spit out the sand. If you are using a larger mussel, remove the outer skin of the piece that sticks out of the shell and rinse it clean, otherwise it is quite sandy.

2 Cut off both ends of the scallions and finely chop.

3 Crush the garlic with the flat side of a cleaver or knife, discard the skin, and finely chop.

4 In a bowl, mix all the ingredients except the mussels. Remove the mussels from the soaking water and rinse a couple of times with clear water, drain and mix them in a metal mixing bowl with the other ingredients using your hands.

5 Fill the steamer pot with water and bring to a boil. Place the pot of mussels in the steamer rack and

steam over high heat for 15 minutes. Remove the pot from the steamer rack. Serve hot or at room temperature.

If you can get an oyster or a scallop in a shell, black bean sauce is perfect to steam it with. You can also simply add finely chopped scallion and fresh ginger to the shellfish with a few drops of white wine and steam each one individually in its own shell. This is a delicacy in fine Chinese restaurants. You can find these dishes in Boston Chinatown's East Ocean City Restaurant (醉瓊樓) on Beach Street.

Easy Squid Salad
涼拌墨魚 (liang ban mo yu) *

Squid available in the U.S. are about 2-3 inches long. Sometimes, the seafood sections of Chinatown grocery stores carry larger squids. In the other parts of the world like Japan and Taiwan, squid comes in many shapes and sizes, with the larger one called cuttlefish. Here, squid is pretty inexpensive. Squid sold in supermarkets is mostly pre-cleaned, so they are easy to use.

Yield: 2-3 servings

6 cleaned squid, about ½ lb. *(See instructions below for how to clean squid.)*

2-3 lettuce leaves, shredded

Dressing:
1 Tbsp. soy sauce

½ tsp. balsamic vinegar (or rice vinegar)

1 stalk scallion, finely chopped

½-1 Tbsp. sesame oil (or olive oil)

1 tsp. sugar

1 *How to Clean Squid:* If the squid has not been cleaned, pull off the purple-grey film covering the body, clean out the innards, cut through the eyes to remove the hard eyeballs, drain the purple-black colored liquid and rinse clean.

2 Butterfly the squid by slicing it open lengthwise. Clean out the slimy stuff and discard. (I usually boil the squid discards, so it does not smell as

bad when I throw it away.) Score the inside of the squid—the side that has no purple skin with a diagonal cross-hatch, then cut each one into 4 large pieces

3 Trim off both ends of the scallion and cut off the lower half of the green end, then cut into one-inch sections. Gather the sections together and finely chop.

4 In a pot, combine the ingredients for the dressing.

5 Bring 3 cups of water to boil, add a pinch of salt, drop the squid slices into the boiling water for only 1-2 minutes. It's not necessary to wait for the water to boil again after putting in the squid. Overcooking will make the squid tough. When pieces curl up and float to the top, skim them out with a ladle. Drain the water and toss the squid in the dressing.

6 Serve the squid on a layer of shredded lettuce on a plate. Serve at room temperature. This is a great appetizer.

Jellyfish Salad
海蜇皮 (hai zhe pi) ****

Jellyfish looks like a large piece of thick parchment paper, which is translucent and hard to break apart. It is usually packed with a lot of salt in a 14 oz. plastic bag package. To rinse off the salt, it has to be soaked in clean water for an hour or more.

Jellyfish is considered an exotic delicacy even in Chinese food. Imported jellyfish from China, called "溫州蜇皮" (Wen Zhou Jelly Fish), is well priced, but the texture is not as firm as the better kind that I remember. A better grade jelly fish should be available somewhere, but I cannot find it here in Boston Chinatown. It is my favorite. There is also a ready-to-eat prepared jellyfish in a pouch in the Chinatown refrigeration section, which comes with a small pack of oil and one pack of hot oil that you can mix in.

In a banquet, jellyfish is usually among the items presented in the first course cold platter (冷盤). It takes some skill to prepare well, such as boiling the jellyfish for the right amount of time to get the best crunchiness out of the jellyfish.

Yield: 4-5 servings/One plate presentation

> One 14 oz. package of jellyfish, reconstituted for three hours in all
>
> One small pickling cucumber (about 8" long), peeled and julienned
>
> 3 Tbsp. sesame oil or extra virgin olive oil
>
> 3 stalks scallion, finely chopped
>
> 1 Tbsp. soy sauce
>
> 1 tsp. sugar
>
> A few drops of balsamic or rice vinegar
>
> A few drops of red chili oil (optional)
>
> A pinch of salt
>
> A pinch of MSG
>
> A pinch of freshly ground black pepper

1 Rinse the salt off the jellyfish and soak in clear water for 1 hour or longer. Rinse about three times and soak for another hour. Drain the water. Roll the jellyfish sheet into a cylinder and cut into thin, long strips. Rinse and soak in water for one more hour. Drop jellyfish into a pot of boiling water (about 5 cups water) for 1 minute then take it out right away and immerse the jellyfish into a pot of icy cold water until they have cooled down. Then drain the jellyfish in a sieve for about 15 minutes.

2 Peel the cucumber and cut it into four sections, each roughly 2-inches long, then julienne each section. Add a pinch of salt, mix well, and let it drain for 30 minutes in a sieve. (This last step makes the cucumber crunchy, but you can skip it for convenience.)

3 Cut off the tops of the scallions and half the green part, and then finely chop.

4 Mix all the ingredients together except for the cucumber and jellyfish. Taste and adjust salt. Add jellyfish and cucumber and mix well. Serve at room temperature.

Red Cooked Sea Cucumber
紅燒海參 (hon shao hai shen) ****

After the sea cucumber has been reconstituted, it is cooked with pork butt, or pork or chicken stock to soak in the flavor of the meat. It takes seven days to reconstitute dried sea cucumber. Some are easier to soften, and some require a longer soak.

Gourmet diners prefer to soak sea cucumbers without the baking soda, but it will take longer to soak through. Around the third day, some sea cucumbers will become soft and sometimes you can smell an odor, which is the innards of the sea cucumbers. Slit the sea cucumber open from top to bottom and open it like a butterfly. Remove the innards, rinse clean, and immerse in the water again. Some innards contain small to good-sized, fish bone-like, rock pieces. There is also some slimy substance on the skin. Clean it off with a sponge. After all the sea cucumbers are softened and cleaned inside and outside, they are ready to cook.

In Taiwan, sea cucumbers which have already been soaked, cleaned, and ready to cook are readily available in the market. Some Chinatown groceries carry the already cleaned, reconstituted, frozen sea cucumbers. It is available in Boston's Chinatown at Ming's Market (平價市場) at 1102 Washington Street.

The Fu Yuan Restaurant on Lin Yi Street in Taipei (台北市臨沂街馥園餐廳) is well known for its Scallion-Flavored Sea Cucumbers (蔥燒海參). They have two full-time employees just taking care of the sea cucumber soaking process, according to the 100 Best Restaurant Dishes Guide in Taiwan written in Chinese by LEE Ze-Zhi, 1995, Eating All Chinese Publisher, Taipei ("台灣100　種最美味的佳肴", 李澤治著, 1995, 台北 吃遍中國出版社). The best sea cucumbers are from Japan where they are called Ci Shen (刺參 namako in Japanese). I have checked with a fish vendor in a Hsin Chu traditional market about how they soak the sea cucumber. He told me that the vendor he gets the soaked sea cucumber from would not say how they reconstitute the sea cucumber as that would be revealing their trade secret.

One time my friend Grace Lee (李懿真) took me to Tong's Pavilion (山王飯店), a restaurant located in Manhattan, New York, when she was working for the Taipei Economic and Cultural Office. She ordered Red Cooked Sea Cucumber (紅燒海參). That was the most gorgeous and tasty sea cucumber dish I have ever tasted. The entire sea cucumber was gleaming with brown sauce. Grace told me that the restaurant was owned by the chef who used to cook for Generalissimo CHIANG Kai-Shek (蔣委員長).

Yield: 3-4 persons

- ½ lb. pork butt or pork with some fat
- 2-3 cleaned sea cucumbers (The reconstituted weight is about 1-1¼ lbs. It takes about seven days to reconstitute dried sea cucumber.)
- 3½ tsp. baking soda, divided
- 3 tbsp. canola oil
- 4-5 slices fresh ginger
- 3 cloves shallots, peeled and thinly sliced
- 2-3 cloves garlic, smashed
- 1 Tbsp. Cognac, brandy or Chinese Shao Xing wine 紹興酒
- 2 Tbsp. soy sauce
- 1 tsp. balsamic vinegar
- ½ tsp. rock sugar (冰糖) or sugar. Rock sugar makes the surface of the sea cucumber gleam.
- 1 tsp. Sichuan Bean Paste 四川豆瓣醬
- A pinch of five spice powder 五香粉
- A pinch of salt
- A pinch of black pepper

1 **Reconstituting Dried Sea Cucumber:** In a large pot add 1 tsp. baking soda to plenty of water to completely immerse the sea cucumbers, about six small ones at a time, and let soak overnight. The next day, rinse clean and soak overnight again with plenty of water and 1 tsp. baking soda. It is better to keep the soaking sea cucumbers in the refrigerator, changing the water once a day, each time adding ¼ tsp baking soda. After the seventh day, rinse clean and soak in cold water for one more day without any baking soda.

2 After the sea cucumbers are reconstituted, they will be soft but not very soft. Slit open each one lengthwise. It looks like there is a slit, but it isn't

really open. Remove the string-like substance and small rock-like substances inside and rinse clean. There is no need to cut the sea cucumbers further.

3 Drop the pork into boiling water for 10 minutes, then remove and cut into two-inch cubes.

4 Peel the shallots and slice thinly.

5 Smash the garlic cloves with the flat side of a knife and remove the skin.

6 Heat up a pot, and add 3 Tbsp. canola oil, shallot, garlic and ginger. When they have turned golden brown, add pork and stir a little. Add 1 Tbsp. Cognac, brandy or Chinese Shao Xing Wine with 1¼ cup water. Add 2 Tbsp. soy sauce, 1 tsp. balsamic vinegar, ½ tsp. rock sugar (or sugar), 1 tsp. Sichuan bean paste, a pinch of salt, five spice powder and black pepper. Mix well and adjust the salt to taste. Bring the water to a boil, and add sea cucumbers. Turn heat to low and simmer for 40-50 minutes with the cover cracked open. Check the water in between, and if it's about to dry up, add ¼ cup water, and then turn heat to medium and cook for 5 more minutes or until the water has nearly all evaporated. The water becomes a brown-colored sauce. Serve. If the sea cucumbers are small, they can be served whole for a very impressive dish. There is no need to decorate the dish. More than anything, a whole sea cucumber says "luxurious and exotic." The meat is to enhance the sea cucumber taste, so it can be served separately.

Any banquet menu that includes sea cucumber immediately increases the price of the banquet to an upper tier of luxuriousness. It is in the same league as a dish with shark fin.

Seaweed Roll 海帶捲
(hai dai juan) ***

Seaweed sheets come in sheets 7 x 8 inches. They are very easy to wrap and make a roll, and are available in Japanese, Korean, and Chinese food markets. Chinese uses dried tofu sheets, egg roll skins, Shanghai egg roll skins, and egg pan cakes for making rolls. Some rolls are steamed and some are deep fried. Seaweed is a light, tasty, and healthy food. There is a very easy recipe I learned from my son-in-law Katsuya. He uses a quarter of a full seaweed sheet to wrap up a small amount of white rice with one slice of avocado and then dipped in a little soy sauce. It is great as a quick snack or for breakfast.

Yield: 8 rolls/8-10 persons

8 seaweed sheets 7" x 8"

Filling Ingredients:

12 oz. fresh shrimps with shells (8 oz. after shells removed)

12 fresh water chestnuts (or substitute with 4 stalks celery heart, finely chopped)

4 stalks celery heart (*Even if you can find water chestnuts, you can still add celery hearts as they add texture to the filling.*)

4-6 oz. ground pork

2 stalks scallion, finely chopped

A pinch of salt

A pinch of black pepper

1 Tbsp. sesame oil

1 Tbsp. cornstarch

3 Tbsp. flour

¼ cup water

1½ cups canola oil

1 Shell the shrimp and devein (see steps **4** and **5** in Shrimp with Broccoli on page 121). Add 1 tsp. salt, mix and rinse clean with water. Drain the water. Sprinkle with a pinch of salt. Put shrimp into a plastic bag (to avoid splattering) and crush shrimps with the flat side of a cleaver into paste-like texture.

2 Peel the skin of the fresh water chestnuts, removing any yellow portions inside. Put peeled water chestnuts in a pot of cold water with some salt. One at a time, place each chestnut inside a plastic bag and use the flat side of a cleaver to smash them.

3 Peel the strings off the celery stalks and then finely chop.

4 Cut off and discard the tops of the scallions and half the green part, and then finely chop.

5 Mix all the filling ingredients together. Stir in one direction and the mixture should become sticky. Mix no more than five minutes.

6 Mix 3 Tbsp. flour with ¼ cup water in a bowl. You will use this to seal each roll.

7 On each seaweed sheet, put about 2 Tbsp. of the filling along the bottom edge of the sheet in a cylindrical shape. At the far edge of the sheet, use a brush or the back of a spoon to paste the flour/water mixture along the edge. Roll the seaweed over the filling to create a long cylinder. Lightly press the edges to make sure they are sealed. There should be enough filling to make about 8 rolls. Do not stack the finished seaweed rolls.

8 Pour 1½ cups canola oil into the wok, and heat over medium high about 3 minutes. Drop in a small piece of seaweed; if it sizzles, the oil is hot enough.

9 Reduce heat to medium, and gently *slide* 4 rolls in one-by-one. Use chopsticks or a spatula to turn the rolls so they are evenly deep fried. Rolls may splatter halfway through the frying if some fillings break out of the seaweed sheet. (It's okay if a little filling breaks out.) Use a tong or spatula to move around seaweed rolls. The total frying time is about 5 minutes. Remove the four rolls and drain in a sieve.

10 Let the oil heat up again, about 1-2 minutes before sliding in the other 4 rolls into the oil. Deep fry 5 minutes. Remove. Let cool down a little about 5-10 minutes. Slice rolls ¼-⅓ inches thick on a bias cut. Serve hot or at room temperature. This dish makes a good appetizer.

CHAPTER 10

牛肉主菜

Beef Entrees

Beef Entrees

Red Cooked Beef Shank, Beef Tendon, and Brown Eggs

紅燒牛肉/牛筋/滷蛋

(hong shao niu ro/niu jin/lu dan) ***

This easy and delicious dish is a typical "bachelor's dish." It can be served hot or cold. Chicken liver, gizzard, or heart can be added to the sauce and cooked for about 30 more minutes. The one pound beef shank or shin (or "leg meat,") is cut into two large chunks. It is not necessary to remove the bone. (Ask the butcher for this special meat cut; most of the time there is shank with bone available in supermarkets.) The sauce is great with fluffy white rice.

Yield: 4-6 servings

- 1-2 lbs. beef shin or shank with bone, or a "leg meat" *(Keep the bone in the middle. You may have to ask the butcher for this special meat cut. Ask to have it cut into two large chunks.)*
- 3 beef tendons *(Beef tendons are white, and available in Chinatown grocery stores, such as Ming's Market on Harrison Ave. in Boston Chinatown packed three pieces in a package.)*
- 6 eggs (to hard boil)
- 5-6 Tbsp. soy sauce
- 1-2 Tbsp. sugar
- 1-2 Tbsp. Cognac or Sauvignon Blanc
- ½- 1 tsp. five spice powder
- 1½ tsp. salt
- 2-3 cloves shallot, peeled and thinly sliced
- 2-3 cloves garlic, peeled and crushed
- 3-4 whole cloves

- 2-3 stalks scallion, cut into one-inch length
- ½-1 Tbsp. black pepper
- 2 cups water

1 *Beef Tendon Preparation:* Place the tendons in a pot of water and bring it to a boil. Do not cover the pot or the water will boil over. Discard the water to remove the wild, raw smell and rinse clean. Place the tendons in a fresh pot of water and bring to a boil. Reduce heat to low, cover, and simmer for 1-1½ hours. If you have more than one tendon, keep one to use in this recipe, and the rest can be kept frozen for later use. Beef tendon is quite tough, and needs a total of about 2-3½ hours cooking time to be done right. Some like it chewier and some like it softer. You can adjust the cooking time to suit your taste. If you have a pressure cooker, you can test to see how long the cooking time should be. With a pressure cooker it should be possible to reduce the cooking time to 30 minutes. If it is still not soft enough for your liking, you can simmer it a little longer on a regular stove top. Since the tendon will also cook with the beef later, it's okay if it's still slightly hard at this point.

2 *Hard Boiling Eggs:* Before boiling the eggs, use a thumb tack to gently push a tiny hole into the fat end of the eggs. This tip is from the French chef Jacques Pépin. Check his cookbook ***Complete Techniques*** for a detailed explanation. Bring a pot of water to boil (enough to cover all eggs). "Place the eggs in a sieve and lower into boiling water. Bring to a boil and simmer for about 10 minutes. Immediately run the eggs under cold water until cold. Crack the shells on the side of the sink and 'roll' gently on a hard surface so the shells are cracked all around." This way it is very easy to remove the shells without them sticking to the egg whites.

3 Peel the shallots and slice thinly.

4 Crush the garlic and discard the skin.

5 Cut off the scallion tops and any damaged ends, and then cut into one-inch lengths.

6 Place beef chunks in a pot; pour a pot of boiling water over; drain the water; and rinse clean to get rid of the wild fowl smell.

7 In a pot, place the beef chunks, cooked beef tendon, hard boiled eggs, the rest of the ingredients, and 2 cups water or just enough to cover the meat and tendons. Don't use too much water or it will dilute the taste. Taste the broth. Adjust the taste to your liking but leave it more on the salty side. Leave the pot only partly covered and bring the mixture to a boil. Reduce heat to very low. Once in a while skim off the foam that will appear on the surface. Cover and let it simmer for 60-80 minutes.

8 Remove the beef and tendon from the pot. Let the beef cool down for 15-30 minutes. Cut both beef and beef tendon into thin slices or small chunks and serve at room temperature. This dish is one of the cold platter items served first in a banquet dinner.

9 Leave the eggs in the pot and simmer for 30 more minutes and serve the next day. Continue simmering the eggs for 15-20 minutes each day for 2-3 days in the same fashion. If needed, add more water so it barely covers the eggs. The extra boiling time will enhance the flavor of the eggs and they will turn into an even more beautiful dark brown color. The browner the eggs, the better they will taste. Slice the eggs into four wedges and serve at room temperature. Use a sharp knife to slice or use an egg slicer. There is an old ingenious way to slice eggs. You wrap a piece of string around the egg, and then scissor the ends of the strings and the egg will split neatly.

10 Chicken liver and chicken hearts can be added to the leftover sauce and cooked for about 20-30 minutes. It is then ready to serve.

11 *Variations:* You can add pork chunks, pork stomach and so forth. As you add more ingredients, you can add more soy sauce, water, or five spice powder to taste. The whole pot will be full of aroma. The ingredients and sauce from this dish can top simply cooked rice or noodles. However, don't add any vegetables; they will spoil the sauce. Fried tofu can be added, but fresh tofu may spoil the sauce.

Beef with Oyster Sauce
蠔油牛肉 (hao you niu ro) **

This typical Cantonese dish appears in every Chinese restaurant. All it takes is beef and oyster sauce. However the beef is very important. Slice the beef when it is totally defrosted, otherwise the slices will break into shreds if it is still partially frozen. The best beef to use is rib-eye steak. If you use sirloin or flank steak, mix it with a little meat tenderizer. Papain from papaya or a tiny pinch of baking soda can be used to tenderize the beef. The oyster sauce is supposedly made out of oysters, but with modern day technology, a taste enhancer is usually added instead. Do not add too much. The oyster sauce is quite salty, so you don't need any other salt.

Yield: 3-4 servings

10 oz. flank steak or rib eye steak

> ### Beef Marinade:
>
> 1 tsp. soy sauce (*The marinade uses less soy sauce because oyster sauce is quite salty.*)
>
> 1 Tbsp. Sauvignon Blanc
>
> A pinch of black pepper
>
> 1 Tbsp. cornstarch

3 Tbsp. canola oil

1 Tbsp. oyster sauce (*Keep the oyster sauce bottle refrigerated after opening although the bottle may not say so.*)

3 cloves garlic, peeled and crushed

1 Tbsp. cornstarch with ½ cup water (optional)

A pinch of salt

1 bunch watercress or ½ stalk of broccoli, peeled and cut into florets

1 If you are using flank steak, cut it lengthwise into three strips, and then slice at an angle into thin slices. To make the meat more tender, use the spine of a cleaver to pound both sides of the meat. Marinate in marinade ingredients for 30 minutes or longer, inside the fridge.

2 Crush the garlic with the side of a cleaver and remove the skin.

3 Rinse the watercress clean in a large pot or in a sink filled with water. Briskly stir the water in one direction to get rid of sand. Lift the watercress out of the water and drain.

4 Heat up the wok over high heat, about 3-4 minutes. Add 3 Tbsp. canola oil to the wok, reduce heat to medium high and add garlic cloves. Stir until garlic turns golden brown. Discard the garlic. Add the marinated beef slices and stir until the beef changes color to pale pink. Turn heat to medium high, and add 1 Tbsp. oyster sauce to the beef, stir well for about 2-3 more minutes. If it's too dry or you like to have more sauce, add ½ cup water mixed with 1 Tbsp. cornstarch. Stir well and remove from heat. Place beef in the center of a large plate.

5 If using watercress, bring a pot of water to boil, and add a pinch of salt. Add watercress to the boiling water and cook about 2 minutes. It is not necessary for the water to boil again. Remove the watercress from the water and drain. Cut the watercress into about two to three inch lengths. Ring the watercress around the outer edge of the plate, surrounding the beef in the middle.

6 If using broccoli, bring a pot of water to boil and blanch in the boiling water for 2-3 minutes, then ring the outer edge of the plate with broccoli florets around the beef in the middle.

Beef with Sha Cha Sauce

沙茶牛肉 (sha cha niu rou) **

Sha cha barbecue sauce is made with peanuts, soy beans, shallot, garlic, chili oil, dried fish, dried shrimp, and other spices. It is a very tasty sauce. In the dipping sauce for hot pot, it is mixed with soy sauce and a raw egg. The best brand is "Bull Head" Barbecue Sauce (牛頭牌沙茶醬) from Taiwan. It can be kept in the refrigerator for a few months. I always keep a can or a jar in my refrigerator. This dish tastes good when it is spicy. With the sha cha sauce only, it is not too spicy, so add more chili sauce or chili oil if you like it spicy.

Yield: 3-4 servings/One plate presentation

12 oz. flank steak

2 Tbsp. crushed or minced papaya or a pinch of baking soda.

Beef Marinade:

1 Tbsp. soy sauce

1 Tbsp. Cognac

1 tsp. canola oil

1 Tbsp. cornstarch

3 Tbsp. canola oil

1 clove shallot, peeled and sliced

2 Tbsp. "Bull Head" sha cha sauce
(牛頭牌沙茶醬)

½ tsp. chili sauce or chili oil *(optional)*

Vegetable Variation: This dish is usually cooked with beef only. If you like vegetables, mix in some sort of vegetable like celery, broccoli, bell peppers or snow peas.

1 Cut flank steak into strips 2-inches wide, and then slice each strip thinly at an angle. Mix in a tiny bit of tenderizing agent such as papaya or a very tiny pinch of baking soda to make the beef more tender. Then, mix the meat with the marinade ingredients, and marinate for 30 minutes or longer in the fridge.

2 Peel the shallot and slice thinly

3 Heat up the wok over high heat for about 3-4 minutes. Add 3 Tbsp. canola oil, turn heat to medium high and add shallot slices, stir until golden about 1-2 minutes. Add marinated beef slices. Don't disturb the beef for 1-2 minutes, and then stir until the beef changes color. Turn heat to medium. Add 2 Tbsp. sha cha sauce, spread and mix well with the beef for about 2 minutes. Add chili sauce/chili oil here if you like it spicier. Serve hot.

4 *Vegetable Variation:* If using vegetables, blanch the vegetables separately and then add them to the beef at the last minute and mix well. .

Sichuan-Style Beef

四川水煮牛肉

(si chuan shui zhu niu rou) ***

A travel show from Taiwan TV visited a restaurant in Sichuan, China. A chef demonstrated this very interesting and easy-looking dish. He first stir fried the beef, and then removed the beef to a plate, and sprinkled it with a lot of chili pepper and Sichuan peppercorn powder. Finally he poured the piping hot oil over the mixture of chili pepper and Sichuan peppercorn. If you can stand the spiciness, you can do the last step. I modified the recipe a little below to reduce the spiciness.

The name of this recipe in Chinese literally translates to "water-cooked beef." This dish has become quite popular nowadays, so if you visit Sichuan China, there is also "water-cooked fish" and "water-cooked meat." Although the name makes it sound like a mild dish, it's actually a very spicy Sichuan dish. It's a historically well-known traditional dish from Sichuan with a distinctive heavy Sichuan taste—spicy and palate numbing. Originally this dish was for coolie laborers who want a dish with a saltier and spicier taste so that they would not have to spend more on another dish to accompany their rice. One dish of Sichuan-Style Beef has enough flavor to accompany a few bowls of rice for a complete meal. In the old days, coolie laborers made a very meager income doing hard labor. "The beef used usually came from a cow who had worked in the fields, so the beef would have some unpleasant taste. To hide that funny taste, more spices and chili peppers were added." [6]

Yield: 4-5 servings/One plate presentation

- 12-14 oz. flank steak *(If frozen, be sure to totally defrost the beef before cutting.)*

Beef Marinade:

- 1 Tbsp. soy sauce
- 1 Tbsp. cornstarch
- 1 egg white
- A few drops canola oil
- A pinch of black pepper
- 3 Tbsp. canola oil
- 6 stalks scallions, finely chopped

Mix the Following Ingredients Together:

- 2-3 cloves garlic, peeled and finely chopped
- 4 slices fresh ginger (if available), finely chopped
- 1-2 Tbsp Sichuan spicy bean paste
- 2-3 stalks celery, stringed and cut into slices against the grain
- 1-2 leaves Napa cabbage, shredded
- 4-6 oz fresh bean sprouts
- 1 Tbsp soy sauce
- A pinch of salt
- 1-2 pickling cucumbers, peeled and julienned *(optional)*
- 1 tsp. chili pepper powder *(optional)*
- ¼ cup canola oil
- 2 Tbsp Sichuan peppercorn or black peppercorn
- 4 whole and fresh chili peppers or dried chili peppers

1 **Beef Preparation:** Make sure the beef is thoroughly defrosted before you slice it. If it is still half frozen, after stir frying, the slices will fall apart into shreds. Cut the flank steak lengthwise into 3 long pieces along the meat's grain, then hold the knife at about a 30 degree angle and slice each long piece thinly against the meat's grain into ⅛-inch thick slices about 1½ by ½ inches. Mix with marinade ingredients and let sit for 15 minutes or more.

2 Cut off the ends of the 6 stalks of scallions and half the green part and finely chop.

3 Using the flat side of a cleaver, crush the garlic, remove the skin, and finely chop.

4 Rub the skin off the 4 slices of ginger using the back of a small knife and finely chop.

---

6 From *Guo's Idea, the New Szechwan Style* by GUO Zhu Yi, page 46, Sai Shang Publishing Co. Taipei, 2008; "郭主義招牌川菜" 作者郭主義，台北賽尚圖文事業有限公司出版，2008 年)

5 Heat up the wok over medium high heat for 2 minutes and add 3 Tbsp. canola oil, half of the chopped scallion and all the chopped garlic and fresh ginger mixture. Cook until golden brown. Add 1 Tbsp Sichuan spicy bean paste and stir for 1 minute to let the bean paste aroma come out. Then add chopped cabbage, celery, stir and add ¼ cup water and let cook in medium high heat for 5 minutes. Add another ¼ cup of water if it's too dry.

6 Add bean sprouts and enough water to barely cover the vegetable mixture. Add a pinch of salt. Bring to a boil and add marinated beef pieces. Separate and spread the beef slices over the top of the vegetable mixture until the beef has changed color. Do not mix the vegetables and beef together. Let the beef stay on top. Put the 1 Tbsp soy sauce into the spatula to sprinkle it evenly over the beef. Remove the whole mixture to a bowl-like dish. Make sure the beef is on the top, Sprinkle with the rest of the chopped scallion, julienned pickling cucumbers, and, optionally, sprinkle with some chili powder.

7 Wash the wok clean, turn on high heat and heat up ¼ cup canola oil, add 2 Tbsp Sichuan or black peppercorn and 4 whole fresh or dried chili pepper to the oil and cook until the peppercorn and chili pepper turn brown. Turn off the heat. Discard peppercorn and chili pepper. Use a Chinese spatula (with the ridge on the back rim to hold liquid) to scoop up the piping hot oil and drizzle all over the beef. Serve. (The purpose of heating up the oil with the peppercorn and chili pepper is to give the oil a spicy aroma.)

Hot Pot 火鍋 **

Each region in China has its own local hot pot flavor and uses different ingredients. This recipe uses the ingredients from the hot pot our family makes. My family's tradition is to have hot pot on Chinese New Year's Eve. The hot pot symbolizes the family's togetherness around a "stove" (圍爐)—symbolized by the hot pot—that is round, just like the moon during the Mid-Autumn Festival when it is the roundest of the whole year. That's the time when family members all come home to celebrate. The famous Chinese poet LI Bai's poem is about this time. "床前明月光 / 疑是地上霜 / 舉頭望明月 / 低頭思故鄉 ; The bright moonlight shines over my bed/Let me mistaken it for the frosting on the ground/ Raise my head to look at the moon/Dip my head feeling homesick."

On Chinese New Year's Eve, my father used to prepare the wood charcoal until it was red hot, and then he placed it inside the hot pot with a chimney, much like the Mongolian hot pot sold in Chinatown. For New Year's, some families eat dumplings, which are shaped like an old-style golden nugget to symbolize fortune for the year to come.

Although Taiwan has sweltering summers with temperatures over 100°F, surprisingly enough the hot pot is one of the most popular dishes. It can be eaten in a single serving hot pot like Japanese shabu shabu, in a yin/yang hot pot (鴛鴦鍋), which is a hot pot with two compartments, one side filled with mild stock soup, the other with a red-hot spicy stock soup. Sometimes it is served as an individual serving dish with a small metal hot pot filled with food with the pot heated with a portable burner.

Arriving in Taiwan after a long stay in the New England area, my husband and I couldn't understand the popularity of the hot pot. But then we suddenly realized that when we lived in Boston during the cold winter days, our freezer was always packed with different flavors of ice cream. People crowd into the tiny space at Toscanini Ice Cream in Cambridge not too far from MIT even when it is 20° degrees or snowing outside.

A pot over a table top portable gas stove is pretty easy to operate; however, it is imperative that you open the window when using a gas stove to let in fresh air for ventilation. Once I was eating shabu shabu at a restaurant in Taiwan that used gas, and all of a sudden

I felt sick, as if I was going to pass out. I felt like I was gasping for air and went outside right away. The poor ventilation of the restaurant was the cause. You have to be really careful to check that the restaurant has the proper equipment for adequate ventilation before eating hot pot heated by gas.

Yield: 5-6 servings

- 10-12 oz. country style pork
- 10-12 oz. rib eye beef
- 2-3 pieces of tofu, in one-inch cubes
- 8-10 oz. shrimp with shells
- Half a Napa cabbage (*about 1¼ lbs. or more*)
- 1 package (7 oz.) cellophane noodles (also called mung bean or green bean noodles)
- 5-6 eggs (*one egg per person*)
- Some Bull Head BBQ Sha Cha Sauce (牛頭牌沙茶醬)
- 5-6 tsp. soy sauce
- 1 lb. or less chicken thighs with bones and ½ tsp. salt (optional)

Equipment:

A table top electric frying pan or a portable gas stove available in Chinatown and Japanese grocery stores.

1 Soak the cellophane noodles in warm water for 10-15 minutes, and then pull it apart with your hands to shorten the noodles.

2 Thinly slice the pork and beef into slices about 1" x 2".

3 Cube the tofu into one-inch cubes.

4 Shell the shrimp and devein (see steps **4** and **5** in Shrimp with Broccoli on page 121).

5 Cut the Napa cabbage into one-inch wide pieces.

6 *Chicken Broth Preparation (optional):* Boil the chicken thighs in a pot with about 7 cups of water. Add ½ tsp. salt, bring to a boil, and then reduce heat to low and simmer for 20-30 minutes. This broth will be the soup stock for the hot pot. Skim off the foam and grease that will appear at the top of the soup when the pot is boiling. Remove the chicken thighs for another use.

7 Put the chicken broth (or just water) into the hot pot, and bring to a boil. Place some of the cabbage and tofu in the pot, cover and let cook about 5 minutes. Uncover and turn the heat lower, but keep the soup at a bubbly simmer. Now you are ready to start the hot pot.

8 In a cereal-size bowl, each person mixes one raw egg with 1 Tbsp. BBQ Sha Cha Sauce (沙茶醬) and 1 tsp. soy sauce. Sha Cha Sauce contains fish, dried shrimps, garlic, shallot and other spices. Then each person dips pieces of meat or shrimp into the hot soup. Let the meat cook for a few seconds until it's done or changes color (usually in less than 1 minute), and dip the meat into the egg mixture in the bowl to cool the food so it won't burn your tongue. If you prefer, you can use a sieve or ladle to pick the meat out of the hot pot.

Ingredient variations include using thin slices of tuna, salmon, tilapia, or other fish. Spinach and watercress are good, too. After the meal is done, the soup is the best part. Tofu and cellophane (mung bean) noodle are two of the best ingredients for the hot pot. By the end, the tofu and cellophane noodles will have soaked up all the tasty soup, becoming the best part of the hot pot meal.

CHAPTER 11

Rice & Noodle Dishes

Rice & Noodle Dishes

Taiwanese-Style Glutinous Fried Rice (Sweet Rice)
台式油飯 (tai shi you fan; yu beng in Taiwanese) ★★★★

Sweet rice is also called glutinous rice or sticky rice (糯米). It comes in long and short grain varieties, but in the U.S., Japanese and Chinese markets only carry the short grain variety. The texture is very pleasantly soft but chewy; however, it is pretty filling. The other ingredients may include shredded pork, Chinese black mushrooms, or dried shrimps.

Glutinous rice is usually cooked for special occasions, such as celebrating the birth of a child, an anniversary or a Buddha festival. A family announces the birth of their newborn when the baby is one-month old. For the occasion, they make a plate of sweet fried rice shaped into a dome to present to their neighbors. Neighbors will then return the same plate filled with regular uncooked rice to wish for the baby to have a "hard head" (i.e., a healthy and smart brain). This kind of tradition is no longer practiced in Taiwan as far as I know.

This dish is one of my children's favorite. When my daughter Tina returned from Japan after a few years there, the first thing she wanted to eat was sweet fried rice. The sweet rice is hard to cook perfectly with a rice cooker. The steps have to be followed exactly to get the best result. My third sister WU Shu Shu (吳淑姝) taught me how to make it. There is another easier way to cook the rice in the rice cooker. My college classmate Stella Weng gave me her recipe. It is explained at the end of this recipe.

Yield: About 6-8 serving

2$^1/_3$ cup sweet rice (糯米) or 3 rice cooker cups[7]. Sweet rice is sold in 5 lb. bags. The one from Koda Farm, S. Dos Palos, California is the best.

10 oz. pork tenderloin (*Often sold in the supermarket as an individually packed strip or two pieces in one plastic-wrapped package.*)

Meat Marinade:

2 tsp. soy sauce

1 tsp. sesame oil

Black or white pepper

1 tsp. cornstarch

4-6 dried Chinese black mushrooms

2-3 Tbsp. vegetable oil

2-3 Tbsp. soy sauce

2-3 large shallots (about ¾-1 cup sliced) *I prefer more and use 1 cup.*

1 tsp. sesame oil

1-2 tsp. sugar (optional)

Salt and black pepper to taste

A pinch of MSG (optional)

Chopped cilantro or coriander (as garnish)

Taiwanese-style gooey soy sauce (醬油膏) for dipping (optional)

Equipment:

A metal or bamboo steamer with at least two racks. Line two racks with damp cheesecloths at least twice the size of the steamer rack

---

7 Each rice cooker comes with a small cup for measuring rice that is actually smaller than a measured cup.

1 Soak the sweet rice overnight or for at least four hours. Rinse the rice before using and drain.

2 Rinse the dried black mushrooms, and in a covered container, reconstitute the dried black mushrooms in one cup of hot water for 1 hour or longer. Then, cut off the stem and discard. Slice the mushrooms thinly. As the mushroom water may have sand inside, filter the mushroom soaking water through a paper towel-lined sieve and reserve for later.

3 Peel the shallots and slice thinly. While completing the next few steps, you can bring the water in the steamer to a boil and turn it off if you are not done stir frying the rice in the next step.

4 Cut pork strips against the grain into slices and then stack a couple of pieces and slice into thin strips about 1½ inches long. Marinate with 2 tsp. soy sauce, 1 tsp. sesame oil, and black pepper or white pepper. Then add 1 tsp. cornstarch and mix well.

5 Heat up 2-3 Tbsp. vegetable oil in your wok (or a 12-inch skillet) and stir fry half of the shallot slices until golden brown. Add the soaked, drained, and rinsed sweet rice, and mix to coat the rice with the oil and shallots. Add the mushroom soaking water from step **2**. Add more water, if needed, until the water barely covers the rice. Add 2-3 Tbsp. soy sauce (to get an even, beautiful light brown color later). Over medium to medium low heat, mix with a spatula, stirring constantly until the water disappears and the rice becomes tacky, about 5 minutes.

6 Divide the sticky rice between two steamer racks lined with damp cheesecloth. Make sure the bottom of the steamer rack is not totally blocked by the sweet rice. Fold the corners of the cheesecloth over the rice to cover it. In the two racks, leave four corners of the steamer uncovered by cheesecloth and rice, so the steam can rise up.

7 Over medium high heat, steam for 5 minutes. If using two steamer racks, rotate the racks top-and-bottom to even out the steaming. After 10 minutes

total steaming time, check for doneness by placing a couple of grains between two fingertips and pressing. Or, if you taste it, it should be chewy, but lack a hard center when done. If it is still hard, steam another 3-4 minutes over low heat and check the doneness again. Do not overcook.

8 When done, move the steam rack away from the steam, and let cool for 5 minutes. Remove the rice from the cheesecloth. Do not leave the rice on the cheesecloth too long; the rice will stick to the cheesecloth after it cools. Spread out the rice with a rice spatula so it will be easier to stir fry in the wok.

9 Heat up the wok over high heat for about 3-4 minutes. Add 3 Tbsp. oil and 1 tsp. sesame oil. Add the remaining shallots and brown them.

10 Add pork and stir fry until the meat turns color. If the meat sticks to the wok, don't worry, the caramelized bits will add flavor to the dish. Turn the heat to medium low. When all the meat has cooked, add the sliced mushrooms and mix briefly. Turn heat to low. Add the steamed sweet rice to the wok and mix well. It will be kind of sticky, but that is OK. Add a pinch of sugar, a pinch of MSG (optional), and salt to taste. Add a pinch of black pepper if you like it a little spicy. Mix everything until well combined and serve with coriander sprinkled over the top. On the side, offer Taiwanese-style gooey soy sauce (醬油膏), which is very thick in texture but not too salty, and quite tasty.

If you have an automatic rice cooker, here is an easier way to cook the sweet rice:

1 Soak **3 rice cooker cups** of sweet rice (**NOT regular cups**) 8 hours or overnight in the rice cooker pot.

2 Wash the rice and drain the water until there is almost no water inside the pot.

3 Add **½ rice cooker cup of water** and 2 Tbsp soy sauce (to add color) to the rice.

4 Place the rice cooker pot inside the rice cooker and press down the cook button. (Turn off the "keep warm" button if there is one in your rice cooker.)

5 When the "cook" button pops up, do not open the lid and let it sit covered for at least 30 minutes to let the leftover steam thoroughly "steam" the rice.

6 Open the lid and thoroughly mix the rice from bottom up with a rice paddle. Cover and let it sit for another 15 minutes. Proceed to step **9** above and finish cooking.

The texture of sweet rice is very different from regular rice. It feels sticky when compared with regular rice. If the cooked sweet rice is pounded with a heavy wooden mallet, it becomes a massive sticky lump and can be made into a desert called "mochi" (麻糬), which is served coated with coarse sweet peanut powder or filled with sweet bean paste. (Pounding mochi is a Japanese festival ritual for the New Year. There are two people, with one holding a wooden mallet and pounding the cooked sticky rice while the other turns the mass of rice.) Mochi is very popular in Japan and Taiwan.

The sweet fried rice is quite filling, but very delicious, so go easy at first when you eat it so you don't become overly full.

Dan Dan Noodles 担担麵
(dan dan mian) ***

This Sichuan dish is very popular outside of Sichuan, too. Its sauce makes this dish unique. The name originated from a vendor selling noodles who shoulders his wares on a bamboo stick, called a dan zi (担子).

Yield: 3 servings

- 4 oz. angel hair pasta
- 1 Tbsp. canola oil
- 6 oz. pork, ground or coarsely chopped (Skip the pork for a vegetarian version.)

  Pork Marinade:
- 1 Tbsp. soy sauce
- 1 tsp. Sauvignon Blanc
- A pinch of black pepper
- 1 Tbsp. cornstarch
- 1 tsp. sesame paste 芝麻醬 or Sichuan bean paste 四川豆瓣醬
- 3 Tbsp. canola oil
- 1 clove shallot, peeled and thinly sliced
- ½ lb. fresh bean sprouts

  Sauce Mixture:
- 2 Tbsp. soy sauce
- ¼ tsp. sugar
- 4 Tbsp. chicken stock or water
- 1 tsp. chili oil
- 1 stalk scallion, finely chopped
- 4 cloves garlic, finely chopped
- ¼ tsp. chili paste
- 2-3 Tbsp. unsalted, roast peanuts

1 If using, mix the pork with marinade ingredients and set aside.

2 Follow the cooking instruction for the angel hair pasta. Drain the water, add in 1 Tbsp. canola oil, and mix, to prevent noodles from sticking together.

3 Peel the shallots, and thinly slice.

4 Cut the tops off and half of the green part of the scallions, and then finely chop.

5 Hit the garlic with the flat side of a cleaver, remove the skin, and finely chop.

6 Grind up the peanuts by putting them in a plastic bag and run a rolling pin over the peanuts until almost powder-like.

7 Heat up the wok over high heat, about 3-4 minutes. Add 3 Tbsp. canola oil and shallot slices, stir, and add marinated pork. Stir until the meat changes color to a pale white. Reduce heat to low and keep stirring. Add 1 tsp. sesame paste or Sichuan bean paste, and cook until the meat is quite dry and a beautiful brown color, about 3 minutes.

8 Bring a pot of water to boil, drop bean sprouts in and drain after one minute. Place bean sprouts on a plate.

9 Mix the sauce ingredients together and serve with the other ingredients (noodles, pork mixture, bean sprouts, and ground peanuts).

10 When serving, in each individual's bowl, spoon some sauce mixture, add bean sprouts, and pick out a small serving of noodles and top with the cooked pork and a sprinkle of ground peanuts. Mix and eat. The serving portion should be on the small side to get the flavor of the sauce, bean sprouts and the noodle fully mixed.

11 This dish tastes better if it is spicy. Experiment with different proportions of the ingredients to get the best results.

Taiwanese-Style Fried Sweet (Glutinous) Rice Wrapped with Bamboo Leaves "Zong Zi"

台式粽子 ★★★★

Zong zi uses the glutinous sweet rice of the previous recipe and wraps it up in bamboo leaves. The bamboo leaves give a very distinctive aroma to this dish. There are many regional styles for folding zong zi with different shapes and ingredients. Shanghai-style wraps uncooked rice in bamboo leaves into a rectangular pillow-like shape. It is then boiled in water to finish cooking. After trying many styles, I think Taiwanese zong zi tastes the best—specifically, northern Taiwanese style. Southern-style Taiwanese zong zi is boiled rather than wrapped with pre-cooked rice. In southern style, after being wrapped in bamboo leaves, the zong zi are tied with a string. In the old days, we used a sturdy straw called "salty straw" 鹹草 (used commercially for woven mats). The bundles are then tied in small bunches and steamed in a steamer. Nowadays, a bundle of strings replaces the hard-to-find straw.

Every year on the fifth day of the fifth month of the lunar calendar (around June) every Chinese family makes zong zi in memory of the poet QU Yuan (屈原) who lived around 300 B.C. during China's Warring States Period. He drowned himself in the Milo River. As a court official, QU Yuan fell victim to the conspiring of the concubine and followers of the Chu Lord (楚王) to have QU exiled from the court. Unfortunately the Chu Lord believed this concubine and corrupt followers, and QU Yuan's idea to strengthen the country was not accepted, and he was exiled.

Because the Chu lord listened to his concubine and corrupt followers, QU's native country Chu (楚) was defeated and wiped out by Qin around 300 BC. So, QU Yuan did not have a country and home to go back to. In a desperate move, he tried to rouse the people and made a statement by drowning himself in the Milo River (湖南省汨羅江), which flows through present day Hunan Province (MAO Zedong's hometown).

The Qin Lord united the Seven Warring States into one empire and called himself the First Emperor of Qin, Qin Shu Huang Di (秦始皇帝) ending 500 years of battles between regional lords around 221 B.C. Qin is the shortest Chinese dynasty. It had two emperors and lasted only seven years because of Qin's brutal rule over his people. He was the first one to erect the Great Wall of China.

Before QU Yuan died, he wrote a poem: "The whole world is muddy/I am the only one whose mind is clear/ The whole world is drunken/I am the only one who is awake." (舉世皆濁啊，而我獨清；舉世皆醉啊，而我獨醒。) *In order not to let his spirit go hungry, the local people made* zong zi *wrapped in bamboo leaves so the fish could not eat the rice. The story goes that in order to scare the fish away, people devised a boat with the head of a dragon—the king of all fishes—and the person sitting at the head of the boat banged a gong to scare away the fish. From that tradition came the custom of the annual Dragon Boat Festival (端午節或端陽節划龍船) to commemorate QU Yuan's sacrifice.*

It is rather tricky to make zong zi. *You need to make a few before you get the hang of it. When serving* zong zi, *each person can take one and open it up on their plate. It is fun to eat, especially for kids, but also for adults. One time my daughter Tina came home with her friend Elizabeth. I showed them how to make* zong zi, *and after a couple awkward ones, they did very good job of wrapping all the* zong zi *for me!*

Yield: 22 zong zi 粽子

3 cups uncooked sweet rice (equivalent to 4 rice cooker cups) (糯米) *Sweet rice comes in 5 lb. bags. The one from Koda Farm, S. Dos Palos, California, is the best.*

4-5 or more dried Chinese black mushrooms (香菇)

¼ cup dried shrimp (乾蝦仁) (optional) *You can find dried shrimp sold in plastic bags in Chinatown grocery stores.*

10 oz. pork loin

Pork Marinade:

1 Tbsp. soy sauce

1 tsp. Sauvignon Blanc or Cognac

A pinch of black pepper

1-2 Tbsp. sesame oil

1 Tbsp. cornstarch

3-5 or more shallot cloves

7 Tbsp. canola oil, divided

2 Tbsp. sesame oil (麻油) or cooking oil *Buy the sesame oil sold in Chinese, Japanese or Korean grocery stores. Do not get the kind sold in supermarkets as it is not aromatic at all.*

1 bunch bamboo leaves, available in Chinatown grocery stores

3 Tbsp. soy sauce

½-1 tsp. salt

A pinch of MSG

A pinch of sugar

A pinch of black pepper

Condiments (optional): Thick Chinese soy sauce (醬油膏), soy sauce, chili sauce.

Equipment:

Chinese steamer with two to three racks, aluminum or bamboo

A ball of kitchen twine

1 Soak the sweet rice in water overnight, and the next day, rinse clean and drain dry.

2 *Bamboo Leaves Preparation:* **Fill the sink with lot of water, place bamboo leaves in the sink to soak. Then using a clean sponge, wipe clean each leaf separately on both sides. You can do this by placing each leaf against a chopping block inclined in the sink, or other flat surface, then put the washed leaves in a large sieve to drain dry for a couple of hours.**

3 Rinse clean the dried Chinese black mushrooms and soak in boiling water for 1 hour. Then remove the tough stem in the center, and slice thinly. Save the soaking water.

4 Rinse clean the dried shrimp, and soak in boiling water for 30 minutes, and then coarsely chop. Save the soaking water.

5 Peel the shallots and slice thinly.

6 Cut the pork loin into thin strips and then combine with the marinade ingredients and set aside.

7 Heat up the wok over high heat, about 2-3 minutes. Add 4 Tbsp. canola oil and 2 Tbsp. sesame oil. Add about half the shallot to the wok and stir until golden, but not brown. Add drained sweet rice to the wok, the soaking water of the dried shrimp, and the Chinese black mushrooms. The water should barely cover the rice. Add more water if necessary. Add 3 Tbsp. soy sauce and ½-1 tsp. salt, and mix well. Check the saltiness of the liquid; it should be slightly salty. Turn heat to medium and stir constantly with a metal spatula until the water has evaporated and the rice becomes tacky, about 8-10 minutes.

8 Bring the steamer pot water to a boil. Line each steamer rack with cheesecloth. The tightly woven cheesecloth from art shops are the best. The cheesecloth sold in supermarkets have a too loose weave. In each steamer rack, spread half of the sticky rice over the cheesecloth. Spread out the rice using a spoon. Fold the edges of the cheesecloth over the rice so the rice is covered with the cheesecloth. Lift the four corners of the cheesecloth so the steam can come up from underneath. When you put the racks over the steamer pot, turn off the burner so that you will not be burned by the steam. After the racks are in place over the steamer pot, turn heat to medium high and steam for about 6-8 minutes in all, or until the rice is soft and there is no hard center, but it is not mushy.

9 About halfway through the steaming—about 4 minutes or so—check the doneness. If you want a softer texture, swap the top and bottom racks so that the rice will steam evenly on both racks. Steam another 3-4 minutes. Turn off the heat and remove the steamer racks from the steamer pot. Open the cover and the cheesecloth on top. Use a rice paddle to pull the steamed rice away from all sides and off the cheesecloth. Let the rice cool down, about 10 minutes. Do not leave the rice on the cheesecloth too long, otherwise the rice will stick to it. Scoop the cooked sweet rice into a pot or mixing bowl. The rice does not have to be cooked until it is fully soft like in the recipe for "Taiwanese Style Fried Sweet Rice," because in this recipe, the rice is steamed again after being wrapped in bamboo leaves.

10 Wash the wok clean and heat up over high heat, about 3 minutes. Turn heat to medium high and add 2 Tbsp. canola oil and the rest of the shallot, and stir until golden. Add the chopped Chinese black mushrooms and dried shrimp and mix well. Remove to a plate.

11 Without washing the wok, heat it up again, add 1 Tbsp. canola oil. Add marinated pork strips and stir until they change color to a pale white, and reduce heat to medium high. Add the mushroom and shrimp mixture from step **10** add a pinch of salt, sugar, and MSG (optional), and adjust to taste.

12 *Wrapping the Zong Zi:* Make 11 loops of kitchen twine about 2½ feet long. Cut the top and bottom ends of the loops and you should have 22 strings. Take 5 or 6 strands in a bunch, and make a loop in the center of the strands that you can hang over a doorknob. With a 5 strand bunch, you should end up with 10 loose ends.

13 Within easy reach, have the cooked rice in a pot and the pork, shrimp, mushroom mixture in another pot with a spoon for each so that you can scoop filling into the bamboo leaves. Now you are ready to start making *zong zi*. See page 163 for photos demonstrating the process.

14 Take two bamboo leaves and hold them parallel, but overlapping about ⅓ of the width in the center and the two leaves also offset a little vertically to form a longer leaf combination. Fold and twist the leaves to form an ice cream cone shape. In the triangular opening, put about 1 Tbsp. cooked sweet rice, and then add 1 Tbsp. pork mixture on top, cover with another tablespoon cooked sweet rice. Fold the bamboo leaves sticking up over the filling to cover the triangular cup, and then fold the ends of the leaves that go beyond the cup and fold them to one side. The final *zong zi* should be shape like a diamond with four corners.

15 Take one string from the bunch hanging off the doorknob, and wrap it around the wrapped bamboo leaf package two times, then tie a knot to secure the package onto the string. Continue to wrap the *zong zi* until you have used up the filling. Cut more string bundles if needed.

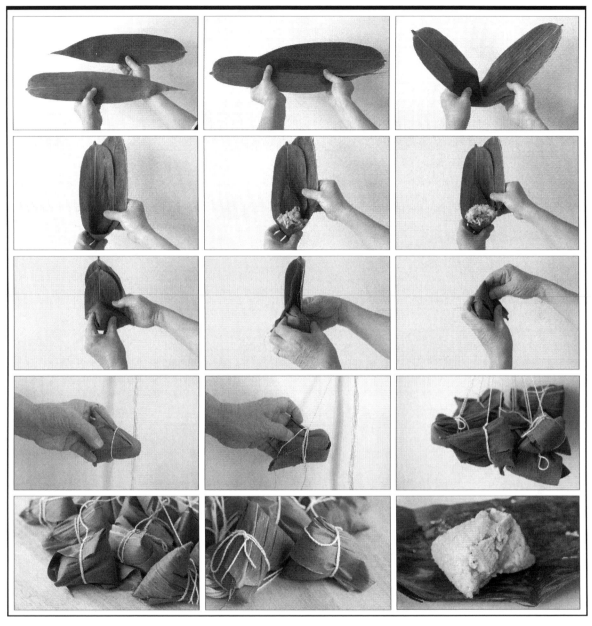

16 Before serving, bring the steamer pot of water to a boil. Place one bunch of *zong zi* on each steamer rack and steam for 6-8 minutes over medium high heat. Serve with Taiwanese thick soy sauce (醬油膏) or with soy sauce mixed with chili sauce. Or serve at room temperature as is. Commercial *zong zi* vendors in Taiwan usually serve *zong zi* with thick Taiwanese soy sauce mixed with chili sauce on the side and topped with a bunch of coriander.

This style of zong zi is popular in the northern part of Taiwan. For zong zi made in the southern part of Taiwan and in other parts of China, the uncooked rice is wrapped in bamboo leaves, and then boiled in water. The shape is also different; it is shaped like an elongated pillow with strings wrapped around it. In a way that style is easier to make, but not as aesthetically pleasing.

Fried Rice Sticks 炒米粉
(chao mi fen) ***

Rice shows up in many forms in Chinese food. There is steamed rice, rice porridge, rice cake, rice powder, rice sticks, rice crackers, and now the very popular new version of a rice bun in Taiwan, which replaces the hamburger bread bun at some McDonald's branches and the Japanese fast food chain Mosburger.

During my childhood in Taiwan, I remember noodles being made fresh daily. On my way to school, there was a noodle maker who used a long wooden pole to knead a big chunk of dough for noodles. He would sit on the pole and press and press the dough until the dough became flat. Again he folded the dough and pressed it in a different direction and so on.

My mother would send me to buy about one pound of fresh noodles, a very soft, yellowish, plump, Taiwanese-style noodle. She would add various vegetables and strips of meat and pan fry them together. It was really delicious.

There was no dried spaghetti available in those days. The only dried form of noodles was rice sticks. Rice sticks are white, and originally were available in a thin and thick version only. The thick version was the specialty of my hometown, Sing Zhuang (新莊). My father liked it cooked in soup. It is not easy to break into short pieces. The texture is more slippery, similar to Vietnamese pho.

The regular skinny rice sticks are more like angel hair pasta. There are not many Chinese restaurants offering dishes cooked with rice sticks. It is not an easy dish to make. In the U.S., the most well-known rice stick dish is Singapore Curry Fried Rice Stick (星洲炒粉). When we visited Bainbridge Island, Washington near Seattle during the Red Sox 2004 World Series Championship, we had to go to a pub, Island Grill, to watch the games. And Voilà! There was Singapore Curry Rice Stick on the menu. I ordered one and it was the best Singapore Curry Rice Stick that I have ever tasted in the U.S. cooked by an American chef.

Singapore has immigrants from southern China, the way Taiwanese have ancestors from Fu Jian (福建). We love rice stick noodles. My eldest sister WU Shun Hua (吳舜華) only eats rice stick noodles. She does not touch spaghetti noodles at all. Picking up the local

flavor of India—since Singapore is close to India—Singapore Fried Rice Stick has a curry flavor with some spicy twists. When I was in Singapore in the summer of 2010, I didn't see Singapore Fried Rice Sticks on the hotel restaurant menu. It turns out that their "black pepper crab" is a favorite for locals as well as tourists. In it, crabs are cooked with tons of spicy black pepper as the sauce. They have some fantastic black pepper from India, which is spicy and aromatic.

Rice sticks are usually packed in a 12 oz. package with two to three flat, rectangular bundles of rice sticks about 8 x 11". There are many brands available in Chinese grocery stores. They are imported from Taiwan, China, Thailand, and Vietnam. Hsin Chu (新竹) in Taiwan has the best rice stick noodles. They are a popular souvenir for tourists visiting, in addition to the pounded meatball (貢丸). It is a windy city, so it's great for drying rice sticks on a bamboo stand. If you visit Hsin Chu, you can find stores with signs advertising rice sticks (新竹米粉) on every commercial block.

There are two kinds of rice stick, one is "water boiled" (水粉) and the other one is "steamed" (蒸粉). They are then dried accordingly. The water-boiled rice sticks have a more gleaming look; while the steamed rice sticks are thinner and dull looking. So the rice sticks sold at the market are actually fully "cooked." In fact, rice sticks do not require much water to cook. I found freshly made rice sticks at the farmer's market in Hsin Chu, which only need 2-3 minutes to cook without much water.

There are many ways to do this dish. This method cooks the fried rice sticks without the rice stick breaking into small pieces. The key is NOT to soak rice sticks in water beforehand. I got this rice stick cooking tip from my friend Linda Chen from my UMass days.

Yield: 3-4 servings

- Half a bundle of rice stick noodles (about 3-4 oz.)
- 3-4 leaves of Chinese Napa cabbage, shredded
- 4-6 oz. fresh bean sprouts (optional)
- 4-6 oz. sirloin ground pork (or a piece of pork cut into thin strips 1½ inches long)

Pork Marinade:

1 tsp. soy sauce

A few drops sesame oil

One pinch of black pepper

1 tsp. cornstarch

1-3 shallot cloves

5 Tbsp. canola oil, divided

Salt

1-1½ cups chicken stock or water

Variations: The vegetable does not have to be cabbage, you can substitute bok choy, bean sprouts (for bean sprouts, add them at the last minute to keep their crunchiness), spinach, broccoli (cut into small florets, and blanched in boiling water for 2 minutes before adding), mushrooms etc. Or if you prefer seafood, scallop and shrimp are good choices. It will take a few times to master this dish. The added vegetables should be blanched or cooked first, except for the bean sprouts.

1 Rinse the rice sticks under the faucet and drain in a sieve. (Do not soak them in water.) They will become limp after 10-15 minutes.

2 Stack two Napa cabbage leaves at a time and cut crosswise into thin pieces.

3 Mix the pork with the marinade ingredients and set aside.

4 Peel the shallots and slice thinly.

5 Heat up the wok over high heat, about 3-4 minutes. Add 3 Tbsp. canola oil in the wok. Turn heat to medium high, add half of the sliced shallots, and stir until golden. Add the marinated pork, and break up the pork with your spatula, stirring until the meat turns pale white. If the wok is not hot enough, the meat will stick to the bottom. That is all right. Use a metal spatula to scrape off the sticky part, but do not discard it.

6 Add shredded Chinese Napa cabbage to the pork mixture, sprinkle with a little salt, and then add ¼-½ cup water, stir, and cover. Turn heat to medium and let cook about 5 minutes.

Uncover and stir well. If the wok looks too dry, add some more water. Turn heat to medium high and cover again and cook for another 4-5 minutes, occasionally removing the cover and stirring. Cook until the cabbage looks translucent and soft. Remove from the wok. Make sure to remove everything including any liquid if there is any left, but ideally the moisture would have all evaporated. Turn off the heat. Rinse clean the wok.

7 Turn heat to medium high and add 2 Tbsp. canola oil to the wok. Add the rest of the sliced shallot, stir and let it turn golden. Add 1-1½ cup chicken stock or water. Bring the water to a boil, salt to taste. Then break apart rice sticks into shorter strands. You can use your hands to pull apart the rice sticks into shorter strands. Reduce heat to medium low. Add the rice sticks to the water (or stock), and using chopsticks in one hand and a spatula in another, stir and turn for 2 minutes. Add cabbage/pork mixture to the wok. Turn and mix slowly. Add bean sprouts and cover for 2-3 minutes. Taste to see if the rice sticks are soft. If not, cover for a few more minutes. If it's too dry, sprinkle some water. Remove the cover, and stir until all the liquid is almost gone. Serve hot.

Yun Nan Rice Noodle Over the Bridge 雲南過橋米線

(yun nan guo qiao mi xian) ***

This is a well known dish from Yun Nan Province (雲南), which literally means "south of the cloud," and is located in the southwestern part of China. The area produces a great variety of Chinese medicinal herbal plants. Quite a few ethnic minorities are scattered around the region and still retain their unique cultures, costumes, and customs. Those groups are well known for producing pretty girls. The rice noodles used in this dish are a little different from regular rice sticks. The texture is like rice sticks, but it is more elastic, slippery and as easy to break apart as regular rice sticks. It is closer to Vietnamese pho.

There is a beautiful story behind this dish. The legend has it that during the Qing Dynasty (清朝 1776-1911 AD) in Yun Nan Province (雲南), a young man was preparing for the national exam which was held once every three years. If he successfully passed this exam, he would be guaranteed a position as an officer of the high court, and his life would be transformed from rags to riches. In order to concentrate on his studies, he studied alone on a small island connected by a bridge to the continent. His wife wanted to give him nourishment to build up his strength, so she killed their home-raised chicken and duck. Slowly she cooked the whole chicken, duck and some pork bones with bone marrow for a long time. When the soup was ready, she also prepared some fresh vegetables and rice noodles to bring him.

The young man was asleep when his wife got there. When he woke up and found what his wife had brought him, he mixed the noodles and vegetables into the soup and discovered that the soup was still hot. The soup had been kept hot by the floating layer of chicken fat, which acted as insulation. Every time she took the dish to her husband, she had to cross over a bridge, hence its name.

The version here is a simpler one. But if you want to try the complicated one you can. Use a large heat-resistant ceramic pot or a stainless steel pot to slow cook the chicken, duck and pork bones with marrow for at least 2 hours. After one hour you can remove the chicken and duck for other uses, but leave the pork bones to simmer for another hour or longer.

Note that there is no need to remove the skin from the chicken bones. The main idea of this dish is to have

the chicken fat float on the surface to prevent the soup from getting cold. When the dish is presented, it does not look like it's hot because there is no steam coming through the film of chicken fat. It may sound greasy, but you have to taste the real McCoy before trying any variations. Of course you can remove the chicken fat after the stock is made.)

Yield: 6-8 servings

One whole chicken carcass & 1 pound pork bones or pork with bones. *You can get bones in Chinatown. If they are hard to find, ask the supermarket butcher for help. They should have some bones. If not, get a game hen or ½ a chicken. Prepare the chicken the same way as you would the bones for soup.*

1-1½ bundles of rice sticks (about 8-10 oz.) *You can substitute with the same quantity of Vietnamese pho, half a package of angel hair pasta, or thin egg noodles. Flour-made pasta tends to swell if it's soaked in soup for too long, but Vietnamese pho or rice sticks will not swell so much.*

8-10 oz. country style pork

8-10 oz. boneless chicken breast

½ head of iceberg lettuce, shredded

2 small pickling cucumbers, peeled and julienned

One piece of tofu (hard or soft) or dried tofu skin (only available in Chinatown in packages of 2-3 pieces). *Dried tofu skin is yellowish and thin.*

One bunch coriander

One bunch scallions (about 5-6 stalks), finely chopped

8-10 squab eggs (available in Chinatown) (optional)

4 oz. fresh bean sprouts

Condiments:

Chili oil or chili sauce

1 If using rice sticks, drop them into boiling water and cook over low heat for 2-3 minutes, then drain and set aside. If using Vietnamese pho, drop into warm water for 2 minutes, then drain and set aside. If using angel hair pasta or thin egg noodles, follow the cooking instructions on the package, boil about 5-6 minutes then rinse in cold water, drain and place on a plate.

2 Slice the pork and chicken into very thin, wide slices about 1"x2". If it's partially frozen, the meat will be easier to slice.

3 Peel the pickling cucumbers and julienne, and then place on a plate.

4 If using tofu, slice thinly. If using dried tofu skin, soak in hot water for 30 minutes and then cut into 1"x2" pieces and place on a plate.

5 Cut off the tops of the scallions and half of the green part. Clean the scallions then finely chop and place on a plate.

6 Cut off the roots of the coriander, and in a sink filled with water, swish the coriander in the water to get rid of the sand. Take the coriander out and then repeat, rinsing one more time. Coarsely chop and place on a plate.

7 If using, gently boil the squab eggs for 6-7 minutes. Peel the shells and place on a plate.

8 Drop the chicken and pork bones into the boiling water, stir one minute, and discard the water. Place the bones in a colander and run clear water all over to get rid the wild fowl smell and the foam from cooking. Place bones in a fresh pot with about 7 cups of water with a pinch of salt. Bring to a boil and simmer for 30-60 minutes or longer.

9 Remove the bones and discard. Save the soup. Drop pork slices, chicken slices and squab eggs into the hot soup, and cover for 5 minutes. Turn off the heat. Transfer the piping hot soup to a large ceramic pot with a fitted cover (or CorningWare) and very carefully bring to the dining table. Open the cover, and add vegetables and the rest of the ingredients, including rice sticks or thin noodles, stir up all the ingredients to get them cooked. Serve hot, but be careful as the soup is quite hot. Each person can ladle soup into their own individual bowls. Add chili oil or chili sauce if anyone likes it a little spicy.

10 Traditionally, when serving, there is an assortment of 10 or more plates with one ingredient on each plate. In this version, these ingredients are the rice sticks, cucumbers, tofu/tofu skin, and squab eggs. Each person is served a ceramic bowl filled with piping hot soup in which each person adds ingredients, and then sprinkles with coriander, scallion, chili paste, etc. In this version, I add meat before bringing it to the dining table, to make sure the meat is fully cooked. This is a dish with a lot of ingredients; it's not practical to prepare a small amount. Preparing a big pot for a party is ideal. Of course the number of servings varies depending on how much each person eats. The servings here are just a rough estimate.

Cold Noodles 涼麵 (liang mian) ***

There is no set rule for what kind of ingredients should be added to cold noodles except the noodles. The noodles can be any kind or shape like Italian pasta. Every Chinese has his or her own recipe. One of our chorus members, Wendy Lou (譚先哲) once brought a cold noodle dish to our regular Greater Boston Chinese Cultural Association (GBCCA) choral group rehearsal. She added mayonnaise, cheese and other seasonings to the cold noodles, and it was really good.

Yield: 4-5 servings

> 3 servings of angel hair or other pasta
>
> 1 Tbsp. canola oil
>
> 6 oz. pork or chicken
>
> **Meat Marinade:**
>
> 1 tsp. soy sauce
>
> 1 tsp. cornstarch
>
> 1 tsp. sesame oil
>
> A pinch of black pepper
>
> 3-4 oz. snow peas
>
> 3 sticks celery heart
>
> 6 slices low-salt ham
>
> 3 oz. fresh bean sprouts
>
> 3 oz. oyster mushroom or other mushrooms
>
> 2 cloves shallot, peeled & thinly sliced (optional)
>
> 2 Tbsp. canola oil
>
> 1 tsp. salt
>
> 3 Tbsp. sesame oil
>
> 2 Tbsp. soy sauce
>
> A pinch of black pepper
>
> 2-3 Tbsp. heavy cream or half & half
>
> A pinch MSG (optional) or 3 Tbsp. cream

Variation: You can substitute other kinds of vegetables like shredded carrots, shredded zucchini, shredded cucumber, etc.

1 Cut the pork or chicken into thin strips and combine with marinade ingredients and set aside.

2 String the snow peas by breaking off the tip at each end and pulling off the string on each side of the pod. Start stringing from the fatter end and pull through to the leafy end which you then snap off. If the snow peas are fresh and you do it right, the string will come off in one complete piece. Soak in cold water for 1 hour or longer to enhance the crunchiness.

3 Cook the pasta according to the directions on the package. Drain the water, run cold water over the pasta until totally cooled. Or, drain the water, and add 1 Tbsp. cooking oil and mix to coat evenly to prevent the noodles from sticking together

4 Peel the tough strings off the celery and then cut into 2-inch lengths and then slice into thin strips lengthwise. Soak in cold water.

5 Cut the ham into thin strips.

6 Cut off the tough center stem of each mushroom and then slice, but not too thinly.

7 If using shallots, peel and slice thinly.

8 Heat up 2 Tbsp. canola oil, add shallot slices and stir until they become golden brown, but not too brown. Remove from heat and set aside.

9 Bring a large pot of water to boil with 1 tsp. salt. Add snow peas, celery, and fresh bean sprouts for one minute. Drain the water and soak vegetables in a pot of icy water for 2 minutes. Drain thoroughly.

10 In a pot, bring ¾ cup water to a boil. Add marinated meat, and stir until the color changes. Add mushroom slices and stir for 1 minute. Turn off the heat. Remove the meat and the mushrooms. Save the cooking water. (The water can be used for Egg Flower Soup.)

11 In a large mixing bowl, add the cooked noodles, the cooked meat and mushroom mixture with the cooking water, snow peas, celery, bean sprouts, ham and 3 Tbsp. sesame oil, 2 Tbsp. soy sauce, a pinch of black pepper and the golden brown shallot from step **8**. Mix well. Sprinkle with a little more soy sauce if it is too bland. Add 2-3 Tbsp. cream and mixed well. The cream adds sweetness to the noodles. Or, you can add a pinch of MSG.

Fried Rice 炒飯 (chao fang) ***

Almost all Chinese restaurants in the States use long grain rice for their fried rice. The Cantonese restaurants started the tradition since they eat long grain rice at home. I don't like long grain rice. To me, it is dry and hard. In Taiwan and in the Northeastern part of China, short grain rice is a staple as it is in Japan. The best rice is the sushi rice. It is more starchy and chewy with larger size grains. If possible, get the Kokuho rice (meaning national treasure 國寶) brand of short grain rice. Sometimes, it is possible to get from some supermarkets. If not, go straight to Chinatown, a Japanese or Korean grocery, or order online.

Using the right rice is the key to making the best fried rice. The second thing is to get an automatic electric rice cooker. It can be purchased at any kitchenware store or online, and is priced between $40-$120. The most basic one is good enough for a beginner. The more expensive models have features like built-in timer and different cooking settings for cooking soft or chewy rice.

In traditional home cooking, fried rice usually is made from leftover cooked rice. I would crack one or two eggs, add a little meat, and some chopped vegetables. Preferably, use vegetables that don't produce much liquid. Green peas, carrots, or snow peas are fine, but avoid spinach or cabbage. After 15 minutes, voilà, I have a plate of fried rice. Kids love it and it's easy to prepare.

After the rice is cooked in the rice cooker, stir the rice with a rice paddle so it becomes loose and fluffy. This way when you cook the fried rice, it will be easier to mix the fried rice evenly without too many lumps. Restaurants usually use cold rice and sprinkle with some water to break it apart before making fried rice.

This is the most basic fried rice recipe. You can add whatever leftovers you have on hand. This is a basic dish but not easy to cook perfectly. The secret is to start with a hot wok, and then cook over low heat. This method results in a clean wok and beautiful fried rice. The rice is delicious and retains its chewy grains.

Yield: 2-3 servings

- 2-3 cereal bowls of cooked rice (about 1 rice cooker cup of uncooked rice)
- 4-6 oz. pork loin, cut into thin strips

Pork Marinade:

1 tsp. soy sauce

1 tsp. cornstarch

A pinch of black pepper

8 Tbsp. canola oil, divided

1 clove shallot, peeled & thinly sliced

A pinch sugar or MSG

1 egg, beaten

Variation: *Pan fried salmon (about 4-6 oz. chopped into small pieces) is a great ingredient to add to the fried rice. It is very tasty. Salmon is very flaky and easy to break up and mix with the rice.*

1 Cut the pork loin into thin strips and mix with marinade ingredients and set aside.

2 Peel the shallot and slice thinly. Shallots really add aroma to simple fried rice.

3 Heat up 2 Tbsp. canola oil in the wok over medium heat, about 2 minutes. When the wok is fairly hot, add the beaten egg, letting it sit for about 1 minute before stirring the egg with a spatula to break it up into small pieces. Remove to a plate.

4 Without cleaning the wok, heat it up over medium high heat, about 3 minutes. Add 3 Tbsp. canola oil and shallot slices until it turns golden. Then, add pork slices and cook until it turns a pale pink color. Remove pork to a plate. The wok may have a tasty meat residue (faun) left on the surface if the wok was not hot enough before the pork was added. Use a metal spatula to scrape the wok clean, but leave the faun there.

5 Without washing the wok, heat it up over medium high heat, about 3 minutes, add 2 Tbsp. oil, add rice to the wok and using a spatula, break up the rice then reduce heat to low. Keep stirring and add a pinch of salt, a pinch of sugar or MSG, and mix well. Add cooked pork and eggs and mix well. Over low heat, mix everything together for at least 5 minutes. The longer the rice is mixed over low heat, the more blended the taste will be. Serve hot.

Egg Fried Rice 蛋炒飯
(dan chao fan) **

This recipe is the basic in fried rice. In the 1960s movie "The World of Suzie Wong," William Holden plays an American author writing stories in Hong Kong. With limited financial resources, he goes to the same restaurant every day to order Egg Fried Rice. To give himself some variations, he orders the same dish but gives it a different name each time, such as Egg Fried Rice (蛋炒飯), Fried Rice with Egg (炒飯加蛋), Fried Egg Rice (炒蛋飯).

Home-made fried rice is all white. Some Chinese restaurants use molasses or dark Karo syrup to make the fried rice quite brown. Chinese restaurants use rice that's been kept in the refrigerator overnight. The rice is separated with a little water before it is added to the wok to cook the fried rice. At home, I don't do it that way, because when the cooked rice is kept in the refrigerator overnight, it becomes hard and is not as fluffy and chewy as just-cooked rice or rice simply left at room temperature for a few hours. You can use rice leftover from lunch to make fried rice for dinner.

Japanese sushi rice is best. After the rice is cooked, use a fan to cool down the rice, separate it, and then use it for fried rice. The results will be superb. Adding other ingredients to this basic fried rice recipe can make it colorful and delicious. You can add cooked shrimp, snow peas (blanched in boiling water for 1 minute) or frozen peas (dropped into hot water for 3-5 minutes).

Yield: 2-3 servings/One plate presentation

- 2-3 cereal bowls of cooked rice (preferably short grain rice)
- 2 eggs, beaten with a tiny pinch of salt (to make the egg easier to beat evenly)
- 1-2 cloves shallot, peeled & thinly sliced
- 2 stalks scallion, in ½-inch lengths
- 5 Tbsp. canola oil, divided
- 1 Tbsp. soy sauce
- ½-1 tsp. sugar (optional) — skip sugar if using molasses or dark Karo syrup
- ½ tsp. molasses or 1-2 tsp. dark Karo syrup (optional) — if using, skip the sugar
- A pinch of salt

A pinch of MSG (optional)

1 Peel the shallots and slice thinly.

2 Cut off and discard the tops of the scallions and half the green part, then cut into half-inch lengths.

3 Heat the wok over medium heat for 2-3 minutes; add 2 Tbsp. canola oil; and swirl the oil in the wok to coat it all over. Add a little beaten egg, let it set for a few seconds and stir briskly with a spatula to break the egg into little pieces. Remove to a plate. Repeat the previous step until all the beaten eggs have been cooked. Add a little oil between batches if needed. Alternatively, you can pour all the beaten eggs into the wok, let it sit for 1 minute, and then use a spatula to briskly stir the egg around to break the scrambled egg into smaller pieces. Remove to a plate.

4 Without washing the wok, heat the wok over medium high for 3-4 minutes; add 3 Tbsp. canola oil. Add shallot and scallions; stir until the shallot and scallions turn golden. Reduce heat to medium low. Add cooked rice, stir a little and chunk up the rice, pour 1 Tbsp. soy sauce onto a Chinese spatula (which has a ridge in the back) and drizzle over the rice, and add a pinch of salt, Ajinomoto (MSG) and sugar (or molasses/dark Karo syrup). Mix well until the color is evenly distributed and the rice is all separated. Add the cooked egg. Mix well and serve hot. At this point, the wok may have rice stuck on the bottom if the wok was not hot enough at the beginning. Scrap it all off if you can. This is the original "poppy rice" that is used in the Poppy Rice Soup in some restaurants. I loved it as a child. It is very tasty even when it's a little burned.

Fancy Fried Rice 什錦炒飯
(shi jin chao fan) ***

This fancy fried rice is called "Ten Delicacies Fried Rice" in Chinese. Figuratively, it means "many" kinds of fancy ingredients. The only important thing is to make sure to use ingredients that do not produce liquid, like spinach, etc. Otherwise, the rice will become moist and stick to the wok or frying pan. The best fried rice should be dry, fluffy, and chewy with glistening rice grains.

Yield: 4-5 servings

- 1 cup uncooked rice (about 1.8 rice cooker cups)
- 2-3 dried Chinese black mushrooms
- 3-4 fresh water chestnuts (optional) or canned if fresh is not available. *Russo's in Watertown, MA carries fresh water chestnuts.*
- 3 oz. snow peas
- 2-3 oz. chicken, cut into thin strips,

    Chicken Marinade:
    - 1 tsp. rice wine or Sauvignon Blanc
    - 1 tsp. cornstarch
    - A pinch of salt
    - A pinch of black pepper

- 2-3 oz. pork loin, cut into thin strips

    Pork Marinade:
    - ½ tsp. soy sauce
    - 1 tsp. rice wine or Sauvignon Blanc
    - 1 tsp. cornstarch
    - A pinch of black pepper

- 3-4 medium-size shrimp with shells

    Shrimp Marinade:
    - Pinch of salt
    - Pinch of cornstarch

- 1 egg, beaten
- 2 cloves shallot
- 2 slices ham, cut into small thin strips
- 6-7 Tbsp. canola oil, divided
- Salt to taste
- 1 Tbsp. soy sauce

Variation: Crab meat and fried salmon are also great ingredients to add to the fried rice at the very end to cook for just 3 minutes.

1 Cook the rice in the rice cooker. When it's done, use a rice paddle to mix up the rice and break it up, and then let it cool down to room temperature.

2 Soak the dried Chinese black mushrooms in hot water for 60 minutes, and then cut off and discard the tough stem in the center and slice thinly.

3 If using fresh water chestnuts, peel off the skin, and slice thinly, or just slice canned water chestnuts thinly.

4 String the snow peas by breaking off the tip of the end (without leaves), and pulling the string down the flatter side, then breaking off the other tip and pulling the string off the other side. Then cut each one into three pieces on a diagonal.

5 Cut the chicken into thin strips and combine with marinade ingredients and set aside.

6 Cut the pork loin into thin strips and combine with marinade ingredients and set aside.

7 Shell the shrimp and devein (see steps **4** and **5** in Shrimp with Broccoli on page 121). Cut into 2-4 pieces, depending on how large they are, and then mix with shrimp marinade ingredients and set aside.

8 Peel the shallots and slice thinly.

9 Heat up the wok over medium heat and add 1 Tbsp. canola oil. Add a little bit of the beaten egg, and then using the spatula, stir up the egg to break it into small pieces, and then remove from the wok. Repeat, working in batches until all the egg is cooked.

10 Heat up the wok over high heat, about 4 minutes. Add 3 Tbsp. canola oil. Add half of the sliced shallots, and stir fry until golden brown, then add the soaked and sliced Chinese black mushrooms, and stir together for one minute. Add marinated

chicken and pork, stir until the meat turns a pale white. Add shrimp and stir for 1-2 minutes. Add thinly sliced ham, water chestnuts and snow peas, sprinkle with some salt and stir well. Remove the mixture to a plate.

11 Wash the wok clean before continuing. Fried rice is easier to make with a clean wok as the rice is less likely to stick to the bottom. Heat up the wok over high heat, about 4 minutes. Add 2-3 Tbsp. canola oil, turn heat to medium high and add the other half of the shallots and stir until golden. Add white rice to the wok, add a pinch of salt and drizzle 1 Tbsp. soy sauce. Turn heat to medium low. Use a spatula to break the rice apart. Add the vegetable and meat mixture from step **10** to the rice, stir until evenly mixed, and add the egg pieces last. Mix everything for 3-5 minutes until it is all well mixed. Adjust the salt to taste. Serve hot.

Cantonese Porridge 廣東粥 (guang dong zou) **

Using leftover cooked rice, this is a great dish to enjoy without too much effort. It is especially good on a cold winter day. A bowl of Cantonese porridge will warm your heart and soul. In Hong Kong, there are all kinds of Cantonese porridges, with various kinds of ingredients.

Yield: About 3-4 servings

- ½ cereal bowl of cooked rice (*long or short grain rice, but not the processed Uncle Ben-kind of packaged rice*)
- 3 cups water or more
- 3 cups chicken or pork stock (*For homemade stock, boil chicken with bones for about 1 hour or longer. Do not add too much water or it will dilute the flavor.*)
- 4 oz. ground pork

   Pork Marinade:

   1 tsp. soy sauce

   1 tsp. cornstarch

- 2 Tbsp. soy sauce
- 1 egg, beaten
- A pinch of salt
- A pinch black or white pepper

   Garnishes:

   2-3 stalks scallion or American chives, finely chopped

   One small bunch of coriander, coarsely chopped

   2-3 Tbsp. unsalted, roasted peanuts

   A few drops sesame oil

1 Cut off the tops of the scallions and half the green part, and then finely chop.

2 Mix pork with marinade ingredients and set aside.

3 In a large pot, add the cooked rice, 3 cups water and 3 cups stock (or water). Do not cover and bring the mixture to a boil, about 5 minutes. Do not leave the pot alone during the first boil, as it might boil over. Reduce heat to medium low.

Occasionally stir with a wooden spoon, making sure you scrape the bottom so it does not stick or burn. Reduce to low heat, cover partially, and cook for 30 minutes. Stir occasionally. Add the marinated ground pork into the porridge pot gradually and stir evenly. Break up the meat with a wooden spoon. Add 2 Tbsp. soy sauce, a pinch of salt and taste. Mix well and cook for another 30 minutes. Cover halfway so the liquid will not burst out and make a mess. Turn to low heat and cook for another 30 minutes. Total cooking time is about 1½ hours.

4 Turn off the heat. With one hand add the beaten egg in a thin steady stream while gently stirring the egg in one direction with a wooden spoon, Mix slowly and sprinkle with white or black pepper. To serve, garnish with coarsely chopped coriander, finely chopped scallion or American chives, and a few roasted peanuts in each individual's bowl with a few drops of sesame oil.

Cantonese Rice Porridge with Fish Slices 魚片粥
(yu pian zhou) **

A few years ago when I was vacationing with my husband in Hong Kong, I tasted the best Cantonese rice porridge with fish slices there. Next to our hotel, there was a Cantonese rice porridge eatery in a shopping mall opened 24 hours a day. They would place a few very thin slices of fresh fish at the bottom of a bowl and then pour the piping hot porridge over it. We just stirred and ate. It was delicious beyond description.

Unlike other types of rice porridge, Cantonese-style rice porridge is quite watery, almost like soup. It is distinct from other styles of rice porridges in that the rice is cooked until it is falling apart into a paste. It has many different versions. Some mix in pig liver, beef, peanuts, etc. Most of the time, the ingredients are very thinly sliced and then the piping hot rice porridge is poured over the ingredients to cook them so they taste very fresh.

The traditional way to cook Cantonese rice porridge starts with rice and water. Some cook the porridge as long as 4 hours. Here I start with cooked rice to save time.

Short grain rice from California, Kokuho brand (國寶牌) or other similar type brand like "Nishiki" (錦) is the best rice for this dish. They are sold in Chinese, Japanese, or Korean groceries, and some area supermarkets also carry it. You can also order it online. Do not use processed rice like Uncle Ben's.

Yield: 4-5 servings/One pot

> 1 cup short grain rice cooked
>
> 4½ cups water
>
> ¾-1 cup tuna fish (about 5-6 oz.)
>
> 2-3 cleaned squid (optional)
>
> 3 stalks scallion, finely chopped
>
> 1 bunch of coriander, coarsely chopped
>
> A pinch of salt
>
> 1 Tbsp. soy sauce
>
> 1 tsp. balsamic vinegar
>
> A pinch of fresh ground black pepper
>
> One egg, beaten (optional)

1 Rub the tuna with some salt, rinse clean, and sprinkle with some salt. Slice the tuna very thinly into pieces about 1½-inch square.

2 Score the inside (the side without the purple membrane) of the squid with diagonal criss crosses, and then cut into one-inch square pieces.

3 Peel off damaged layers of scallion and cut off and discard the scallion tops and half the green part and finely chop.

4 In a large pot, add cooked rice and 6 cups water (or more). Use a rice paddle or a large wooden spoon to break apart the rice chunks. Turn heat to medium high and bring to a boil. Do not cover, otherwise it will boil over. Reduce the heat to low and cover, leaving a crack and simmer for 90 minutes. Stir the rice porridge once in a while so it won't stick to the bottom.

5 Turn the heat higher until the porridge is bubbling, but not really boiling, and add the thin fish slices and squid pieces, and stir for 2 minutes. Turn heat to low, add 1 Tbsp. soy sauce, 1 tsp. balsamic vinegar, and salt to taste. Cover and let simmer for 2 more minutes. Turn off the heat. Add the beaten egg in a stream while stirring in the egg in one direction.

6 Sprinkle with coriander or chopped scallion or both. Sprinkle with some fresh ground black pepper, and serve hot.

Cantonese Rice Porridge with Pork and Thousand Year Egg
皮蛋瘦肉粥 (pi dan shou rou zhou) **

This Cantonese rice porridge dish is one of the most popular in the Cantonese restaurants especially in Hong Kong and U.S. Chinatowns where there is a concentrated Cantonese population. The egg white of thousand year eggs (皮蛋) looks like a solid dark black or green jello (or sometimes a little whitish), and the egg yolk looks like a gooey dark green. People who love this kind of egg are like people who love smelly blue cheese. It is a very acquired taste.

There is a popular tofu appetizer sprinkled with a chopped thousand year egg and drizzled with a specially made sauce of soy sauce, vinegar, sugar, and fried shallot bits. This appetizer is very well done on the weekend Dim Sum menu at Chung Shin Yuan Restaurant (中興園) in Newton, MA on California Street.

Yield: 4-5 servings/one pot

> 1 cup cooked short grain rice
>
> 1-2 thousand year egg
>
> 8-10 oz. ground pork,
>
> > **Pork Marinade:**
> >
> > 1 Tbsp. soy sauce
> >
> > 1 tsp. sesame oil (optional)
> >
> > A pinch of black pepper
> >
> > 1 tsp. cornstarch
> >
> > **Garnish:**
> >
> > 3 stalks scallion, finely chopped
> >
> > 1 bunch coriander, coarsely chopped
> >
> > 1 Tbsp. soy sauce
> >
> > A pinch of salt
> >
> > A pinch of freshly ground black pepper
> >
> > ½ cup unsalted roasted peanuts

1 Crack and peel the shell of the thousand year eggs (no need to cook them), and dice into ¼-inch cubes.

2 Mix the ground pork with the marinade ingredients and set aside.

3 Cut off and discard the tops of the scallions and half the green part, and then finely chop.

4 Cut off one inch of the coriander root, and then swish the leaves and stems in a sink filled with water. Rinse clean, remove, drain the coriander, and then coarsely chop.

5 Cook the rice the same as the Cantonese Rice Porridge with Fish Slices in step **4**.

6 Turn heat to medium, gradually break up and add the marinated ground pork to the rice mixture. Stir well and simmer over low heat for about 15-20 minutes. Add 1 Tbsp. soy sauce and salt to taste. Add the thousand year egg.

7 Turn off the heat and sprinkle with finely chopped scallion, chopped coriander and some black pepper. Ladle one bowl for each person, and sprinkle with some roasted peanuts.

Savory Rice Porridge
Taiwanese Style 台式鹹粥
(tai shi xian zhou) ***

Farmers in Taiwan eat five meals a day when they work in the rice field. The two extra meals are served with Savory Rice Porridge. This custom is called "Eat Five Meals" (吃五頓) (jia go deng in Taiwanese pronunciation). The farmer's family will cook up a huge pot of Savory Rice Porridge to bring to the field for farmers to eat during their mid morning break and the mid afternoon break. Kids love to join them as it is such a fun and delicious meal to eat.

Everybody gathers around the piping hot Savory Rice, each with a bowl and a pair of chopsticks eating and chatting, and having a delightful time in the middle of the rice field. I used to join in the occasion when I was little.

After the meal, kids will run around the small paths dividing the rice field and chase after each other. At home, we did not often have Savory Rice Porridge as it takes time to simmer the various ingredients so that they all blend into one cohesive taste. This dish is a complete meal which satisfies one's appetite without any other dishes.

There are quite a few eateries and restaurants well known for this dish in Taiwan. The ingredients are very flexible. Some are cooked with fish bone broth and fish meat, clams and so forth. It can start with the uncooked rice or cooked rice. With the uncooked rice, bring a pot of water to boil before adding rice to it, to keep the rice grains from break up too easily.

Rice porridge is especially good for people who are recuperating from an illness and cannot take too much solid food. Rice porridge is reserved especially for patients in Japan according to my son-in-law, Katsuya.

Yield: 3-4 servings

> 2 cups cooked rice (*Do not use processed rice like "Uncle Ben"*)
>
> 6 oz. ground pork,
>
> **Pork Marinade:**
>
> 1 tsp. soy sauce
>
> 1 Tbsp. cornstarch
>
> Pinch of black pepper

1 regular size carrot (about 5 oz.) or 1 tomato

2 stalks scallion

4-6 oz. fresh bamboo shoots (or canned bamboo shoots) or substitute with 3 stalks celery heart

6-8 of your favorite mushrooms (oyster, regular, crimini, shiitake etc.)

1 tsp. salt

1-2 Tbsp. soy sauce

1 Cut the carrot into thin strips or shred with a box shredder

2 Cut off both ends of the scallions, and then slice into tiny pieces.

3 If using bamboo shoots, cut off the coarse part at the bottom, leaving only the tender part, and then cut into thin strips. If using celery, peel off the tough strings and slice crosswise into small pieces.

4 Cut off the stems of the mushrooms and slice into two or into thin pieces.

5 In a large size pot, add 8 cups of water. Use a pot large enough so that the water does not fill more than ¾ of the pot. Bring to a boil.

6 Add marinated ground pork, reduce heat to medium low, and skim off the foam.

7 Add shredded carrots (or tomato), bamboo shoots (or celery heart), and mushrooms. Bring to a boil and simmer over medium low heat for 20 minutes.

8 Add 2 cups cooked rice. Use a large spoon to break apart the rice lumps. Add 1 tsp. salt, 1½ Tbsp. soy sauce, and mix well.

9 Reduce heat to low, and cover only half way. If the pot is all covered, the porridge will boil over and make a mess. Simmer for 20 minutes. Stir occasionally. Turn off heat, stir in finely chopped scallions, mix and serve hot.

10 *Variation Using Uncooked Rice:* If you want to start with uncooked rice, wash the rice in water first.

11 In a large pot add 8 cups of water and bring to a boil. Add ½ cup uncooked rice and reduce heat to low. Let it simmer for 40 minutes, stir once in a while, and then add ground pork, carrots, bamboo shoots, celery heart, mushrooms, etc. and simmer for 20 more minutes until all the flavor of the ingredients have blended together. Add salt or soy sauce to taste. It's all right to cook this dish a little longer; however you have to start with more water in that case. If you add water later on, the taste will be diluted, and the dish is not as tasty as if the extra water had been added at the start.

The Taiwanese rice porridge is not as watery as Cantonese rice porridge. Cantonese porridge is cooked until the rice grains have broken down and are nearly indistinguishable from each other, but Taiwanese porridge is simply cooked with meat and other ingredients until the flavor of everything is blended together.

Rice Balls 飯糰 (fan tuan) ***

Rice balls used to be simply a ball made of cooked rice and filled with the dried fluffy pork or fluffy dried fish (see page 205). It is every Taiwanese child's favorite food, much like the Asian version of a sandwich.

Now with the availability of different kinds of rice in Taiwan (short grain, long grain white rice, jasmine rice, brown rice, sweet rice, black sweet rice (really a deep purple color), organic rice, wild rice, and ten grain rice 十穀米etc.), rice balls have become a creative, artistic cuisine.

I was back in Taiwan in the winter of 2004, and as I strolled through the local farmer's market, I saw an old lady with a piece of plastic wrap in her hand, skillfully scooping cooked rice, topped with different cooked ingredients, like five spice tofu, shredded dried pork, pickled cabbage, pickled daikon, and local pickles. She then covered the fillings with another layer of rice and folded the plastic wrap over the ingredients, and with a twist of her hands she squeezed the mixture into a neat ball of rice.

The ingredients used in the rice ball can be anything that you prefer as long as they are cooked and dry. Using vegetables that exude a lot of water make it difficult to hold the rice ball together. For making rice balls, sushi rice is the best. Take hot cooked rice mixed with rice vinegar and sugar, and then fan dry the rice.

Here is a simple version of rice balls with readily available ingredients.

Yield: 3-4 rice balls depending on the size

   3 cups cooked rice, mixed with 1 Tbsp. vinegar and 1 tsp. sugar

Filling Ingredients:

   1 cup fluffy dried fish (see page 205)

   2-3 pickles (use your favorite pickles)

   2 pickling cucumbers, peeled & julienned

   3 slices bacon fried and crumbled into bits

   2 slices coarsely chopped ham

1 Peel the pickling cucumbers and cut into 1" lengths, then slice thinly and stack slices to julienne into thin strips.

2 Spread a piece of plastic wrap on a plate. Spread out about ½ cup rice, topped with a little bit of each filling ingredient, and then spread another ½ cup of rice on top. Gather up the edges of the plastic wrap and tie it together at the top. Twist and shape the rice into a ball. Remove the plastic wrap and put the rice ball on a plate and serve.

CHAPTER 12

鮮蔬素食

Vegetarian Dishes

Vegetarian Dishes

Tender Cabbage with Cream
奶油菜心 (nai you cai xin) **

This easy Chinese dish with a slightly Western flavor is an especially great vegetarian dish. The Chinese cabbage shrinks quite a lot during cooking. A combination of any two fresh mushrooms works fine for this dish, or you can even skip the mushrooms. For a more luxurious dish, add a few dried Chinese black mushrooms. Right after my daughter Tina's wedding, I prepared quite a few dishes for our new in-laws from Tokyo, and they loved this dish the most.

Yield: *4-5 servings/one plate size*

   One Napa Cabbage (about 1½ lbs.)

   1 clove shallot

   4-5 dried Chinese black mushrooms

   ¼ lb. fresh Japanese shiitake or regular button mushrooms (optional)

   ¼ lb. oyster mushrooms (optional)

   3 Tbsp. canola oil

   Salt

   ¼ cup heavy cream or half-and-half (can be substituted with light cream)

1 Soak the dried black mushrooms in hot water for 1 hour, and then remove the tough stem and cut each mushroom in half.

2 Peel off the 3-4 outer leaves of the Napa cabbage and use the tender, inner leaves for this dish. Cut the leaves crosswise into one-inch slices.

3 Peel the shallot and slice thinly.

4 If using fresh shiitake or button mushrooms, cut off the tough stems and cut mushrooms into halves or quarters.

5 If using oyster mushrooms, cut them in two.

6 Heat up 3 Tbsp. canola oil in a wok over high heat, about 2-3 minutes. Add shallot slices and stir until golden. Add reconstituted black Chinese mushrooms and stir a little bit. Add cabbage, sprinkle a pinch of salt, add ¼-½ cup water, stir and cover for about 5 minutes over medium high/ medium heat.

7 Open the cover, stir well and turn the heat to medium and cover again for 5 more minutes or until cabbage is tender and looks kind of translucent. Add about ¼ cup water if the cabbage looks dry. Add all the fresh mushrooms (if using) and stir and cook 2-3 more minutes. Salt to taste

8 Turn heat to low, add ¼ cup heavy cream, mix and serve. The heavy cream adds body and sweetness to the dish.

Fried Green Beans 乾煸四季豆 (gan bian si ji dou) ***

This well-known Sichuan dish can be cooked with ground pork. However, just the green beans themselves are very good and are a vegetarian's delight. People who are tired of the usual boiled green beans should try this recipe for a delightful surprise. The big difference is that this dish does not use any water to cook the beans.

Most restaurant deep fry this dish, I just go along with it for the best results, even though regularly some pan fry it. I've tried it but the result is not always satisfactory. The following method was worked out by my husband Leo. He loves this dish. He cooks it regularly whenever we can get fresh green beans.

The original dish is cooked with garlic, Sichuan pickled cabbage (四川搾菜), some ground pork and chili pepper for spiciness. You can try it. Simply sautée the crushed garlic and shredded Sichuan pickled cabbage together with the cooked green beans. This dish is not easy to master. I tasted this dish cooked to perfection in Taipei's Ji Pin Xuan Restaurant (極品軒). The green beans retained their fresh green color yet were very wrinkly and sweet. The restaurant is located on Heng Yang Road (衡陽路) near 228 Peace Park (新公園, 現改為"二二八和平公園").

Yield: 4-5 servings/One plate presentation

> 1½ lbs. green beans
>
> 2-3 cloves garlic, peeled, crushed and finely chopped
>
> ½ cup canola oil
>
> ½ tsp. salt

1 Prepare the green beans by snapping a little off each end and discarding the ends. If it is longer than three inches, then snap it in half. When buying green beans, snap off a couple beans, if they snap crisply, they are fresh, otherwise the green beans are too old. From my own experience, you have to purchase green beans the day you want to cook them. If you let them sit even one day, they become old and fibrous quickly. Perhaps this is so since most green beans at the market are not freshly picked the same day from a local farm.

2 Rinse and soak the green beans in cold water for 30 minutes before cooking. The string beans will become fresher and crunchier. I learned this tip from Iron Chef CHEN Keniji (陳建一). Drain the water and pat dry with paper towels.

3 Heat up ½ cup cooking oil in a wok over medium-high heat for 2-3 minutes. Add green beans and turn heat to medium. Sprinkle ½ tsp. salt over the green beans. Stir well and fry for 3-4 minutes until you see some green beans have become somewhat wrinkled. Remove the green beans to a sieve and let them drain for a short while, then place the green beans onto a plate lined with paper towel.

4 Pour out oil from the wok, leaving about 3 Tbsp. and turn to medium heat for 2-3 minutes. Sautée garlic until golden brown. Discard the garlic if the garlic is overcooked to dark brown as it will be bitter. (If you want to add some ground pork, you can add here, stir and when pork has changed to pale white, add Sichuan pickled cabbage, and stir well. Add the cooked green beans from step **3** back to the wok and stir well and serve.

5 After being deep fried, the green beans will shrink in quantity. Try cooking 1½ lbs. first, and if you like it a lot, next time try 2 lbs.

How to Make Gluten (vegetarian meat substitute)
麵筋作法 (mian jin zuo fa) ***

Besides tofu, gluten is the second main ingredient in Chinese vegetarian dishes. Though gluten is commercially available in large quantity bags and is not commonly sold in smaller quantities in supermarket, I found packaged gluten powder at Shaw's at Porter Square in Cambridge, MA. Here is a simple way to make gluten. It can be cooked with soup or stir-fried. Gluten is quite chewy; it can sit in hot soup without falling apart.

I prefer to use flour with a higher gluten content like King Arthur brand. Flour with less gluten content will produce less gluten. Chinatown groceries sell flour labeled as low gluten (cake flour) 低筋麵粉, medium gluten (regular all-purpose flour) 中筋麵粉 and high gluten (flour for bread making) 高筋麵粉.

Using this recipe with 5 cups of Gold Medal brand flour and letting the dough sit for 3 hours, I collected 8 oz. of gluten. Then using 5 cups of King Arthur Unbleached All Purpose flour and letting the dough sit for 4 hours, I collected 13 oz. of gluten.

Yield: 13 ounces of gluten

Dough Ingredients:

5 cups King Arthur unbleached all-purpose flour

1¾-2 cups water, depending on the temperature and humidity

1 Tbsp. canola oil

1 tsp. salt

¼ tsp. baking soda

1-2 cups canola oil (for frying)

1 Mix flour, baking soda and salt together. Mix in the oil and water with the flour. Knead into a smooth dough, like bread dough. Knead with the palm of you hand, turn, and knead for 5 minutes or longer. If it is sticky, sprinkle with more flour. You are looking to make a smooth, not tacky dough. At the end your hands should be clean. Place the dough in a pot and cover with a piece of plastic wrap and let it sit at room temperature for 4-5 hours.

2 Remove the dough from the pot and divide into two equal parts. Washing half at a time, it is easier to hold the dough when you wash it in the next step.

3 Place half of the dough into a smooth stainless steel colander ready (not a wire mesh colander, but the kind with a smooth stainless steel surface with holes). Using two hands rub and squeeze the dough under running water for 7-10 minutes to wash off the starch. When the starch is all gone, the water will run clear, leaving just a rubbery-like substance with a honeycomb texture and pale light gray in color. That is the gluten. Repeat this step with the other half of the dough. The total amount of the gluten collected will be about 13 oz.

4 *Frying the Gluten:* Put 1-2 cups canola oil in the wok, and heat over medium high. The oil is hot enough when a little piece of gluten dropped into the oil sizzles. Break the gluten into half-inch globs and deep fry. Smaller is better, so it will fry through. The added baking soda makes the fried gluten puff up like a small balloon. Without baking soda, the fried gluten will have a denser texture. I like it with a little baking soda; it makes the gluten's texture more interesting. It can be served as is or mixed with salad or stir fried with vegetables as a vegetarian meat substitute. It also can be added to soup.

5 *Boiling the Gluten:* Instead of frying, you can also cook the gluten by boiling. Boil 3-4 cups of water in a pot. Break off half-inch pieces of gluten and drop them into the boiling water and boil about 2 minutes until the gluten floats up. Scoop out the cooked gluten and cook with vegetables like vegetarian meat.

In the refrigerator, fried or boiled gluten will keep well for about a week. Gluten can also be frozen after it's been deep fried or boiled.

Buddha's Delight 羅漢齋
(lo han zhai) ***

Inside Chinese temples on either side of the Buddha, which sits in the center, there are "Eighteen Lo Han" (十八羅漢 "the bachelor gods"), holding different kinds of weapons to guard the Buddha. Since all Buddhas are vegetarians, the food they eat is called Lo Han Vegetables (lo han zhai 羅漢齋). This dish originates from the temple where monks and nuns are all vegetarians. Later it became popular among the common folks.

PU Jie (溥傑), the brother of the Qing Dynasty's Last Emperor PU Yi (溥儀), had a Japanese wife SAGA Hiro (嵯峨浩). Their marriage was arranged by the Japanese military government at the beginning of Japan's aggression toward China. They got married in 1937 in Northeast China, then-called Manchuria by the Japanese government. Japan wanted to strengthen the relationship with China after the Last Emperor was forced out of the Forbidden City (紫禁城) in 1924. It started as a political marriage, but they fell dearly in love with each other. After World War II, Pu Jie became a political prisoner and was detained in Russia because he collaborated with Japanese. SAGA Hiro went back to her family in Japan, but later rejoined Pu Jie in China. She wrote a book Cuisine in the Palace ("食在宮庭") describing how Buddha's Delight was cooked by the Qing Royal Family (清皇室):

> Cut cabbage to 3 cm square
>
> Carrot and common yam rhizome (山藥, shan yao, tastes like taro root), rolling bias cut into 3 x 1.2 cm size
>
> Tofu cut into 3 x 1.5 x 0.6 cm cubes.
>
> Clean up tree ears and tiger lilies.
>
> A few slices fresh ginger finely chopped
>
> In a wok, deep fry carrot, common yam rhizome, and tofu cubes.
>
> In another pot, add some soy sauce, add finely chopped ginger, cabbage, water and bring to a boil. Add the rest of the ingredients. Bring to a boil and simmer for 40 minutes until all well blended, soft but not mushy.

The Qing Dynasty royal family (清皇室) that SAGA Hiro married into had a custom of serving only vegetarian dishes during the Lunar Chinese New Year (usually around February), which ran from the first day to the fifth day of the first lunar month.

The ingredients for Buddha's Delight vary a lot. Each chef has his or her own combination of vegetables. The dish is much like Buddhism, which is practiced "as you like it" or in a "laissez faire" (隨緣) fashion. You can put together your own assortment of vegetables, but do not use vegetables which turn yellow after being cooked a long time, such as green beans, spinach, bell pepper, broccoli, lettuce, and bok choy. When you cook this dish, you have to know the order to cook the various kinds of ingredients. The ingredients that take longer to cook should be added first; mushrooms and quickly cooked vegetables are added last. This way the whole dish will come out harmoniously even though some ingredients are very different in nature.

The ingredients combined in this well-known Chinese vegetarian dish use more exotic Chinese vegetarian ingredients. The cooking method is not that hard, just combine everything and let it simmer for a while (40 minutes or so) until the flavor of all the ingredients are well blended. The main ingredients are tofu products, such as fresh tofu, tofu sheets, fried tofu, five spice tofu, and gluten. (See **How to Make Gluten** on page 183). The fancy banquet-style version of Buddha's Delight has more than 10 ingredients, as there are 18 Lo Han Buddhas.

Yield: 5-6 servings

- 1 sheet of dried tofu or 2 sticks dried tofu (腐竹), soaked. *Dried tofu comes in sheets and sticks.*
- ¼ cup dried tree ears (about 1 cup when reconstituted)
- ¼ cup tiger lilies, soaked & knotted
- 1 onion, sliced
- 1 regular size carrot, peeled & shredded
- ½-1 cup crimini or oyster mushrooms
- 2 leaves Napa Chinese cabbage, in ½-inch slices
- ½-1 cup fried gluten (see *How to Make Gluten* on page 183)
- 1 small bunch of "hair" vegetable (髮菜 fa cai) (optional) *Fa cai is very light and grows at the edge of the Gobi desert in China. It looks exactly like fuzzy black hair. Its name in Chinese sounds exactly like "get rich" (發財) so a lot of banquet dishes require this ingredient to bring good luck and*

wealth to the host. Because of its high price, in China people flock to the desert to harvest it, however, that is an ecologically damaging act. When this "hair" vegetable is overharvested, it causes the desert to spread. The Chinese government has prohibited people from picking it anymore. Now industry in China is developing a technique to cultivate fa cai indoors because of the high demand from restaurants in China, Hong Kong, and Taiwan. Fa cai is considered the caviar of Chinese vegetarians.

6-7 sticks bamboo fungus, a.k.a., bamboo pith (竹笙 zhu sheng) This fungus is off-white in color and has a crunchy texture, and is shaped like a hollow, net-like cylinder about four inches long. Some chefs stuff it with a meat filling and steam. It is a very interesting ingredient at a reasonable price. They are sold in a plastic bag with a bamboo and panda design on the cover for about $3.50 per 100g.

3 Tbsp. canola oil

2-3 Tbsp. soy sauce

1 Tbsp. balsamic vinegar or regular black vinegar

1 tsp. sugar

1 Tbsp. sesame oil

A pinch of salt

A pinch MSG (optional)

1 Soak the dried tofu sheet or sticks in hot water for 1 hour, and then cut sheets into large, two-inch squares or the sticks in two-inch lengths. Tofu sheets are packed with a few sheets in one plastic package, yellowish in color, and is about 7" x 12". It can be stored for a while, but do not leave it too long otherwise it might get a stale oily smell. This is one of the main ingredients for Chinese vegetarian dishes. It is a very reasonable priced item, one package costs around $1.00 - $2.00

2 Soak dried tree ears in hot water for 30 minutes, and rub the tree ears with two hands to get rid of the sand. Remove the hard part where tree ears attached to the wood. Rinse clean, and then coarsely chop or leave it whole.

3 Soak tiger lilies in cold water for 30 minutes or warm water for 15 minutes, and then remove the tough tips. Tie each lily into a knot to prevent the flower from falling apart.

4 Peel the onion and cut into 4 wedges. Soak the wedges in cold water for a few minutes to prevent tears when you cut it. Slice the wedges.

5 Peel the carrot and shred with a box shredder.

6 Slice the crimini mushrooms. If using oyster mushroom, just cut each one in half.

7 Slice the Napa cabbage crosswise into half-inch slices.

8 If using "hair" vegetable, soak it in cold water for 15 minutes.

9 Soak the bamboo fungus in water for 10 minutes, cut off the tip and stringy bottom.

10 Heat up the wok over high heat for about 3 minutes. Add 3 Tbsp. canola oil and sliced onions and stir. Reduce heat to medium and stir the onion once a while. Cook the onion for about 10-15 minutes over low heat until it softens and becomes golden. Add shredded carrot, Napa cabbage, tree ears, tiger lilies, bamboo fungus, tofu sheet/stick, and fried gluten. Add ½ cup water. Turn heat to medium high and stir. Add 2-3 Tbsp. soy sauce, 1 Tbsp. balsamic vinegar, a pinch of salt, 1 tsp. sugar, 1 Tbsp. sesame oil, a pinch of MSG and mix well for 2 minutes. Turn off the heat.

11 Transfer the mixture from step *10* to a pot. Add enough water to barely cover the mixture. Turn heat to high and bring to a boil. Reduce heat to very low, cover and simmer for 40 minutes. Occasionally stir the pot so the ingredients do not stick to the bottom of the pot. Add mushrooms and the "hair" fa cai 髮菜 vegetable; mix and simmer for another 5-10 minutes. Taste and serve hot.

The amount of the ingredients can be adjusted. Sometimes if you have too many kinds of ingredients there is a tendency to cook more than you need. You can start with a small amount of everything first.

Deep Fried Soft Tofu
炸嫩豆腐 (zha nen dou fu) ★★★★

There is a saying among the Chinese that the master always keeps a little secret from his disciples (留一手). Restaurant recipes and family herbal medicines are also two things that people keep secret. I have asked quite a few friends how to make this dish. Nobody seems to have a clue. After reading many Chinese cooking story books, I finally work out this recipe with great success. Our family has ordered this delicacy many times from a restaurant called East Ocean City (醉瓊樓) on Beach Street in Boston Chinatown.

Yield: 3-5 servings/One plate presentation

- 2 pieces of soft tofu (*Use the soft tofu, not the silky one. I prefer the traditional type of Chinese tofu which is sold by the piece, and not pre-packaged in a plastic container, but that may only be available from a Chinese or Japanese market.*)

- 2 egg whites, beaten (*Do not overbeat them into a froth. They should just be a little foamy but still watery.*)

- 2 level Tbsp. of cornstarch

- 1½-2 cups canola oil

- Soy sauce, chili sauce, and chopped coriander (as condiments)

1 Cut each tofu into 4 square pieces. Drop them into a pot of boiling water and let them cook for 1-2 minutes. Drain the water, and let the tofu cool down. Cut each square tofu in half and let drain in a sieve.

2 Using a handheld egg beater, mix the egg whites with cornstarch. Do not overbeat, just incorporate the cornstarch with the egg whites.

3 Put the boiled tofu cubes in a pot and drizzle with the egg white mixture. Do not mix egg white mixture with the tofu cubes or the tofu will break apart. Slide the tofu and egg white mixture from one pot to another pot to mix them while keeping the tofu whole. Slide the tofu into the first pot one more time.

4 Place 1½-2 cups canola oil in a wok and heat over high until the oil is quite hot, about 5 minutes. Use a spatula to pick up each tofu one by one and gently slide them into the hot oil. Place about half of the tofu cubes into the hot oil and deep fry until golden brown. Gently turn over to the other side after the tofu looks golden. Fry a few more minutes on the other side, and remove. Turn heat to medium high and wait for about 2 minutes to let the oil temperature go up again before adding more tofu to fry. Finish frying the rest of the tofu cubes.

5 Serve the deep fried tofu with soy sauce and chili sauce. Or place deep fried tofu on a plate, garnish with chopped coriander and drizzle with a little soy sauce and chili sauce and serve hot.

This is a true vegetarian delicacy. It is a simple dish but hard to execute perfectly. There is a pale yellowish "egg tofu" 雞蛋豆腐 on the market in Taiwan, which can be deep fried successfully easily. Simply cut the egg tofu and fry in hot oil and it turns a beautifully deep fried golden color. However, this kind of tofu is not available in U.S.

Eggs Three Ways 煎蛋
(jian dan) **

Following are three ways to pan fry eggs for fried rice or for adding to egg rolls.

A. Egg Pancake

This is a kid-pleasing dish that is simple and easy. It can also be tossed over salad to add texture and color. This ingredient is a must-have for making genuine "egg rolls" (春捲).

Yield: 2 egg pancakes

> 2 eggs
>
> A pinch of salt
>
> 4 Tbsp. canola oil

1 Beat one egg with 2 chopsticks or a fork. Add a pinch of salt. Use a non-stick frying pan. Turn heat to medium high. Swirl 2 Tbsp. canola oil around the frying pan so that the surface is all coated with oil. Wait about 2-3 minutes or until the surface is fairly hot, but not too hot.

2 Add the egg mixture and reduce heat to medium. Swirl the frying pan to coat the bottom of the pan.. Wait for about 2 minutes, and then using a flat spatula, gently lift the sides a little bit; the sides will be a little flared up. Slide the spatula underneath the egg, and gently flip it over and let it cook 1-2 minutes on the other side. Remove the egg pancake to a chopping block with the spatula, or simply flip the frying pan over a large plate. Let it cool.

3 Repeat the above steps with the second egg to make another pancake. Stack the egg pancakes and let them cool down a little. Roll the egg pancakes into a cylinder. Cut into small strips. Place on a plate and serve hot or at room temperature.

B. Mini Scrambled Egg Pieces

Prepare eggs for fried rice in this easy method.

> 2 eggs
>
> A pinch of salt
>
> 2 Tbsp. canola oil

1 Beat two eggs and add a pinch of salt.

2 Heat up a wok over medium high heat and add 2 Tbsp. canola oil. Wait about 2-3 minutes, then reduce heat to medium, and add about 1-2 Tbsp. of beaten egg to the wok. It's not necessary to measure. Let the egg sit a little bit, about 30 seconds. Use a spatula to break up the egg and stir it briskly until cooked, about 1 minute. It will come out in a stringy irregular shape. Remove to a plate.

3 Repeat the above step until all the egg is used up.

C. Deep Fried Egg

> 1 egg
>
> 1 cup canola oil

1 Scramble one egg in a bowl.

2 Heat up the wok (medium heat) with 1 cup canola oil for 2-3 minutes. Drop a little of the beaten egg, if it curls up and floats to the top, the oil temperature is good.

3 Pour the beaten egg through a sieve—while gently shaking the sieve—into the oil until it forms a layer of stringy looking egg. Ladle out the egg and drip dry in a sieve.

4 The deep fried egg can be added to soup or stir fry with other vegetables (like in T*he Best Shark Fin Soup—Taiwanese-Style* 台式魚翅湯 (tai shi yu chi tang) ***** on page 53). It is also good to mix into salads.

Tea Eggs 茶葉蛋 (cha ye dan) ***

On the sidewalks of Taiwan in the old days, you could see vendors with a pot of brown sauce swimming with brown-colored eggs with cracked shells. Those were tea eggs. When the shell is removed from the egg, the surface of the egg has a pretty marbled design. The taste is quite subtle.

Nowadays, in the 7-11 convenient stores in Taiwan, one store may sell hundreds of tea eggs everyday. When hunger strikes, one tea egg can temporarily satisfy the stomach. When you make it at home, you can leave the eggs soaking in the sauce inside the refrigerator for about two to three days to get more flavorful and tasty tea eggs. This dish is a party favorite.

Black tea has dark amber color which enhances the design. Other kinds of tea like Oolong tea are fine but you have to use more tea to enhance the color. This recipe is a variation on plain hard boiled eggs. I got this recipe from my fellow GBCCA chorus member Judy Wang in Boston.

Yield: 4-6 eggs/one egg per person

> 4-6 large or extra large eggs
>
> 1 tsp. five spice powder 五香粉
>
> 3-4 slices fresh orange peels (optional)
>
> 3 star anise 八角 (optional)
>
> 3 Tbsp. red wine
>
> 1 Tbsp. dark vinegar
>
> 2 sticks cinnamon or 2 tsp. cinnamon powder 肉桂皮/肉桂粉
>
> 3 Tbsp. loose black tea or oolong tea or 8 tea bags (*The loose tea leaves are more aromatic.*)
>
> ½ tsp. whole black peppercorns or ground black pepper
>
> 4 Tbsp. sugar
>
> 1¼ cup soy sauce
>
> ½ tsp. salt

1 Use a thumb tack to gently make a hole in the wider end of each egg. Bring 8-9 cups of water to a boil or enough water to cover all the eggs. Reduce heat to medium and gently add eggs and the rest of the tea egg ingredients to the water. Cook for 30 minutes, and turn off the heat. Use a slotted spoon to remove the eggs from the pot. Reserve the tea sauce mixture inside the pot. Let the eggs cool down at room temperature for about 60 minutes. Holding an egg in one hand, lightly hit the egg shell with a spoon or chopsticks to crack the shell, but not hard enough for the shell to come off. Repeat with all the eggs.

2 Put the eggs back into the pot with the reserved tea sauce mixture inside the pot from step **1**, and bring the pot to a boil over high heat, and let boil about 10 minutes. Reduce heat to low and simmer for 20 minutes. Remove from heat and let the whole pot cool down to room temperature before refrigerating the whole pot overnight.

3 The next day, heat the pot over medium low heat to simmer for 20 minutes. There is no need to bring the pot to a boil before simmering. Let the whole pot cool down to room temperature and refrigerate the whole pot overnight.

4 The next day, heat the pot over medium low heat and simmer for 20 minutes. Ladle out one egg and let it cool down. Remove the shell from the egg. The surface of the egg will have a marble-like design. If you let it simmer longer, the taste will be stronger and better, however the surface may look more like brown eggs with less of a marble design.

Eat the egg with your hands. It's not necessary to cut it or anything. It is traditionally a picnic or finger snack food. No utensils are needed. Of course, you can also slice it with a sharp knife and serve it on a plate as an appetizer. You can also cut it with a piece of sewing thread. Wrap the thread around the egg and holding both ends, cross them like scissors to cut the egg. This recipe is a little different from the recipe for traditional brown eggs. It has a marbled design, so when serving, they are usually presented whole to let people admire the design. The taste is milder than that of the brown egg.

It is all right to leave eggs in the sauce for a few more days to one week in the refrigerator. When it's time to serve, simply heat up the whole pot over low heat for about 15-20 minutes. Serve the eggs unshelled on a plate, so each person can pick one and peel it. It adds to the fun of eating like a little kid again.

CHAPTER 13

麵餃點心

Dim Sum Dishes

Dim Sum Dishes

Pan-Fried Savory Beef Pie
牛肉餡餅 (niu ro xian bing) **and**
Savory Chive Pie 韭菜盒子
(jiu cai he zi) *******

There are a few traditional versions of savory pie. The one filled with beef is Savory Beef Pie (牛肉餡餅). The larger size vegetarian version, Savory Chive Pie (韭菜盒子), is filled with a mixture of cellophane noodles and chives or green cabbage. For extra flavor, mushroom slices are added. Both pies usually use the same kind of dough but are traditionally shaped differently to differentiate between the beef and vegetarian pies. However, here I combine the ingredients to make the fillings light and delicious with a homemade touch.

Yield: 12-16 savory pies.

Pie Dough Ingredients:

3½ cups all purpose flour

1⅛ cup lukewarm water

1 tsp. canola oil (optional)

A pinch of salt

1 Mix salt with flour; add oil and water to the flour; and mix. Knead for 5 minutes or more until the dough is very smooth without any stickiness. The Chinese call this consistency *san guang* "three shines" (三光) meaning the hand is *guang*, the dough is *guang* and the kneading board or kneading counter is *guang*, that is, all three are smooth and bare without any dough sticking to them.

2 Place the dough in a pot and cover with a piece of plastic wrap or a few layers of moist cheesecloth. Let it sit at room temperature for 30-60 minutes to relax.

Pie Filling Ingredients:

1 lb. ground beef (omit for vegetarian version and replace with 4-5 leaves Napa cabbage)

2 leaves of Chinese (Napa) cabbage or Bok Choy

2-3 oz Chinese green chives, yellow chives or American chive (optional) for flavoring

One 1.75 oz. package of dried cellophane noodles (Also called mung bean noodle (龍口粉絲) which are sold individually wrapped with six in each package)

4-5 regular white mushrooms or crimini mushrooms (optional)

2½ Tbsp. soy sauce

¼ tsp. salt

⅛ tsp. black pepper

1 Tbsp. sesame oil

1 tsp. Cognac, Sauvignon Blanc or your favorite wine

Making the Filling:

1 Finely chop the cabbage and sprinkle it with a little salt. Let it sit 20-30 minutes to let the water in the cabbage come out. Squeeze out the water and set aside.

2 Soak the cellophane noodles in hot or warm water until soft, about 15 minutes, and then chop into 1-inch lengths.

3 Mix all the filling ingredients, stirring in one direction for a few minutes until the ingredients are uniformly blended.

Assembling the Pie and Cooking:

3 Tbsp. cooking oil (for cooking)

1 Roll the dough into a one to 1½-inch diameter cylinder and cut into one-inch sections. Flatten each piece, cut side down to create a round circle. Dip both sides of the disc in flour. Then with a rolling pin, roll each piece into a 3-inch round skin, turning the dough as you roll it out to achieve an evenly thick, round shape.

2 Put about 2 Tbsp. of filling in the center of the skin. To make the round shape of Savory Beef Pie, gather the edges together and seal at the center into a round shape about 3 inches in diameter and ½- to ¾-inch thick. For the half moon shape of Savory Chive Pie, fold the skin in half over the filling into a half moon and firmly press the edges together, and then fold edges into a pleated design.

3 In a non-stick pan, heat up 3 Tbsp. cooking oil over medium high heat and arrange the pies in the frying pan in one layer. Pan fry each pie over medium heat, about 2-3 minutes per side or until golden brown. Add ½-¾ cup water, cover and turn the heat to medium high. Let it simmer for about 5 minutes or until the water has all evaporated. Remove and serve hot. Repeat this step with all the pies until they are cooked.

Savory Buns 包子 (bao zi) ****

Steam buns are made with many different fillings and come in many styles. It is a sweet bun when filled with sweet red bean paste (红豆沙). Cantonese savory buns are filled with cha shao pork (叉烧肉). Below, I include meat and vegetarian versions. Steamed buns are sold everywhere Chinese people live. Nobody really bothers to make their own, as it is time-consuming like bread making. However, it is fun to make, as you can choose your own fillings. The following recipe is a surefire version for keeping the buns plump after steaming—the buns will not deflate after the steamer lid is removed.

Making the Dough:

Most commercially made steam buns use a starter (麵種), which gives the bun a finer texture without too many air holes. Here I use a fail-proof method for making steamed bao zi.

Yield: 30-35 buns

> 1 tsp. dry yeast
>
> 1 tsp. sugar
>
> ⅓ cup warm water
>
> ¼ tsp. baking powder
>
> 3½ cups all-purpose flour, sifted
>
> ¼ tsp. salt
>
> 1 cup warm water for proofing yeast (~100°F) (= 1/2 cup cold water + ½ cup boiling water) + 3 Tbsp. cold water
>
> 2 Tbsp. canola oil or vegetable oil
>
> 1 egg white, beaten
> *(Reserve the egg yolk for the filling.)*
>
> **Used Later When Forming the Buns:**
>
> ¼ tsp. baking soda mixed with 1 Tbsp. water

1 In a small bowl, dissolve the yeast and sugar in ⅓ cup of warm water, about the temperature of comfortable bath water. Let the mixture stand about 10 minutes or until about ½ to ¾ inches of foam form on top. (This activity proves that the yeast is alive.)

2 In a separate bowl, mix the sifted flour, baking powder, and salt.

3 To the flour mixture, add 2 Tbsp. cooking oil and the yeast mixture from step **1** with an additional ¾-1 cup warm water, and the beaten egg white. When it becomes too stiff to mix, turn it out onto a clean counter and knead.

4 Knead about 5 minutes until smooth, and shape into a ball. Cover with plastic wrap or a few layers of moist cheesecloth and let the dough rise at room temperature for 1-2 hours or until doubled in volume. While the dough is rising, prepare the filling.

Fillings:

The amount of filling is not exact as each cook uses a different amount in each bun. Cook any leftover filling with another dish or add it to soup.

Choose one or more fillings for the buns.

Pork Filling

- 1 lb. and 12 oz. ground pork (*For a very juicy filling, use pork with a higher percentage of fat. If possible, grind the pork with some pork fat.*)
- 10-12 dried Chinese black mushrooms (pre-soaked for one hour)
- 5-6 cloves shallot, peeled & thinly sliced
- 3 Tbsp. canola oil
- 1 egg
- 1 Tbsp. sesame oil
- 3 Tbsp. soy sauce
- ¼ tsp. salt
- ½ tsp. black pepper
- 1 Tbsp. Sauvignon Blanc or other favorite wine
- 1 reserved egg yolk (optional) *Use the egg yolk leftover from making dough.*

1 Rinse and soak the dried mushrooms in hot water for one hour. Then cut off and discard the stems. Slice the mushrooms thinly then coarsely chop them.

2 Peel the shallots and slice thinly. Stir fry the shallots with 3 Tbsp. canola oil until golden. Remove and combine with ingredients in step **3**.

3 Mix all the ingredients together in a bowl, stirring in one direction until the meat develops a sticky texture. The raw pork will be stuffed in the buns before steaming.

Cha Shao Pork Filling

- 1-1½ lb. cha shao pork, coarsely chopped into ¼-½-inch cubes (*These strips of roasted pork, usually colored red on the outside, are sold in Chinatown stores where they sell roasted ducks.*)
- 1-2 Tbsp. Hoisin sauce (optional)

1 If you like, mix the Hoisin sauce with the cha shao. Try 1 Tbsp. first. Too much sauce covers the pork's flavor. I prefer it with less Hoisin sauce.

Vegetarian Filling

The vegetarian filling consists of a variety of sautéed mushrooms. You don't have to have the exact combination of mushrooms listed below, but it's tastier with two or more kinds of mushrooms. The filling will still work if you only have one kind of mushroom.

- 1 cup fried gluten, cut into small pieces (*See How to Make Gluten (vegetarian meat substitute)* 麵筋作法 *(mian jin zuo fa) *** on page 183.*)
- 10 Crimini mushrooms
- 10 white button mushrooms
- 10 Oyster mushrooms (cut off and discard the tough stem)
- 10 fresh shiitake mushrooms or dried Chinese black mushrooms (pre-soaked for one hour)
- 1 package (7 oz.) cellophane noodle
- 4-5 stalks celery
- 2 cloves shallots
- 2 small pieces of five spice tofu (the light or dark brown kind, optional)
- 1-2 carrots
- 2 Tbsp. soy sauce
- Black pepper
- Pinch of salt

1 If using dried Chinese black mushrooms, reconstitute them by soaking in a bowl of boiling water for at least 1 hour. Cut off and discard the tough stem.

2 Soak cellophane noodles in warm water for 15 minutes, drain, and cut into roughly 1-inch lengths.

3 Score the surface of shallot and peel off and discard the surface layer of brown skin, and then slice thinly.

4 Rinse the dirt off the fresh mushrooms and slice thinly.

5 Peel off the tough stringy layer of the celery and then finely chop.

6 Dice the five spice tofu into tiny cubes.

7 Peel and shred the carrots using a box grater.

8 Add 3 Tbsp. cooking oil to the wok and turn the heat to medium high. Brown the shallots and add fried gluten, five spice tofu cubes, celery heart, and carrots.

9 Turn heat to medium high. Add all the mushrooms and cellophane noodle with ½ to 1 cup water and mix well. If the mixture sticks to the wok, add about ¼ to ½ cup more water. (The cellophane noodle soaks in a lot of water.)

10 Let the mixture cook for about 3-5 minutes or until the mushrooms are soft. The cellophane noodle soaks in juices from the mushroom and binds the flavors together. Add a pinch of black pepper and 2 Tbsp. soy sauce. Mix vigorously and well until the water is almost gone, but the mixture is still wet looking. Salt to taste. The juice from the mushrooms makes the filling delicious.

Forming the Buns

1 Mix 1 Tbsp. water with ¼ tsp. baking soda and add it to the risen dough. Knead again for 5 minutes or longer until smooth.

2 Shape the dough into a fat cylinder and cut into three equal pieces. While working with one piece, place the other pieces back in the bowl and cover.

3 Shape the dough into a long cylinder about 1½ inches in diameter and cut into roughly ½-inch sections, for about 11-12 pieces.

4 Sprinkle flour over the board and both sides of the cut dough pieces. Flatten each piece, cut-side down with the palm of your hand. Then with a rolling pin, roll each piece into a 3½-4 inch diameter round. If possible, make the center thicker and the edges thinner. Place about 1 Tbsp. of filling in the middle. The size of the cut dough can be adjusted. If you want to make it bigger, then cut the pieces bigger. Don't cut it too small, otherwise it's hard to handle.

5 Take one edge between your thumb and forefinger. Keeping your thumb pointed downward over the center of the filling, gather the edges up and pleat them as you press the pleats against your thumb, as you work your way around the entire edge of the skin. Be sure to leave a pea-sized opening on top (where your thumb was).

6 Cover the finished buns with a piece of moist cheesecloth and let sit at room temperature for about 50-60 minutes to rise again before steaming or pan frying.

7 Proceed to *Steaming Buns* or *Pan Frying Buns* below.

Steaming Buns

When the first batch goes into the steamer, work on the second batch, allowing each batch to sit at least 50 minutes before going into the steamer. To steam, you will need an aluminum or bamboo Chinese steamer plus 2-3 leaves of Chinese cabbage (or enough to cover the bottom of a steamer rack) or four or more layers of heavy, moist cheesecloth. If using Chinese cabbage, be sure to wipe the leaves dry with a paper towel before placing the buns on top of them.

Yield: about 35 savory buns

1 Bring the steamer's water to a boil. In the meanwhile, place the buns in a steamer rack lined with Chinese Napa cabbage leaves or four layers of moist cheesecloth. It is important to use four layers of cheesecloth. If only one layer of cheesecloth is used, it will dry out and make it hard to remove the steamed buns.

2 Steam over high heat for 10-12 minutes. Remove the steamer racks from the steamer pot before you turn off the heat and let them sit uncovered at room temperature for less than 3 minutes. Remove the steam buns while they are still warm and the cheesecloth is still moist, otherwise the buns will stick to the cheesecloth when the cheesecloth dries out. If the buns do stick to the cheesecloth, place the whole rack back over the steamer and steam for 3-4 minutes to loosen the buns so they can be removed easily. Repeat the steaming process until all the buns have been steamed.

After being steamed, leftover bao zi *can be frozen. When heating up frozen buns, do not defrost them, but steam them frozen over high heat for 15-20 minutes. Or place them on a plate and steam inside the rice cooker with a rack at the bottom filled with ¼ cup water.*

Pan Frying Buns

Pan-fried buns are usually called "Water Fried Bao Zi" (水煎包 Shui Jian Bao) or "Raw Fried Bao Zi" (生煎包 Sheng Jian Bao).

Yield: about 35 savory buns.

> 2-3 Tbsp. canola oil
> ¾ c. cold water mixed with 1 Tbsp. flour
>
> **Dipping Sauce:**
> 1 Tbsp. soy sauce
> 1 Tbsp. white vinegar or Japanese rice vinegar
> Chili sauce or Tabasco to taste (optional)

1 Heat a non-stick frying pan (with a cover) over medium high, with 2-3 Tbsp. canola oil for about 2 minutes. When the pan is fairly hot, place buns in the pan, and pan fry about 1-2 minutes, or until the bottom looks golden brown when you lift the corner of a bun with a spatula.

2 When it turns golden brown, pour in ¾ cup cold water mixed with 1 Tbsp. flour and immediately cover the frying pan. (Adding flour to the water gives the buns a very lacy, thin, crunchy layer of flour which both looks good and tastes good. The flour is optional.)

3 Reduce the heat to medium and let cook about 8-10 minutes or until the water has all evaporated.

4 Turn off the heat, remove 2-3 buns at a time with a spatula, and place on a large plate upside down, so that their golden brown bottoms face up.

5 For dipping sauce prepare 1 Tbsp. soy sauce mixed with 1 Tbsp. white vinegar (or Japanese rice vinegar). If you like it spicy, add a little bit of chili sauce or Tabasco.

Steamed Black Bean Sauce with Spare Ribs 豆豉排骨 (dou chi pai gu) *

This dish is a dim sum favorite at Chinese restaurants. Dim Sum (點心) literally means "touch of heart," but refers to Cantonese-style appetizers. It is easy and delicious. The black bean sauce is quite salty, so no salt or soy sauce is necessary for this dish.

Yield: 6-8 servings.

> 1½ lbs. spare ribs (*Ask the butcher to cut the pork ribs into 1-1½-inch lengths.*)
>
> 2 Tbsp. black bean sauce (*Buy the black bean sauce in a glass jar, not the dry fermented beans in a plastic bag. The "Ping Fong Brand Black Bean" 屏豐牌蔭豆豉 from Ping Dong 屏東, Taiwan is the best. It's available in Boston's Chinatown at Sun Sun Grocery on Oxford Street.*)
>
> 1 Tbsp. Cognac, Sauvignon Blanc or your favorite wine
>
> 3 stalks scallion
>
> 2-4 slices fresh ginger (*If you cannot find fresh ginger, just omit. Do not substitute with powdered ginger.*)

1 Peel the damaged layers from the scallion, cut off the tops and the damaged green ends, and finely chop the rest.

2 Mix all the ingredients with the spare ribs in a stainless steel pot or a large heatproof bowl. Put the bowl in a steamer, bring the water to a boil, reduce heat to medium/medium-high and steam for 50-60 minutes. A lot of juices come out of the steaming spare ribs. Save the sauce to serve with hot rice or cook with stir fried vegetables. Place spare ribs on a plate and serve hot or at room temperature.

Pot Sticker Dumplings 鍋貼與餃子 (guo tie yu jiao zi) ***

This version is easy. Prepare the dough and wrap the filling inside. However, making the filling is an art. The Chinese are very particular about the filling. When you bite it, does the chewy texture of the filling bounce back? Is it tender? Is it dry? Do juices flow out of the filling?

In order to make the fillings juicy, tender, and delicious, the traditional filling calls for the pork and pork fat to be chopped by hand. The proportion of fat to pork must be correct for the best filling — usually three parts fat to seven parts pork. Nowadays, fat is hard to find at the market, although some butchers have it. The easiest way is to buy a piece of pork that seems to have some fat on the edge and take it home to chop finely with a cleaver. It takes a little experimenting to get the best result. However, it is really worthwhile to make the best filling possible. To give the meat a "bouncy" texture, often the chef literally throws the pork into a pot, picks it up and throws it into the pot again. The chef repeats this several times to obtain that "bouncy" meat texture.

Jiao zi is a party favorite. Have everyone come early to help make them. While a couple of people roll the skins, the rest can wrap up dumplings. There are directions below for both pan frying and boiling.

Yield: about 35-37 pot stickers.

Making the Dough (餡皮 xian pi)

If you don't have time to make your own wrappers, you can use the thicker kind of commercially made wonton skins as wrappers. When pan fried, the effect is pretty good, but not as good as the freshly made ones.

> 3 cups all-purpose flour
>
> 3 Tbsp.-½ cup canola oil (*More oil makes the dough more supple, allowing the skin to be rolled more thinly.*)
>
> A pinch of salt
>
> 1 cup lukewarm water

1 Make a well in the flour, and add the oil and mix it into the flour a little, and then add some water and mix it well until it forms a dough. It is better to make the dough softer; you can always add more flour to it. If you make the dough too hard, it is hard to mix in more water later.

2 Knead until smooth. If it is kind of sticky, sprinkle some flour and knead it in. Let it sit in a pot covered with plastic wrap or a layer of moist cheesecloth for about 30 minutes or longer to get a consistency similar to bread dough.

Pork Filling 肉餡 *(ro xian)*

1¼ lbs. ground pork

10 fresh water chestnuts *(Available in Chinatown grocery stores and Russo's in Watertown, MA).* If fresh water chestnuts are not available, use canned ones or substitute with 4-5 stalks of celery.

1-2 leaves of bok choy or Napa cabbage, boiled in hot water and finely chopped

2 Tbsp. soy sauce

A pinch of black pepper

4 Tbsp. sesame oil or canola oil

A pinch of salt

2 Tbsp. water

1 Slice off the top and bottom of each chestnut then peel off rest of the skin with a peeler. Place each water chestnut inside a plastic bag and use the flat side of a cleaver or chef's knife to smash the water chestnut. If using celery, peel off the strings with a paring knife and finely chop. If you have *bok choy* or Napa Chinese cabbage, drop 1-2 leaves in boiling water for 1-2 minutes, squeeze out the water, and then finely chop and mix in with the meat.

2 Add the rest of the ingredients to the meat and mix in one direction to get a sticky texture. Salt to taste. It is OK to be a little on the salty side. In order to get the stickier texture, use less vegetable or meat only. However, nowadays with health in mind, fillings usually include more vegetables. Adjust the combination of ingredients to fit your personal preference.

Traditional Pork Filling

A traditional filling uses ground pork mixed with the savory pork broth jelly that comes from cooked pork skin. Follow the directions above for pork filling, but add the jelled broth with the fillings above.

1½ lbs. pork skin or two pig feet

1 Rinse the pork skin or the pig feet and put in a pot with enough water to barely cover the skin. Add a pinch of salt. Bring to a boil and boil for 5 minutes. Then, drain the water and rinse the pork skin or pig feet with clear water in order to get rid of the raw smell of the skin or pig feet. Put the skin or pig feet back into the pot with enough water to barely cover the skin or pig feet, and bring to a boil for 5 minutes, then reduce the heat to low, cover and simmer for 60 minutes. Stir occasionally so that the skin or the pig feet will not stick to the bottom of the pot.

2 Remove the pork skin or the pig feet from the pot. Remove the meat, and let the broth cool down to room temperature and then refrigerate 2 hours or overnight. The broth will jell. Add some of the jelled broth to the fillings above. Don't add too much if the gel is on the liquid side.

The leftover skin or pig feet can also be eaten as separate dishes. The skin can be cut into one-inch square pieces and served with soy sauce and finely chopped scallion as a dipping sauce. The pig feet can be cooked in a fresh pot of water (barely covering the pig feet) with about 5 Tbsp soy sauce and simmered for 30 more minutes until it is tender.)

3 The fillings of "Soup-filled buns" (灌湯包 *guan tang bao*) contain pork broth jelly. When the diner bites into the bun, the delicious broth from the filling comes out. When you eat soup-filled buns, poke a small hole in the middle before biting into it so you can suck out the delicious juice with a straw. The skin of soup-filled buns is very thin and delicate, rolled to about 3 inches in diameter (unlike the thicker skin of the savory buns (包子) presented here). When served, each bun is placed inside an individual small bowl.

Wrapping the Dumplings
(餃子皮 *jiao zi pi*)

1 After the dough has relaxed for 30 minutes or more, divide the dough into three equal portions. Roll each portion into a 1½-inch diameter cylinder. Cut each cylinder into several ½-inch lengths. With the cut side down, flatten each piece into a coin-like shape, and dip both sides into the flour to avoid stickiness, and roll it into a circle about 3½-4 inches in diameter.

2 Place about 1 to 1½ Tbsp. filling in the middle of a skin. Fold the skin in half over the filling into a half moon and pinch just the very top of the arc. On one side, gather the skin into pleats towards the middle pinch, and press it against the other half of the skin. Shape it so it will have a flat bottom to stand on the frying pan. Do not overfill, otherwise it is hard to seal tightly without leaving any openings.

3 At this point, you can freeze some dumplings to save to cook later. (See below.)

Freezing Uncooked Dumplings
Any uncooked jiao zi (餃子) can be stored in the freezer.

1 Line a large plate with plastic wrap and then place the *jiao zi* on top, making sure they don't touch. Cover with another piece of plastic wrap and put it in the freezer. The next day, transfer all the frozen *jiao zi* to a plastic bag to store in the freezer.

Pan Frying Dumplings (鍋貼 *guo tie*)
Traditional pot stickers are made with a rectangular shape skin about 3-4 inches long. The skin is filled and folded up the middle and pressed closed. The two ends are left open. Here we use the jiao zi style dumpling and pan fry.

1 Heat 3 Tbsp. cooking oil in a non-stick frying pan with a fitted cover over medium high heat. Place the pot stickers (fresh or frozen) closely together in the pan in rows. Try not to leave any space between the dumplings.

2 After about 1-2 minutes, lift one to see if the bottom is golden brown. If most of them are, add ¾ cup cold water (or, if you are cooking frozen ones, add 1¼ cup water and cook about 10 minutes over medium/medium-high heat) to the frying pan and cover right away. Reduce heat to medium and let it cook about 5-6 minutes or until all the water has evaporated.

3 Uncover the pan and ready a large plate. Shake the frying pan a little to loosen the pot stickers so none are sticking to the pan. Turn the heat off and let it sit about 3-4 minutes. Cover the pan with the large plate and reverse the pan, flipping all the pot stickers onto the plate so the bottoms are facing up. Be careful when flipping the pot stickers. Use a smaller frying pan at first as it is easier to flip it over. If you are not too sure of the flipping, you can use a spatula to scoop up a few pot stickers at a time and flip them over onto the plate.

4 If the pot stickers were tightly packed together in the pan, they should come out on the plate like one giant, round jigsaw puzzle. The design is impressive and beautiful. Serve hot with dipping sauce, which is equal parts soy sauce and vinegar. Add a little chili sauce or Tabasco if you like it spicy.

Boiling Dumplings
When the dumplings are boiled, they are called jiao zi. *I remember when we were in college near National Taiwan University in Taipei. At lunchtime, four or five of us would go to the* jiao zi *eatery next to our campus and we would order 40 or 50 for us. The waiter would shout out the number across the eatery to the kitchen, and at the same time, their hands would be rapidly wrapping the* jiao zi *at the rate of about one a second, or so it seemed. Sometimes when a group of guys came in, they would order 200!*

1 Bring a large pot of water to boil. NEVER drop *jiao zi* into cold water, or they will fall apart!

2 For fresh *jiao zi*, put about 10 at a time into the boiling water. Do not put too many in the pot at once. When the water starts to boil again, add ½ cup cold water to stop the boiling. When the water boils a second time, add another ½ cup cold water

to the pot. When the water boils for a third time, the *jiao zi* will be floating on the top of the water (a sure sign that the *jiao zi* are done). Remove the *jiao zi* and serve hot. The water is brought to a boil three times (三滾) while the *jiao zi* is in the pot. The hot and cold treatment keeps the *jiao zi* from turning mushy. This method is the surefire, traditional way to cook *jiao zi* to perfection without a timer.

3 For frozen *jiao zi*, follow the instructions above, but boil 4 times.

One time, my husband Leo would not follow the old traditional way and insisted on experimenting like a scientist. He boiled the jiao zi *all the way through and then let the* jiao zi *simmer for 15 minutes without adding any cold water in between. The end result was a disaster. The dumplings were mushy, and the skin turned into an overcooked mess.*

Taiwanese Turnip Rice Cake
蘿蔔糕 (lo bo gao)***

This dish is made for the Chinese Lunar New Year in Taiwan, but also eaten as an appetizer in the morning and afternoon, or as a midnight snack. In the old days, when Chinese New Year was approaching, every family in Taiwan would soak a few pounds of long grain rice (在來米) and bring it to the village stone grinder. There, people pushed and pulled and ground the waterlogged rice. Two people would push and pull the grinder's wooden handle (attached to the ceiling beam with a rope), while the third person would ladle the rice and water mixture into a hole at the top of the grinder. It required some skill to do the job well. While the grinder is moving, the third person has to follow the moving rhythm of the grinder so as not to collide with the poles that are holding the grinder. I used to do this chore with my sisters, taking care of the pushing and pulling.

Either daikon (white turnip) or taro root would be cooked and mixed with the watery rice, then steamed into a large block of rice cake. It can be eaten as is, or cut into ½-inch thick squares of one-inch on a side and then pan fried or deep fried. It is served as a dim sum appetizer in Chinese restaurants.

Nowadays with the availability of rice powder, no grinding is involved. One simply mixes the rice powder with water, which is then cooked and steamed. Daikon (the Japanese word for white turnip) is called chai tao in Taiwanese, which has the same sound as the word for "good luck omen." So it is a must item for Chinese New Year to bring prosperity for the coming year.

Yield: 6-8 servings

- 2 cups long grain rice powder 在來米粉 (usually packed in a 16 oz. paper package). *Ask the store clerk to make sure it is long grain. Chinatown carries rice powder from Thailand. There are many kinds of rice powder: sweet rice powder 糯米粉, regular rice powder 蓬來米粉 and long grain rice powder 在來米粉.)*

- 2 cups water

- 5-6 dried black Chinese mushrooms

- ¾ lbs. or 3 cups shredded daikon (white turnip), about ½ of a medium-sized daikon

- 3 Tbsp. large-size dried shrimp (optional)

(Available in Chinatown grocery stores, packed in plastic bags. Do not get the small ones, which are not tasty and sometimes quite salty.)

6-7 Tbsp. canola oil, divided

1-2 Tbsp. good soy sauce *(I prefer naturally brewed Japanese soy sauce.)*

5-6 cloves shallot *(the more the better)*

2 Tbsp. sesame oil (optional)

A pinch of black pepper

A pinch of salt

5 Tbsp. canola oil

Soy sauce or gooey Taiwanese soy sauce 醬油膏 (as a condiment)

1 Soak the dried black mushrooms in hot water for one hour, then remove the tough stem, cut into thin strips, and coarsely chop. Save the soaking water to be mixed with rice powder. The mushroom soaking water is quite aromatic.

2 Peel the *daikon* and cut in half lengthwise into two long pieces, so it is easier to hold the *daikon* to shred against the box shredder. Shred with a box shredder. You should have about 3 cups.

3 Soak the dried shrimp in hot water for 30 minutes, drain, and coarsely chop. Save the soaking liquid to be mixed with the rice powder.

4 Peel the shallots and slice thinly.

5 Combine the soaking water from the mushrooms and shrimp. If needed, add enough water so that you have two cups of liquid. Mix with 2 cups long grain rice powder and 1-2 Tbsp. canola oil.

6 Heat a wok over medium high for about 3 minutes. Add 5-6 Tbsp. canola oil and shallot slices and cook until golden and slightly shrunken, but not brown. Add black mushrooms, dried shrimp, and 2 Tbsp. sesame oil (optional), and stir about 2-3 minutes. Add the shredded *daikon* with 1 Tbsp. soy sauce, black pepper and sprinkle with a little salt. Stir about 5 minutes or until *daikon* is soft and limp. Remove to a bowl.

7 Wash the wok clean. Turn heat to low and add half of the rice powder and water mixture from step 5 and stir with a spatula while scraping the mixture from the sides of the wok. The mixture will thicken. When it turns into a thin paste-like liquid, in about 2-3 minutes, turn off the heat, and add the rest of the rice powder and water mixture and mix evenly into a liquidy paste. Add the *daikon* mixture from step 6 and mix well. Sprinkle with a little salt and mix. Dip a finger in to taste to check the saltiness. It should just be lightly salted.

8 Grease a ceramic or stainless steel bowl with a paper towel dipped in canola oil. Use a Chinese spatula to scrape the mixture from the wok into the bowl.

9 Fill a steamer pot about ¾ full and bring to a boil over medium/high heat. Remove the steamer pot cover and place the bowl with the turnip cake mixture inside the steamer rack. Be careful not to burn your hands as the steam is quite hot. Cover and steam for 40-45 minutes.

10 To check for doneness, turn off the heat and stick a chopstick into the turnip cake. If the chopstick comes out clean, it's done. Remove the steam racks from the steam pot and leave them uncovered. Let the rice cakes cool down for 20 minutes before cutting. The surface will appear "wet" with steam. Leave the rice cake at room temperature for 20 minutes and the surface moisture will evaporate. For a clean cut, wait until after the turnip cake has totally cooked and cooled down, and then cut and serve.

More frequently, after the cake has cooled, it is pan fried or deep fried to a golden brown on both sides before being served. The additional frying makes it taste much better. Serve with soy sauce or Taiwanese-style gooey dipping soy sauce (醬油膏).

Scallion Pancakes 蔥油餅
(cong you bing) ***

Scallion pancakes are now commercially available in the frozen food section of Chinatown grocery stores next to the frozen dumplings. They are easy to make and can be kept in the freezer. The hardest part is kneading the dough. Everyone has their own way of folding the dough and flattening it into scallion pancakes.

I once visited Da Jue Temple (大覺寺) in the Bronx, New York, and a nun, De En (德恩法師) made some scallion pancakes with a huge amount of oil. She made a very soft and greasy dough, which she separated into smaller pieces and soaked in oil to keep it fresh until the next time she made "scallion pancakes" but without scallions. As a follower of Buddhism and a vegetarian, the nuns as well as monks do not have scallion, garlic, onion and leek in their diet. These foods supposedly stimulate attraction for the opposite sex. To my surprise, the scallion pancake dough used by a few sidewalk food stands in Taiwan now use a similar very oily dough like De En's.

During the summer of 2013, I visited a seaside park in Hsin Chu (Nan Liao 南寮). At the park, there was a food stand operated by a young couple from Indonesia, making very thin Indonesian-style scallion pancakes, which are then deep fried in the oil. When he removes the pancake to drip dry on a rack, at the same time he folds the pancake into a half moon shape and fills it with fried spicy potatoes that look like thin French fries. He has three kinds of fillings: ground pork, corn, and Indonesian spicy potato. I tried one Indonesian style. Even though it was a little greasy, it was sure a delicious snack.

In the summer of 2005, after Typhoon Haitang, there was a scallion shortage in Taiwan. The price of scallion shot up from $1 to $20 a pound. Some scallion pancake eateries had to shut down temporarily until the scallion prices stabilized.

Yield: 13-15 pancakes

 3 cups all purpose flour

 1 cup boiling water

 1/3 cup cold water

 4-5 stalks scallion

 3 Tbsp. to 1/4 cup canola oil (for dough)

 1/4 cup canola oil (for brushing)

 1 Tbsp. sesame oil (optional)

 A pinch of salt

 4-5 Tbsp. canola oil (for cooking)

 Soy sauce, rice or white vinegar, and
  Tabasco/chili sauce as condiments.

1 Cut off and discard the scallion tops and half of the green part, then coarsely chop.

2 Make a well in the flour, add a pinch of salt, 3 Tbsp. (to 1/4 cup) canola oil, and roughly mix in with flour. Make a well in the flour again, and slowly add 1 cup boiling water and mix it in with the flour. Add 1/3 cup cold water. Knead until smooth. It is better for the dough to be on the soft side. Sprinkle with some flour if it feels a little sticky. Place the dough in a pot, cover with plastic wrap or a few layers of moist cheesecloth and let it sit for 30-60 minutes to relax.

3 Knead and cut the dough into 3 large pieces. Roll each piece into a cylinder and cut each cylinder into 4-5 equal portions.

4 In a bowl mix 1/4 cup canola oil with 1 Tbsp. sesame oil and a pinch of salt.

5 Roll each piece of dough into a round disc about 5-6 inches in diameter and brush with the oil mixture, and sprinkle with some chopped scallion. Tightly roll up the dough like a jelly roll into a cylinder. Press both ends of the dough so it is sealed together, and then coil the cylinder tightly into a round shape (like the snake coils its body). Press it flat first with the rolling pin, then using a rolling pin roll it into a thin round disc.

6 Repeat the previous step once more and roll into a round disc. Individually wrap each pancake with plastic wrap or stack them with a piece of parchment paper between each pancake. Repeat with each section of dough.

7 In a non-stick frying pan, heat up 4-5 Tbsp. canola oil over medium high. Reduce the heat to medium, cook the pancakes about 2 minutes on

each side or until golden, but not too brown or too burned. The pancake should fry up with small light brown spots on each side. That is the perfect look.

8 When serving, cut the pancakes into quarters like a pizza. Serve with 1 part soy sauce and 1 part rice vinegar (or white vinegar) with some chili sauce (like Tabasco). Just fry up the amount you want to serve. The uncooked pancakes can be stored in the freezer by individually wrapping each pancake in plastic wrap. Stack them up and freeze. Frozen ones can be pan fried without thawing.

Some restaurants deep fry the whole piece, so it is evenly golden brown. At home, pan frying is better and less greasy. This Chinese breakfast item is also ideal as an afternoon or midnight snack.

Rice Cake with Taro Root
芋頭糕 (yu tou gao)****

Taiwanese-style rice cakes are made using daikon (see Taiwanese Turnip Rice Cake 蘿蔔糕 (lo bo gao)*** on page 199) or taro root (in this recipe.) If you can't get taro root, you can substitute with malanga coco which has a very similar texture, but is not as flavorful as Taiwanese taro root. Russo's in Watertown, MA carries it.

Taro root is very starchy and is almost like a potato, but it's a little purple on the inside and has a stickier, denser texture. It is very popular in Asia where you can find taro root powder, taro root cake, taro root bread, fried taro root, sweet taro root paste, taro root ice cream, etc.

Yield: 6-8 servings

- 2 cups long grain rice powder 在來米粉 (It comes in a 16 oz. plastic or paper package at Chinatown grocery stores. There are many kinds of rice powder: glutinous rice powder, regular rice powder and long grain rice powder. Make sure you get the one that only has rice and water as the ingredients and says 在來米粉 "zai lai mi fen" in Chinese.)
- 6-8 oz. of taro root (about 2 taro roots, only available in Chinatown)
- 5-6 dried Chinese black mushrooms
- 2-3 Tbsp. dried shrimp (optional; available in Chinatown grocery stores)
- 5-6 cloves shallot *(the more the better)*
- 5-6 Tbsp. canola oil
- 2 tsp. sesame oil (optional)
- Salt
- A pinch of black pepper
- 2 Tbsp. soy sauce

1 Soak the dried black Chinese mushrooms in hot water for one hour. Reserve the mushroom soaking water. Remove the center tough stem. Slice the mushrooms thinly and then coarsely chop.

2 *Cooking Taro Root:* When preparing the taro root, wear gloves, because when you peel the skin a slimy substance on the surface may cause an allergic reaction, making your hands feel itchy. The best way to remove the skin is to rinse the

roots without peeling the skin, then cut them in half and boil the roots in a pot of water for 10 minutes (or more for larger roots). Remove from the water, and once it has cooled, the skin can be easily removed. A third way is to steam the root in a steamer for about 20 minutes. Rinse the whole root clean, and boil whole for 10-15 minutes in water. Peel off the skin and smooth out the bumpy surface with a peeler, and then cut into small pieces or half-inch cubes. Some people like to see taro chunks in the rice cake. It's all right if the chunks tend to stick together. Cut taro root into one-inch cubes or smash into a paste, leaving just a small portion as small cubes

3 Soak the dried shrimp in hot water for 30 minutes and reserve the soaking water. Coarsely chop the shrimp.

4 Peel the shallots and slice thinly.

5 Combine the soaking water from the mushrooms and shrimp. If needed, add enough water so that you have two cups of liquid. Mix with 2 cups rice powder and a pinch of salt.

6 Grease a heat-resistant ceramic pot, CorningWare glass pot or a stainless steel pot, by wiping the inside with a piece of paper towel dipped in cooking oil.

7 Heat up 5-6 Tbsp. canola oil and 2 tsp. sesame oil over medium high heat. Stir fry the shallot until golden, but not brown, about 1-2 minutes. Turn heat to medium, add dried shrimp and stir about 1 minute, and then add the mushrooms, and stir well for about 2 minutes. Sprinkle with fresh ground black pepper. Add the cooked, crushed taro root. Use a spatula to break it apart. Add 2 Tbsp. soy sauce. Sprinkle with a little salt. Remove to a dish.

8 Wash the wok clean. Over low heat, add half of the water and rice powder mixture. Use a spatula and stir and scrape the mixture until it becomes a thin paste-like liquid. Some of the mixture may clump on the spatula creating lumps, so keep stirring as it cooks to dissolve the lumps into a smooth paste.

The mixture will become unevenly paste-like in parts, while staying liquid in parts. This uneven texture is OK. The lumpy part will later vanish into the cake. Turn off the heat. Add the taro mixture from step **7** and add the rest of the water and rice powder mixture. Stir and mix evenly. Pour the mixture to the oil-coated pot from step **6** and place the pot on the steamer rack.

9 Over medium high heat, bring the steamer pot water to a boil. Make sure you have enough water to steam for 45 minutes. Place the steamer racks on top of the steamer pot, while being very careful as the steam is very hot. Steam for 40-45 minutes.

10 Check to see if the rice cake is done by turning off the heat and inserting a chopstick into the center. Be careful as the residual steam is very hot. If the chopstick comes out clean, the rice cake is done. Remove the steam rack from the pot and let cool down, uncovered at room temperature for 15 minutes or longer. The surface of the rice cake will be "wet" with the steam moisture. It takes 15 minutes or longer to evaporate.

11 Cut into squares or rectangles and serve at room temperature. Or, cut the rice cake into half-inch thick slices 1" x 2" and pan fry in a non-stick frying pan on both sides until golden brown and serve. You can also deep fry the slices before serving. This dim sum item is served with soy sauce or Taiwanese-style gooey soy sauce (醬油膏) for dipping.

Salted Egg

鹹蛋 (xian dan) **

Salting is a terrific way to preserve eggs. In Taiwan, eggs are coated with a sticky red mud mixed with a lot of salt and then let to sit for about one month. When the eggs are ready to be cooked, the salted mud is removed and the eggs are washed and boiled. You can find red mud-coated eggs at Taiwanese farmers' markets. Nowadays, in the U.S., commercially sold salted eggs all come from China packed in a plastic jar with salty water. In Taiwan, I bought some salted eggs and discovered they were all sold cooked. I had trouble finding uncooked salted eggs there. I asked people why. They told me people nowadays are lazy. They just want to take it home, crack it open, and eat.

One day, I was very excited to find one vendor carrying the red mud-coated salted eggs in Hsin Chu during the Dragon Boat Festival. People wrap the hard-boiled, salted egg yolk with other ingredients, like pork chunks, chestnuts, and black mushrooms in the bamboo leaves with sweet rice, a treat called "zong zi" (粽子).

This version can easily be made at home. In the late summer, the well-known Moon Festival (中秋節) moon cake bean paste fillings contain a salted egg yolk. It is a delicacy that I like a lot.

> One dozen extra-large or jumbo eggs
> (*Eggs with bigger yolks make delicious salted eggs with a brilliant orange/red egg yolk. In particular, the yolk of free range eggs are much more reddish in color.*)
>
> ½ gallon water (64 oz. = ½ gallon, use a ½ gallon milk container for measuring)
>
> 2 cups salt plus extra
>
> ¼ tsp. baking soda
>
> Plastic wrap
>
> One large glass or ceramic jar with a tight-fitting lid. *It should be big enough to hold the eggs and water, and still allow the eggs to float. Do not use a metal container as it will rust.*

1 Bring a ½ gallon of water to boil, then turn off the heat and let it sit for 10 minutes to cool down a little. Add about 2 cups salt and ¼ tsp. baking soda, and mix slowly until they dissolve completely. Keep adding salt until no more salt will dissolve. Let the salted water cool down to room temperature. Pour the water into the glass container.

2 Put the eggs slowly into the salted water, cover with a piece of plastic wrap and screw on the tight-fitting lid. Let the eggs soak for at least 24 days at room temperature .

3 Mark the date on the jar lid and the date in 24 days. To keep the eggs from becoming too salty, remove eggs from the salty water after 30 days. They may be kept in the refrigerator, cooked or uncooked for up to 2-3 weeks.

4 When the eggs are salted, place however many you wish into a pot of cold water. Turn the heat to medium and boil for 25 minutes from the time you turn on the heat. There is no need to bring the water to a boil. Do not use high heat as the shell will crack.

5 When eggs cool down, peel off the shell and serve at room temperature. The egg yolk will have a brilliant orange color.

Serving suggestions:

As an accompaniment to rice: Hard-boiled salted eggs are simply delicious when served with hot rice or hot rice porridge. It is a perfect breakfast food. The egg white is quite salty. It can be crumbled into little pieces and mixed with vegetable salad, too.

Added to dishes: Salted eggs are used in Steamed Pork with Salted Eggs or cooked with bitter melon (苦瓜), a Hakka Chinese specialty dish. [8]

---

8 Hakka is a minority group that lives in Southern China near Canton and in the western and southern part of Taiwan. Their dialect is different from Mandarin, Cantonese, as well as Taiwanese.

Fluffy Dried Fish
魚鬆 (yu song) **

A traditional Taiwanese breakfast is usually hot rice or rice porridge accompanied by fluffy, wispy dried pork, fluffy dried fish, scrambled eggs, Chinese pickles, salted fermented tofu, or fresh-made tofu (still warm from the maker) drizzled with soy sauce. My mother would buy a large piece of fish like tuna, salt fish, or shark and transformed it into the most delicious fluffy dried fish. In the process of making it, the house would fill with an incredible aroma that made everybody hungry. The following recipe is one easy way to make it using canned tuna fish. Chinatown grocery stores sell ready-made fluffy dried fish, it is usually too sweet or too salty—not to my taste. It is fun to make and enjoy the fruits of the hard work afterwards.

*Besides being served with rice and rice porridge, fluffy dried tuna fish is perfect as a filling for rice balls. In the West, people bring sandwiches for picnics, while in Japan and Taiwan, rice balls are the perfect picnic food. In the palm of your hand, hold a piece of plastic wrap, spread out about ½ cup cooked rice on the plastic wrap and fill the middle with about 1 tablespoon of fluffy dried fish and other ingredients like pickles. Sprinkle with toasted white or black sesame seeds. Gather the corners of the plastic wrap and twist it into a ball, folding the filling into the center. (See **Rice Balls** 飯糰 *** (fan tuan) on page 177.)*

Total cooking time: about 60 minutes

> Two 6 oz./170 g cans Bumble Bee solid white albacore in oil *(Do not use other brands, and be sure to buy tuna packed in oil, not in water. Other brands of tuna tend to be more crumbly.)*
>
> 2 Tbsp. canola oil
>
> 2-3 cloves of garlic
>
> 2 tsp. sugar
>
> 1 tsp. Italian balsamic vinegar *(Do not substitute with other kinds of vinegar, the sweet taste of balsamic vinegar makes it perfect.)*

1 Smash the garlic with the side of a cleaver or regular kitchen knife, and remove the skin.

2 Heat up the wok over medium high with 2 Tbsp. canola oil. Add garlic and stir until the garlic turns brown. Discard the garlic.

Add 2 cans of tuna fish including the oil in the can, to the wok with 2 teaspoons sugar and one teaspoon balsamic vinegar to the tuna fish.

3 Use a spatula to break up tuna fish chunks into very fine pieces. Tuna fish is pretty flaky so it should be fairly easy to break up. After 5 minutes, reduce the heat to medium or medium low.

4 Keep stirring until the tuna fish becomes light, fluffy, and dry, about 40-60 minutes. The drier the fish the better, but be careful not to let it burn. If it looks like it's going to burn, turn the heat lower. If the bottom of the wok burns, scrape with a metal spatula and turn the heat even lower. Keep stirring until very light and fluffy. The finished product should be very light in weight and golden brown in color. Make sure it doesn't become too brown.

5 Remove the dried tuna fish, and let it cool down to room temperature. Place in a glass container. It can be kept at room temperature for one week without any problem because the moisture from the tuna fish is almost all gone. For safety, if keeping longer (up to 3-4 weeks) refrigerate the dried tuna fish. This method was how food was preserved in the old days when refrigeration was not available.

CHAPTER 14

臺灣飲品

Taiwanese-Style Drinks

Taiwanese-Style Drinks

Soymilk 豆漿 (dou jiang) **

Soymilk is a very popular drink to have with a Chinese breakfast. Every morning, people flock to eateries to order a bowl of piping hot soymilk (either plain or sweet). It is an especially common breakfast drink for people from northern China who drink a cup of hot soymilk with the flaky, but not sweet, pastry, Shao Bing (燒餅), in which they sandwich a You Tiao (油條), a foot-long, crispy fried dough stick, which looks like a long cruller. Or, they may have a steam bun with their soymilk. Now soymilk is popular among all Chinese, either hot or cold. For the hot climate in Taiwan, a cold one is more comfortable to drink.

In Taiwan, soymilk comes in a paper cup, with the cup machine-sealed with a plastic film. My gynecologist Dr. Robert Shirley of Winchester, MA, now retired, recommended eating more soy products for good health. He kept a jar of roasted soybeans right in his office.

This recipe is easy. Soybeans are very inexpensive. You can get them from Chinatown grocery stores or sometimes in the bulk food section of a good grocery store. There is a commercial brand soymilk "Silk" available in supermarkets. I tried it once, but the manufacturer added some other ingredients (like seaweed) which made it taste very strange to me. Chinatown carries commercially made fresh soy drink from local tofu manufacturers.

Yield: about ¾ quart

- 1½ cup dried soybeans
- ¾ cup to 1 cup sugar (optional; for sweet soymilk)

1 Soak the dried soybeans overnight in a big pot with a lot of water. The soybeans will expand quite a bit.

2 In batches of 1 cup soaked soybeans with 2 cups water, puree in a blender or food processor. Pulse the mixture for about 2 minutes at a time until the beans are well ground up and it is foamy on top. (In the old days, soymilk was made with a stone grinder.)

3 Line a large colander with a large, close-weave cheesecloth, and put it in a larger mixing bowl. Pour each batch of puree into the cheesecloth-lined colander. Do not overfill the cheesecloth. Stop before you are unable to hold all the puree in the cheesecloth. Depending on how large the cheesecloth is, you may need to go to the next step before you've finished pureeing all the soybeans.

4 Carefully gather up all the edges of the cloth and twist them together. Use the twisting pressure to squeeze as much liquid as you can out of the cloth. (Do not oversqueeze so much that the pureed solids come through the cloth.) Discard the soy pulp. If needed, repeat with the rest of the puree. (In the old days, the soybean pulp was a main source of feed for hogs.)

5 Place the filtered soymilk in a very large pot. There should be at least 2 inches of pot above the surface of the soymilk. Over medium-low heat, cook the soymilk for about 50-60 minutes or until it starts to boil. Stir occasionally, so the soymilk will not stick to the bottom and burn. Do not leave the liquid on the stove without watching it. If it boils over, the hardened protein in the milk makes a huge mess that is hard to clean.

6 Remove from heat. If you like, add 1 cup of sugar to make sweetened soymilk. Allow the milk to cool completely, and then keep refrigerated for up to three days. If the soymilk becomes yogurt-like, the taste will also turn bad.

Tea Drink with Condensed Milk and Sugar 奶糖紅茶
(nai tang hong cha) *

Whenever I drink tea brewed from commercial tea bags—regardless of if it's Starbucks, airline tea, or any other coffee shops—they all make me rush to the restroom. However, the tea I make from imported, loose Chinese tea that is distributed and sold through Chinese grocery stores does not have that effect. I wonder if it's the way tea is manufactured here or, if in the process of packaging tea into tea bags, some other agents besides tea are added. In the case of the better teas in Taiwan, the tea comes in the shape of a small ball (from one single tea leaf). It is a pretty long process for the tea to go from picking from the tea tree to fermenting and drying into a small tea ball.

Most of the tea that we drink is made with only boiling water. The only kind of tea we add sugar to, is black tea—which is called red tea in Chinese 紅茶. Black tea has to be fermented first.

The following is a good and delicious recipe. You can use any kind of tea you like: black tea, green tea, oolong tea or jasmine tea. Because the sugar and sweetened condensed milk dilute the flavor of the tea, make the tea a little stronger than usual.

There is a Japanese brand of this kind of drink available commercially that I used to drink all the time. It is called Kirin Afternoon Tea. One day, I ran out of it and decided to make it myself. The end result was fantastic.

Not only does homemade tea taste better, but it has no artificial ingredients and saves money. There are several kinds of tea drinks called "fruit tea" (水果茶) which are very popular in Taiwan today. Hot water is poured over an assortment of fresh fruits, like lemons, apples, strawberry, plums or pears cut into wedges, and some teas add dried flowers like roses. However, the best teas for this recipe are oolong tea and black tea.

  2-3 Tbsp. loose black tea 紅茶 (depending on how strong you like it)

  10 cups boiling water

  ½ can of 14 oz./396 g sweetened condensed milk (Carnation or other brand, available in supermarkets) or substitute with milk

  ¼ cup sugar (Add less if sweetened condensed milk is used. It is quite sweet. Adjust the sweetness to your own preference)

1 In a Pyrex or heat-resistant container, place 2-3 Tbsp. loose black tea. Bring a pot of water to boil. Add boiling water to the Pyrex container (about 10 cups).

2 Let the tea steep for about 30 minutes or longer. Filter out the tea leaves and discard. Since sweetened condensed milk is very thick, dissolve it in a cup with a little hot water before adding it to the tea. You can use milk instead of sweetened condensed milk, but the condensed milk adds a unique aroma and taste to the drink. Mix well. Add ¼ cup sugar to the tea and mix well. Let the tea mixture cool down to room temperature. Refrigerate. It's a great summer drink.

Rice Milk 米乳/米漿
('bi lin' in Taiwanese) ***

In the old days in Taiwan when there was no milk available, rice milk was a substitute for mother's milk to feed the babies. I have a very fond memory of this specialty in Taiwan. I got this recipe from a woman while I was waiting at a Chinese acupuncture doctor's office in Hsin Chu, Taiwan. It is commercially available in Taiwan's breakfast and night market eateries. However, the aroma of the one I make myself is simply divine.

½ cup short grain rice *(soaked in water overnight and drained)*

¼-½ cup commercial roasted peanuts *(grind to a powder by putting in a plastic bag and rolling over it with a rolling pin)*

1 Tbsp toasted black or white sesame seeds (optional)

8 cups water, divided

¾-1 cup sugar (adjust to taste)

A pinch of salt

1 After soaking the rice overnight, drain the water.

2 In a blender, add 2 cups water, the rice, the finely ground roast peanut (and toasted sesame, if using), securely cover the top, and then blend for about 5 minutes or until the mixture looks finely blended and creamy. Add one more cup of water and blend again for 1 minute until you barely see any rice grains left.

3 In a pot, add 6 cups water and the mixture from the blender, also a pinch of salt. Turn heat to medium low. Stir constantly for 20 minutes so that the rice doesn't stick to the bottom of the pot. When you see the bubbles turned to small "lazy" bubbles, it is done. Remove from the pot right away. If you leave it on the stove, even with the heat turned off, rice lumps will form at the bottom of the pot.

4 The mixture will be the color of hot chocolate when using ½ cup roast peanuts. With fewer peanuts the color will be lighter. Let the mixture cool down for 30 minutes. Add ¾ cup sugar first. If you like it sweeter, add another ¼ cup. It's a great creamy drink with the slightly aroma of roasted peanuts. Refrigerate after it cools to room temperature. It will keep up to three days in the refrigerator. Drink warm or at room temperature.

Sweet Green Mung Bean Soup with Tapioca 綠豆西米圓湯
(lyu dou xi mi yuan tang) **

Sweet green mung bean soup (green bean soup) and red bean soup are two of the most common Chinese desserts you will find in Chinese home cooking or in Chinese restaurants. It is easy to make, and kids love it. Here small tapioca pearls are added to make it creamier in taste and look interesting.

I got this recipe from Mrs. Mann-Wen LIU (柯曼雯) when she brought this dessert to a GBCCA chorus rehearsal.

Yield: 6-8 servings

- 1 cup green mung beans (green beans soaked overnight)
- 1 cup small tapioca pearls (soaked in cold water 30 minutes)
- ½ cup sugar or more (adjust the sweetness)
- Pinch of salt
- ¼ cup milk, light cream, or sweetened condensed milk (optional) *(The milk/cream is like a garnish to add a milky flavor to the soup. It can be added to the whole pot or individually added to each serving. It's popular in Taiwan restaurants to serve this sweet dessert with milk.)*

1 Soak the green beans overnight and then rinse clean.

2 Soak the tapioca pearls in cold water for 30 minutes.

3 In a medium size pot, add the soaked beans with 3 cups to one quart of water. Bring the pot to a boil with the cover cracked open. Then reduce heat to medium low and simmer for 60 minutes or until pretty soft—the softer the better. Turn off the heat.

4 Add the soaked tapioca pearls to the hot green mung bean soup and cover for 10 minutes. There is no need to turn on the heat to cook the tapioca pearls. Simply let the heat of the soup cook the tapioca pearls. Add sugar to your taste and a pinch of salt. Add ¼ cup milk, light cream or sweetened condensed milk to make it taste better.

5 Put the pot in the refrigerator when it cools down to room temperature. It tastes very good the next day served cold.

6 Or evenly divide the soup in ice cube trays. Cover with plastic wrap and insert a toothpick in each cube to make green mung bean popsicles.

Flour Tea 麵茶
(mi deh in Taiwanese) **

In the old days in Taiwan, around midnight, the "flour tea" vendor would push his cart which had a tea kettle fitted with a very long spout and go 'whistling' (boiling) through the streets. People would know the flour tea cart was approaching the neighborhood. And from different households, people would dart with bowls to get a serving for a midnight snack. It's an old-fashioned Taiwanese sidewalk snack, popularly categorized as an "old early taste" (古早味) now in Taiwan. As society modernizes, it has almost disappeared from the regular market except in some southern Taiwan countryside areas. It is one of my childhood memories. During the Second World War, Taiwan was under the bombardment of U.S. B-29s, we had to be prepared to run for shelter under dire circumstance, so my mother prepared a bottle for each of us filled with "flour tea" packed in each of our backpacks, ready to be carried with us when we were running from the bombardment. We could just add hot water to this flour tea so we wouldn't go hungry. Most of the time we just ate it dry for fun.

Yield: 6 servings

> 3 cups all purpose flour, sifted
>
> 2 Tbsp. canola oil
>
> 1¼-1½ cup confectionery sugar, super fine sugar or brown sugar
>
> 1 Tbsp roasted white or black sesame, finely ground or as is
>
> 3 Tbsp roasted peanuts, finely ground

1 Heat up a wok (easier to maneuver) or frying pan, over low heat to medium low. Add 2 Tbsp canola oil, sifted flour and keep stirring for 30-40 minutes until the flour turns golden brown or a beige-like color.

2 Turn off the heat, and remove the flour to a pot. Let it cool down for 20 minutes. Add sugar, ground sesame, and ground peanuts; mix well.

3 Scoop out about ½ cup of the mixture to a bowl. Bring water to a boil and immediately add the piping hot water to the mixture gradually and mix briskly. Do not let the water sit in the teapot for even a short while. It will weaken the flavor. Add water little by little, until it is the texture of a Colombo yogurt mixed with a spoon. Make it thicker or thinner depending on personal taste. The dried cooked flour mixture from step **2** can be kept in the refrigerator for a few weeks. It's a great snack for children as well as adults. (This kind of flour tea used to be used as baby food in the old days.)

CHAPTER 15

西菜佳肴

Western Favorites

Western Favorites

Mama's Hamburger 媽媽的漢堡 (mama de han bao) **

Most American-style hamburgers are made with plain meat, cooked, and then seasoned with sauces. The main difference between Chinese food and Western food is that Chinese food does not rely on the sauce to add taste. Chinese food, especially for meat, is usually "marinated" before cooking in order to enhance the ingredient's nature flavor and to make the meat tender.

Following is the basic marinating technique used for almost any ground meat or sliced meat. This hamburger, even without adding tomato slices, lettuce and commercial bottled sauces, is very delicious. One time for a BBQ party, I ordered some rib-eye beef and asked the butcher to grind it for me. Then I marinated it as explained below. Everybody simply loved it.

Yield: 4-6 servings, depending on your appetite

- 1 lb. ground pork (pork loin) or hamburger (rib-eye beef)
- 1½ Tbsp. soy sauce (*Use Kikkoman or a good quality soy sauce from a Japanese grocery store. Some soy sauces are quite salty and have no flavor. Never use the plastic packaged soy sauce from Chinese restaurant takeout; they are awful. It's like water mixed with salt and food coloring.*)

Meat Marinade:

- 1 tsp. sugar
- 1 egg
- ½ tsp. Sauvignon Blanc, Cognac, or your favorite wine
- 2 stalks scallions, keep the top white part and a little bit of the green part, finely chopped
- 2 Tbsp. canola oil
- ¼ lb. regular mushrooms or crimini mushrooms, sliced
- 6 hamburger buns
- 1 Tbsp. cornstarch

1 Peel any damaged outside layers of the scallions then chop off and discard most of the green part. Finely chop the remaining white part and little bit of the green part. Slice the mushrooms.

2 In a large bowl, combine ground meat, soy sauce, sugar, egg, scallions, wine and mix evenly into a uniform mass. Try to mix in one direction and the hamburger meat will develop a sticky texture.

3 Shape the meat into 4-6 hamburgers. Dust your hands with a little cornstarch so that the meat will not be too sticky in your hands as you shape them.

4 Add 2 Tbsp. canola oil to the wok and heat it up until fairly hot. Add the hamburgers, turn the heat to medium, and let them cook for 2-3 minutes before flipping to the other side. Try not to press on the hamburger otherwise the best part—the juice—will come out. Reduce heat to medium low, and let cook another 3-4 minutes on the other side. Use a chopstick or a fork to poke into the center of a hamburger. If reddish juice comes out, it is not quite ready yet, unless you like it a little rare (when making beef hamburgers). Remove hamburgers when they are ready and place on buns. Use the oily juice collected at the bottom of the wok to cook the mushroom slices for 2-3 minutes until soft. Serve mushrooms over hamburgers.

You can use a flat bottom frying pan to do the cooking. However when using a wok, the grease from the hamburger will come out and stay at the bottom of the wok. The grease collected can be used for cooking vegetables or the mushroom slices as explained above.

Thanksgiving Turkey & Sauces

感恩節火雞與滷汁

(gan en jie huo ji yu lu zhi) ****

Each pound of turkey takes about 15 minutes baking time (350° F). I got this recipe tip from our neighborhood store called Petrillo's. The store was tended by a few elderly brothers and one smiling lady. They were in their 70s and 80s and all worked long hours during the 1980s. Customers went there not just to buy groceries, but also to chat with them like an old family. When my son Derek was born, the first stop to show my newborn baby straight from the hospital was Petrillo's. The sauce recipe is from my college classmate Cindy LAI (陳杏仔). The main difference is this sauce uses hard boiled eggs.

Yield: 10-12 servings

> 10-11 lb. turkey (the smallest size available on the market)
>
> One 8 oz. stick of butter at room temperature
>
> Salt
>
> 2 Tbsp. soy sauce
>
> 2 eggs
>
> 1-2 Tbsp. cornstarch mixed with ¼ cup water

1 Leave the butter at room temperature to soften (about 30 minutes).

2 Remove the paper package of neck, gizzard, and liver from inside the turkey cavity. Place the turkey in a large sieve. Prepare a pot of boiling water and, pour the boiling water all over the turkey. Scalding the turkey gets rid of the wild fowl smell. Sprinkle some salt (1-2 tsp.) on both hands and rub all over the turkey inside and out. Have a large baking pan ready, preferably not an easy to bend aluminum pan, but a sturdy metal pan. Place a flat wire rack or a V-shaped wire rack in the baking pan. Use one hand to hold the room temperature softened butter and plaster butter all over the whole turkey. Make a V-shaped roof over the turkey with aluminum foil. Leave some room between the turkey and the aluminum foil roof.

3 Preheat oven to 350° F degree. Place the turkey pan into the oven. Every 30 minutes to one hour, rub some more butter onto the turkey using a brush. (A silicone brush is available on the market for this special use.) Every pound of turkey needs 15 minutes baking time (10 lb x 15 = 150 minutes). In the last 30 minutes, remove the aluminum foil roof and turn up the heat from 375° F to 400° F degrees. This way the turkey will come out golden brown. Baking an extra 10 to 15 minutes more than the calculated time is okay.

4 *For the Sauce:* Bring a small pot of water to a rolling boil. Use a thumbtack, press a tiny hole into the fat end of two eggs. Drop two eggs into the boiling water, reduce heat to a very low boil and boil for 10 minutes. Ladle the eggs into a pot of icy water to cool down thoroughly then crack the eggs all over and peel. Place turkey neck in a separate small pot with about 1½ cups cold water with the gizzard and liver. Add a pinch of salt. Bring to a boil and simmer over low heat for 30 minutes. Discard the neck. Chop the gizzard and liver into tiny pieces. Chop the 2 hard boiled eggs into small pieces. Add the chopped liver, gizzard, and hard boiled eggs into the small pot with the broth from cooking the neck. Add 2 Tbsp. soy sauce, a pinch of black pepper and mix well. Turn the heat to medium and simmer for 10 minutes. When the turkey is removed from the baking pan, there is a lot of meat juices and fat at the bottom of the pan. Remove some of the fat or simply add the whole thing to the small pot, and let the whole mixture simmer for another 5-10 minutes. Salt to taste. Mix 1-2 Tbsp. cornstarch with ¼ cup water; mix well and add to the pot. If you like the sauce thicker, add more cornstarch mixture; if you like the sauce thinner, add less cornstarch mixture.

The leftover turkey meat is great for fried rice, fried noodles or in stir fry with vegetables. With the turkey cut into thin strips, it's especially great with bean sprouts. Place turkey bones in a pot with water barely covering the bones, and simmer for 30-40 minutes. Discard the bones, save the turkey stock for soup or cooking with vegetables.

Mama's Best Cheesecake
起士蛋糕 **

This recipe is from a colleague of my husband Leo when he worked at Mt. Auburn Hospital in Cambridge, Massachusetts many years ago. I have made small modifications, such as reducing the confectionery sugar by about ¼ cup and adding an extra egg. It is the best cheesecake recipe—thick, creamy, and delicious.

- 1 Graham Cracker Ready Crust pie shell (6 oz./170 g size)
- 2 boxes of Philadelphia original cream cheese (8 oz./226 g)
- ¾ cup confectionery sugar (powdered sugar)
- 2 extra large eggs or 3 medium eggs
- Heavy cream or half and half cream (optional)

1 Leave the cream cheese at room temperature for 30 minutes to soften, making it easier to blend. Cut each cream cheese bar into 4-5 smaller pieces to make it easier to blend in a blender or a food processor.

2 In a food processor, add eggs, blend once; add cut up cream cheese pieces and ¾ cup confectionery sugar. Blend well, about 2 minutes. If it's too thick, you can add a little bit of heavy cream.

3 Slowly pour the mixture into the pie shell.

4 Preheat oven to 375° F. When you put the pie shell into the oven, *place a large pan under the pie shell, so if it overflows, the oven will not become a mess.* Bake about 45 minutes, or until golden. Stick a chopstick into the center of the pie. If it comes out clean, it is done. Remove from the oven and let it cool down to room temperature. Cut into 12 pieces. Cover and place in the refrigerator overnight. Serve the next day. It is better when served cold but it is very good from the oven too.

Usually I bake two cheesecakes at a time. It is better served cold. To prevent the cheesecake from cracking on the surface when baking, place the pie shell inside a baking pan filled with water. Doing this will add about 10-15 minutes to the baking time.

CHAPTER 16

Afterword

The Chinese describe the experience of living often using food terms as a most common way of expression. The five words "sour, sweet, bitter, spicy, and salty" (酸甜苦辣鹹 suan tian ku la xian) denote the different kinds of lifetime experiences. "Taking bitterness" (吃苦 chi ku) means a person is able to battle through hardship.

I have been to some elaborate banquets. The banquet which impressed me the most was at the Taipei Ambassador Hotel (國賓大飯店) during the 1960's and the dish was "Stir Fried Eel" (炒鱔糊). I'll never be able to do that dish myself except when the eel is all prepared to be cooked, namely sliced already. The eel looks terrible. It has appeared on the Iron Chef TV show several times with skillful Japanese chefs. The eel is believed to help a person's body regain its "heat," and is also a good for a person who is recuperating. To enjoy some great dishes you have to make a mental note to travel to Asia some day.

In Taiwan, a lot of the food is prepared professionally and commercially. Living in Taiwan, one does not have to think of cooking hard to make dishes like steam buns, red cook beef, red cook pig feet, beef noodle soup, etc. These dishes are readily available everywhere. Living in the U.S. for over 30 years, I have had to learn to make a lot of things, like making tofu, sprouting bean sprouts, and making Shanghai egg roll skins. It may take a while for you to digest some of the recipes in this book, but the cooking methods are universally similar, namely boiling, steaming, frying, and stir frying (pan frying). The only thing that the Chinese are not accustomed to is baking. It is because the traditional kitchens are not equipped with an oven even today. The roasted cha shao red barbecue pork (叉燒肉 cha shao rou) is considered available only commercially as it can't be made in a traditional Chinese home kitchen.

Some of the recipes in this book may sound far out and incomprehensible, but actually they are less strange than some existing dishes in Taiwan and China. Once you are familiar with the Chinese cooking method, you can experiment with ingredients available to you in your area and achieve satisfactory result.

✑ The End ✎

Index

NOTES

NOTES

NOTES

NOTES

23033271R00138

Printed in Great Britain
by Amazon